Sociology and
Social Work

Transforming Social Work Practice – titles in the series

To order, please contact our distributor: BEBC Distribution, Albion Close, Parkstone, Poole, BH12 3LL. Telephone: 0845 230 9000, email: **learningmatters@bebc.co.uk**. You can also find more information on each of these titles and our other learning resources at **www.learningmatters.co.uk**.

Sociology and Social Work

JO CUNNINGHAM AND STEVE CUNNINGHAM

Series Editors: Jonathan Parker and Greta Bradley

LearningMatters

First published in 2008 by Learning Matters Ltd

British Library Cataloguing in Publication Data
A CIP record for this book is available from the British Library.

ISBN 978 1 84445 087 9

Cover design by Code 5 Design Associates Ltd
Project management by Deer Park Productions, Tavistock
Typeset by PDQ Typesetting Ltd
Printed and bound in Great Britain by Cromwell Press Ltd, Trowbridge, Wiltshire

Learning Matters Ltd
33 Southernhay East
Exeter EX1 1NX
Tel: 01392 215560
info@learningmatters.co.uk
www.learningmatters.co.uk

Contents

Acknowledgements

We would like to thank Kate Lodge, Di Page and Jonathan Parker from Learning Matters, for their encouragement and regular prompting.

Thanks also go to the very many students we have taught, past and present, for their never-ending enthusiasm and willingness to share their views and experiences.

And last but by no means least, huge thanks to Harry for his patience while we have been writing this book. Normal parenting will now be resumed with much vigour.

Dedication

This book is dedicated to Mike Riley, a former colleague of ours at the University of Central Lancashire, who was both a passionate advocate of sociology and a skilled social worker. Mike died from motor neurone disease at the age of 46. This book is for Mike with fond memories and much affection, and for his family with our love.

Quite how readers of *The Times* reacted to the revelation that sociologists were, as a species, on the verge of multiplying enormously in number is not altogether clear. Neither do we know what the response was to a second letter to *The Times*, published on 22 September 22 1903, which pleaded for its readers to donate £10,000 for the setting up of a school of sociology in London. The reaction, we suspect, was not one of enormous enthusiasm. Nonetheless, a school of sociology, which went under the name the London School of Economics (LSE), was created very soon after. Of course, the LSE has today evolved into a citadel of first-class social science research and teaching, justifiably attracting plaudits from governments and academics around the world. Its days of having to rely for its funding on pleas for cash in national newspapers are long gone. However, things did not initially go particularly smoothly for this embryonic school of sociology. The LSE's first annual report, for example, talked about the need to *dispel the fog of indifference* that seemed to surround its endeavours. *Sociology*, the report went on, *was not at present popular* and the calibre of the students they were attracting was not altogether good. Many of their students were *inclined to pessimism* and *disillusionment*, unable to grasp the explanatory, liberating potential of sociological research and teaching (*The Times*, 7 December 1904).

These early, passionate defences of the discipline do have something of a contemporary resonance for us. The difficulties the LSE pioneers experienced in getting sociology taken seriously sound familiar to us as sociologists today, for although the discipline is now widely accepted in academia, it has always struggled to get itself taken seriously 'out there' in the 'real' world. Indeed, we sociologists have often found ourselves at the butt of what 'we in the trade' regard as unwarranted jokes and humour. By way of example, some of you may remember the British Telecom 'ology' advert shown in 1988 starring Maureen Lipman as 'Beattie', the doting grandma. She received a phone call from her distraught grandson, who told her that he had failed all his exams. For those of you who did not see the advert, here is an extract from it:

Beattie (receiving the phone call whilst baking a cake): *Anthony? Ooh, congratulations on your exam results.*

Anthony (sat sulking on the bottom of his stairs at home): *Grandma, I failed.*

Beattie (sits down, shocked): *What do you mean, you failed?*

Anthony: *I mean I failed* (he then goes through all the 'real' academic subjects he has failed)!

Beattie: *You didn't pass anything?*

Anthony: *Pottery* (he says this sulkily)!

Beattie (her spirits pick up): *Pottery's very useful ... Anthony, people will always need plates! Anything else?*

Anthony: *Sociology!* (he almost spits this out, the tone of his voice illustrating the lack of 'worth' he attaches to the subject).

Beattie (unaware of the 'uselessness' of a sociology qualification): *An 'ology'! He gets an 'ology' and he says he's failed!? You get an 'ology' and you're a scientist!*

The joke, of course, was on poor Beattie, who was daft enough to even think that an 'ology' was a serious subject, and worthy of congratulation. Indeed, in Anthony's eyes sociology came even further down the pecking order than pottery, as evidenced by the fact that he mentioned it last.

As well as having to respond to ridicule, sociology has also been criticised for contributing to moral breakdown and as being a bastion of unhinged, militant, left-wing revolutionaries. In 1969, for example, the Pope blamed sociology for generating *moral uncertainty*, describing it as *socially very dangerous* and accusing it of undermining the Catholic faith (*The Times*, 4 December, 1969). At the same time, the study of sociology was blamed for encouraging campus riots, anti-Vietnam war protests, and later in the 1970s, it was linked to a propensity to commit terrorist acts. The discipline has been a particular target for conservatives on the 'right' of the political divide, many of whom see it as a destabilising influence. One such commentator, David Marsland, once said that sociology students were being *systematically de-skilled for effective work and trained (by deliberate intent or by default) to be critical saboteurs of Britain as it is, and as most people want it to be* (cited in Bossley, 1987). They were invariably being taught, argued another right-wing commentator, by *an ignorant rabble lost in jargon, fired by doctrine and profoundly hostile to all forms of authority and power* (Scruton, 1985).

Certainly, sociologists have often been motivated as much by a desire to change society as they have to explain it, and in this sense they are often driven by passion and a clear sense of purpose. Karl Marx, one of the 'founding fathers' of sociology, was deeply moved by the exploitation and endemic poverty suffered by the working classes in the nineteenth century, and in his work he sought to set out the path towards a society that would be free of social and economic ills. Many sociologists since, while not necessarily subscribing to Marx's ideas, have been influenced by a similar desire to initiate progressive change. It is perhaps this that often leads to charges of political bias and subjectivity. However, as you will see as you work your way through this text, there is no one 'truth', or 'correct' explanation for social and economic problems. There are different, competing interpretations and there are as many influential sociologists of the 'right' as there are of the 'left'. Rather than this being a handicap, for us as teachers of sociology this is one of the subject's most endearing features. Helping students negotiate these different explanations for social phenomena, watching them grapple with interpretations of social problems with which they were previously unfamiliar, and seeing them challenge their preconceived views is fascinating and rewarding. Indeed, while writing this book, we inadvertently discussed between ourselves our own first encounters with sociology. Although we discovered the discipline at different periods in our lives, its impact and influence upon both of us was the same. Sociology opened up a new outlook on the world for us, challenging taken-for-granted assumptions that we had held for years, and providing interpretations of social phenomena that helped us situate our viewpoints and experiences.

Most of all, though, our passion for sociology stems from the fact that it offers us, as social workers, insights into and explanations for the problems that we have to deal with on a day-to-day basis. Surely, as professionals who are positioned at the 'front

Chapter 1
Developing a sociological imagination: Debunking society

ACHIEVING A SOCIAL WORK DEGREE

This chapter will help you begin to meet the following National Occupational Standards and General Social Care Council's Code of Practice.

Key Role 1: Prepare for, and work with individuals, families, carers, groups and communities to assess their needs and circumstances
- Work with individuals, families, carers, groups and communities to help them make informed decisions.

Key Role 2: Plan, carry out, review and evaluate social work practice, with individuals, families, carers, groups, communities and other professionals
- Apply and justify social work methods and models used to achieve change and development, and improve life opportunities.

Key Role 3: Support individuals to represent their needs, views and circumstances
- Advocate with, and on behalf of, individuals, families, carers, groups and communities.

Key Role 6: Demonstrate professional competence in social work practice
- Implement knowledge based social work models and methods to develop and improve your own practice.

General Social Care Council Code of Practice

Code 1.5: Promoting equal opportunities for service users and carers.

Code 1.6: Respecting diversity and different cultures and values.

It will also introduce you to the following academic standards as set out in the social work subject benchmark statements.

3.1.1 Social work services and service users
- The social processes (associated with, for example, poverty, unemployment, poor health, disablement, lack of education and other sources of disadvantage) that lead to marginalisation, isolation and exclusion and their impact on the demand for social work services.
- Explanations of the links between definitional processes contributing to social differences (for example, social class, gender and ethnic differences) to the problems of inequality and differential need faced by service users.

3.1.4 Social work theory
- The relevance of sociological perspectives to understanding societal and structural influences on human behaviour at individual, group and community levels.

Introduction

This chapter encourages you to understand the concept of the sociological imagination, and develop this in relation to service users' own lives and practice. As the National Occupational Standards for social work acknowledge, social work *intervenes at the points where people interact with their environments,* this chapter therefore will begin to locate social work practice within an understanding of wider underpinning structures. The concepts of structure and agency and their relevance to social work practice will be examined through clear consideration of core sociological theories such as Marxism, functionalism, symbolic interactionism and postmodernism. A range of practice examples and exercises will be used to encourage students to 'debunk society' and question taken for granted, common sense assumptions

The sociological imagination

Arguably, learning to think sociologically is one of the most important skills a social worker can bring to their practice. A sociological perspective enables social workers to step back from taken for granted assumptions about social life and encourages them to critically unpack these assumptions, to develop skills which enable them to link issues in their own lives (and in the lives of service users) to the 'bigger picture'. C.Wright Mills, a flamboyant American sociologist, first used the term *sociological imagination* to refer to the ability to link what happens in individuals' lives, to the social structures of the wider world. He talked about how the 'private troubles of men' effectively trapped them in their lives, as they understood only their immediate personal difficulties rather than understanding what was happening to them with reference to the histories in which they lived.

> *It is the idea that the individual can understand his own experience and gauge his own fate only by locating himself within his period, that he can know his own chances in life only by becoming aware of those of all individuals in his circumstances.*

(Mills, 1959, p12)

It is worth noting that Mills wrote at a time when language tended to be rather sexist. As you will see, Mills talks about 'men' although he is in fact referring to all human beings. He stresses the importance of locating or understanding individual issues with reference to the experiences of others in the same social group. For example, rather than conceptualising in individual terms the specific experiences of a man who is experiencing periods of low mood and depression after he was made redundant, Mills suggests that in order to gain a fuller understanding, we should locate that person's experiences within a broader understanding of the social and historical circumstances that underpin that individual's experience. So, rather than focusing upon the experience of depression and the person's inability to cope as the main problem, this would be understood in terms of the impact of economic and political conditions of the day. This may seem contrary to other teachings in social work which generally tend to begin from the fundamental assumption that social workers should treat all people as individuals. We need to take care here, as one position does not necessarily contradict the other. Clearly, it is extremely important that social workers do indeed relate to service users individually and recognise that everybody's circumstances and experiences are different. However, while ensuring that we are respecting individuals and taking time to understand each person's very particular circumstances, it is also important, as Mills suggested, for social workers to locate service users within an understanding of the *bigger picture* that underlies their lives. In other words, social workers need to use their sociological imagination to situate individuals within analyses of broader social structures and to comprehend the social processes which shape their lives.

By using our sociological imagination then, 'personal troubles' become reconfigured as public issues:

> *It is by means of the sociological imagination that men now hope to grasp what is going on in the world and to understand what is happening in themselves.*

(Mills, 1959, p14)

You may have come across a similar idea from feminist writings, where the phrase *the personal is political* is used to explain how the individual experiences of women's oppression are rooted in the structures, legislation, culture and economics of centuries of patriarchy, or male domination. Whether you agree with this position or not, the point to be understood here is that although the troubles of individuals are inherently personal and unique, they occur within a specific set of political, social and economic circumstances which shape and to some extent define the lives of individuals. Sociologists disagree on the *extent* to which society defines or constrains the lives of individuals and we will give more consideration to this debate later in this chapter. For now however, we wish to turn our attention to thinking sociologically or developing a sociological imagination. Peter Berger (1963) suggests that sociology enables us to *see the general in the particular*. In other words, thinking about how the general categories into which we fall, (for example, white, female, working class) shape our particular life experiences. Berger makes the case for deconstructing or debunking 'the familiar' in order to see the world differently.

ACTIVITY *1.1*

Debunking society

You should do this exercise individually and then discuss some of the issues raised, in small groups. Try and think about the themes that emerged in your group. Thinking about Berger's (1963) view that sociology helps us to see how the general shapes the particular, spend some time debunking the particular of your life from a sociological perspective. As a student who has recently started a social work degree, think about what general factors led to you commencing social work training. How did some or all of the factors listed below influence, help, or hinder you?

- *The social class you were born into.*

- *Area of living/neighbourhood.*

- *Culture.*

- *Socialisation/norms/values.*

- *School – including the school you went to, messages from teachers, peer groups, streaming/ability groups.*

- *Language.*

- *Gender.*

ACTIVITY *1.1 continued*

- *Race.*
- *Religion.*
- *Ability and disability.*
- *Family.*
- *Economy.*
- *Politics/policy.*
- *Groups and interaction.*

By doing this exercise, you will have hopefully had the opportunity to really think about the 'taken for granted' of your life. Very often, the factors that make up our individual biographies are unquestioned by us, as these become the facts of our lives, the things we take for granted. Studying sociology can often have the effect of illuminating our lives in ways that perhaps we have not thought of before. It enables us to ask *why?* Once you have started to develop a sociological imagination, you will probably find yourself becoming passionate about the subject and wanting to learn more and more. As Berger (1963) suggests, *Sociology is ... a passion. The sociological perspective is more like a demon that possesses one, that drives one compellingly, again and again, to the questions that are its own* (p36).

Once you have begun to challenge the familiar of your own life and see beneath the immediate reality that presents itself, you will begin to recognise and understand some of the factors that have shaped or constrained your path through life so far. It is not uncommon for students in our sociology classes who have returned to education after an unhappy time at school, to tell us that they have gone through their lives without really questioning what they have been told about their own academic ability. Once they have begun to deconstruct their lives more, they have been able to recognise how factors such as their social class, their race, their gender or other 'general' categories have significantly impacted upon their particular experiences. Perhaps this is true for you too. Possibly by the time you come to the end of your sociology module on your course, you will feel as though you are looking at your own life in a very different way, almost as if someone had turned the light on for you! You may be wondering why we have asked you to spend so much time thinking about your own lives so far, rather than using examples of service users. Mills is helpful here when he makes the point that those who think sociologically should not split their work from their lives, and implores that they use their life experience in their intellectual work. By understanding our own biographies in sociological terms then, this better equips us to comprehend the lives of those we work with.

Socialisation, values and culture

Sociologists use the term *socialisation* to refer to the lifelong process of learning which takes place to enable individuals to learn the 'rules' and norms of their society. Without this process, human beings simply could not function in their social system.

Culture refers to a way of life; it comprises a vast range of norms about how to act, think and behave. For most of us most of the time, our culture is absolutely taken for granted, as it is the backdrop or 'wallpaper' of our lives, which we are both absorbed by and indistinguishable from. As well as the norms, beliefs and rules that comprise culture, so too do components of living and lifestyle, such as religion, rituals, language, literature, costume, jokes, art, cartoons and other visual images. Our culture is rich and varied, and is transmitted to us throughout life via a range of powerful media. Human beings are socialised, or taught to fit into society, firstly by their parents and families (primary socialisation) and later on via various secondary sources such as the school, the peer group, media, and work organisations. Both primary and secondary socialisation teaches us important aspects of culture, that become our taken for grantedness about life.

ACTIVITY **1.2**

Aspects of culture

In small groups, think about the rules or norms of social life that you take for granted. Try to come up with a list of ten. It may help to imagine you are a creature from outer space: what things would your Martian find a bit strange that we take for granted?

Once you have done this, try to think about how you know about the rules or norms of social life you have listed. How do you know, for example, how to behave in your lecture theatre? How do you know what do in a supermarket, or at a bus stop?

Think points

Are there any differences between norms in one culture and norms in another? What about cultures within a culture? For example, working class culture/middle class culture; cultures based around religion or ethnicity; subcultures such as the hippy movement or the punk movement? Do these generate any differences from 'mainstream culture'?

Think also about specific types of culture, for example, the workplace culture. When you go on your practice placement, you will need to be able to demonstrate your competence around the norms and rules of the agency in which you are placed, in order to pass your placement. It would not be acceptable for example, to dress inappropriately or use the internet for your own purposes. It would be expected that you will behave in certain ways to your colleagues and service users. This latter example shows us that we never really stop being socialised. Although you may know that it is the norm to queue at the bus stop in the UK, or be quiet when you go in a place of worship, or pay for items before you leave the supermarket, you may not be entirely au fait with how to behave in a social work office and you may need to learn the rules of work and professional culture.

Our socialisation therefore, or the process by which we learn all the norms, values and practices of society, is lifelong.

Structure and agency

Sociologists are interested in looking at the patterns, processes and structures of social life, and the relationship between these and members of society. One of the most exciting, yet most daunting aspects of sociology for those who are new to it is that there are many different ways of looking at the world sociologically. Later in this chapter, we will introduce you to different sociological perspectives and consider some of the issues relevant to these. One core issue of debate for sociologists is to analyse the extent to which society shapes and controls what individuals do, versus, the extent to which human beings are the architects of their own lives. This is referred to as the structure/agency debate. At its simplest, this considers whether it is Society that determines, influences and constrains the individual's life over and above all other factors, or whether the Individual creates and shapes their own destiny by making choices, decisions and taking action in order to shape their own path through life.

Structural perspectives are those that adopt a macro level of analysis to emphasise the bigger picture in individuals' lives. In other words, although we go about our lives in various ways, structural sociologists argue that the underpinning structures or formations in society, ultimately shape and constrain individuals. So, although we might make an individual decision to become a student on a social work course, or buy a large house, or stay at home to look after our children, structural sociologists purport that these individual decisions are constrained decisions that are ultimately shaped by structures such as class, gender and ethnicity. Agency perspectives, on the other hand, emphasise the free will of the individual to act upon their environment, to interpret their reality, make decisions and choose their own paths throughout life. Agency perspectives adopt a micro view of the world; therefore they are interested in small-scale individual experiences rather than structures.

The structure/agency debate concerns not only the respective role of individuals in relation to society, but also influences the ways in which sociologists go about their business. Sociologists who engage in a structural level of debate are not interested in the small-scale experiences of individuals as their prime concern, rather they are interested in learning about patterns, structures and formations.

Sociological perspectives

Macro approaches

There are a number of different ways of thinking about society and the way in which it operates. We have already identified the structure/agency debate and the core difference between the two perspectives. It is now important to refine this further as we approach some of the main sociological perspectives. Structural approaches then, refer to sociological perspectives which examine society as a whole and regard the organisation and structure of society as determining, or at least greatly influencing, the lives of individuals. Within this broad approach however, there are two very distinct ways of conceptualising the world; these are consensus and conflict.

In short, consensus perspectives begin from the assumption that there is general agreement between members of society, who live together in co-operation with others. To this end, members of society have a strong sense of shared social values which enables there to be order and stability in social life.

Conflict theories, on the other hand believe that there are vast inequalities of power within society, that significantly determine life chances. Society is divided into different groups, who are essentially in conflict with one another.

Consensus theory: introducing functionalism

Perhaps the best place to begin when getting to grips with understanding functionalism is to borrow a well-rehearsed analogy from biology. Just as biologists understand the ways in which different bodily organs such as the heart, the brain, the kidneys, the lungs and so on, perform a specific function to keep the human body alive, so with society, its different components work in harmony with one common end, the survival and well-being of society. Social institutions such as the family, religion, education, the political system, the economy and the legal system exist because they perform important tasks which contribute to the maintenance and well-being of society. In the same way that the body is considered to be the 'whole' organism, which is maintained by the different parts identified above, so society, according to functionalists, is regarded as the 'whole' – or as a social system which comprises different component parts, working together to maintain the whole. According to Auguste Comte (1798–1857) who is largely credited for the origin of the term 'sociology' in 1839 and who influenced the development of the functionalist perspective, society is a system of interrelated parts each of which relies upon other parts for efficient functioning. For example, the education system is dependent upon the family to produce effectively socialised children who understand the early rules of school; the economy relies upon the education system to produce suitably educated and trained individuals to perform certain tasks so that jobs are filled by appropriately skilled workers; the family depends upon the economy to enable it to earn a livelihood to support family members, and so on.

Just as the main aim of the human body is to stay alive, survival is also the key goal of society. Talcott Parsons (1902–79) used the term social equilibrium to describe the ways in which healthy societies achieve a state of harmony or balance (1951). Parsons was influenced by Emile Durkheim (1858–1917), who argued that social order is crucial for any society to exist. Central to this is the existence of shared values, or value consensus.

ACTIVITY *1.3*

Pause for a minute to think about social order. We tend to take this for granted, only perhaps recognising its existence when things go wrong and stability is disrupted. Try to write down three examples of instances where social order has been disrupted, either locally, nationally or internationally, and think about the consequences. What happened? What was the effect of the disruption? How were things brought under control again?

You may have come up with suggestions such as the situation in Iraq following the displacement of Saddam Hussein in 2003; or protests against the introduction of student tuition fees; or you may have brought to mind more local examples such as race riots or football-related violence in your locality. If we think about the first example, vivid images of violence and confusion come to mind, with looting commonplace and the scenes on television depicting times of chaos and near anarchy. Authority had broken down as it was not clear where power resided. In his day, Durkheim used the term *anomie* to refer to a state where the norms governing social behaviour had broken down. Durkheim made the assumption that for any group to live co-operatively, social order was essential and there needed to be some common agreement among group members on how to behave towards each other, and upon what their priorities were as a group. He suggested that members of society co-operate with one another in order to pursue shared goals. Durkheim noted some differences, however, between pre-industrial and industrial society. In primitive society where people worked together on the land, Durkheim believed that a collective conscience emerged out of tradition, morality, shared beliefs and values that largely emerged from sharing similar lives and roles within communities. He called this *mechanical solidarity*. However, he suggested that as industrial society developed and lives became more complex, mechanical solidarity would inevitably break down and a new social order would develop that he referred to as *organic solidarity*. This reflected the fact that over time as working processes became more complex, individuals began to work away from the home and were involved in an increasingly specialist division of labour. In this way, individuals were forced into a situation where they become dependent upon one another for survival, as nobody could produce everything they needed in order to survive in modern society. Durkheim suggested that such interdependence generated organic solidarity, where bonds were based upon differences and co-dependence, rather than upon similarity and co-existence.

Utilising Durkheim's concept of the 'collective conscience' it is possible to understand the functionalist position that value consensus is fundamental to the survival and smooth running of society. The collective conscience both constrains and obliges individuals to act in certain ways. The understandings that emerge unite members of society in a unified whole and enable them to live co-operatively. Hence the collective conscience is rather like a 'social glue' that binds members of society together. According to the functionalist perspective, social relationships are structured and underpinned by the shared norms and values which constitute the collective conscience, and are transmitted from one generation to the next via the socialisation process that we discussed earlier.

ÅCTIVITY *1.4*

Try to list as many examples as you can which constitute the 'collective conscience' or 'social glue' in contemporary society. In other words, what shared values exist?

You may have identified values such as the value of human life; being safe; loyalty and faithfulness; valuing people's rights to their property; and so on. Depending upon your religious beliefs, you may identify some of these values as being present in religious teachings. In summary, shared norms and values perform a powerful social cohesion function for members of society, acting as a form of social control by perpetuating norms which are designed to curb certain behaviours. This is central in understanding functionalist thinking.

Functionalists do recognise that conflict can occur within society; however, they see it as being the result of temporary disturbances or 'blips' in the system, which are usually quickly corrected. A relatively recent example of such a disturbance would be the anti-war protests, that sociologists from this perspective might regard as a temporary phenomenon, or outlet of emotion or protest, that did not ultimately impact upon or change the system. Functionalists accept differences of interest but see the bigger picture as being one where shared values predominate, believing that all groups benefit if society runs smoothly. Furthermore, if people step out of line, society needs to have adequate means of ensuring that anti-social behaviour is dealt with and conformity re-established. This is important for the 'greater good' and for the equilibrium in society to be maintained.

Functionalism is often criticised for being deterministic in that it denies the existence of free will and choice, preferring to regard individuals as passive recipients of whatever the 'system' serves them. This is contested by social action theorists who, as we shall see later, reject the deterministic stance of structural theories, and contest the idea that systems possess qualities which can act upon individuals, preferring to see individuals as architects of their own lives. Additionally, functionalism has been criticised for its basic belief that shared values exist in society. As we shall see later in this chapter, Marxists argue that shared values are in fact ruling-class or bourgeois values, that serve the interests of the ruling class rather than everyone in society. Furthermore, it could be argued that contemporary Britain is a diverse society in which different values coexist.

A functionalist perspective of social work

The application of a functionalist perspective to the social work profession would conceptualise the profession as constituting one of the parts of society that fulfils certain functions and plays an important role in maintaining society. Martin Davies (1994) uses the analogy of social workers being like motor mechanics who perform an important role in the maintenance of society, and are pivotal in assisting marginalised individuals to be better integrated into society. The emphasis is upon *assisting service users to adjust* by educating them, helping them to change and supporting them to fit into mainstream society more effectively. The social worker is performing a useful role, to all intents and purposes smoothing over the rough edges around the periphery of society. Drawing upon the work of Parsons, social workers can be regarded as assisting those who have been 'incorrectly socialised' to fit back into society, so that they can engage in effective role performance. Individuals who are mentally ill, for example, need help to get better so that they can play a full role in society. Social work should be actively involved in curbing deviant behaviour and thereby contributing to the smooth running and successful functioning of the social system. Similarly, parents who fall short of 'good-enough parenting' should be assisted to perform the parenting role more effectively; their children who have experienced 'faulty socialisation' should be helped to relearn the norms and values of mainstream society in order to become good citizens of the future.

Clearly, this view is open to much criticism as it effectively locates the source of all problems on the individual, requiring him or her to change in order to be a fully functioning part of society, rather than seeing the system as being in any way culpable. However, it could be argued that much state-sponsored social work is premised upon the principle of assisting service users to fit into society, while those who do not are subject to the social control functions of the social work role. This can be seen particularly in the fields of mental health, childcare and youth justice, where social workers are empowered to implement legislation which curtails and controls individual 'dysfunctions'.

CASE STUDY

Paul is a 22-year-old man who works in a packing factory. He works long hours, mostly on night shifts, doing work that he finds largely unfulfilling, for which he gets paid a minimum wage. He has had a great deal of time off sick recently due to being depressed and feeling anxious. His poor mental health began 12 months ago following the death of his parents in a car crash and the subsequent break-up of his relationship six months afterwards. Paul's wife was pregnant when his parents were killed, but after their death, Paul wanted nothing more to do with her or the baby. It was just too painful; he did not want to know the child if his parents could not know their grandchild. Since the break-up however, Paul has felt unable to cope. Recently he has been wandering through town late at night muttering to himself. Last night, he was picked up by the police who found him on a high bridge in a distressed state. He was taken to the local hospital and agreed to be admitted as a voluntary patient.

Adopting a functionalist perspective, think about how Paul's circumstances might be considered. What would be the role of the social worker?

A functionalist analysis to this case would consider that Paul's behaviour is somewhat deviant, because it is preventing him from participating in society. He is unable to fulfil his social roles, of worker, father or husband. Paul's illness is costing society, both in terms of his health care and because he is not contributing to the upbringing of his newborn baby. A functionalist perspective would suggest that Paul must be taken care of by society in order to bring him back into the parameters of normality. The social worker would therefore have a responsibility, along with health care professionals, to help Paul become well again. Effective intervention would hopefully assist Paul to work through his loss and become reintegrated into society. It is hoped that he would return to work, possibly reunite with his wife and baby, or at least contribute to their lives financially.

Although this is a slightly exaggerated analysis, you will hopefully be able to understand how functionalism regards individuals who deviate from socially agreed norms, and understand how social work is regarded as being a key component part of society and performs an important function for the well-being of the whole.

Conflict theories: Introducing Marxism

In contrast to the above, conflict theories regard society as being characterised not by harmony and consensus, but by conflict. It is considered that conflict is a common and persistent feature in society, with some groups having clear and distinct advantages and power over others. Although there are a number of views encapsulated within this perspective, the best known and influential is Marxism.

The work of Karl Marx (1818–83) has been immensely significant in shaping social theory. Marx was a German political activist who dedicated his life to writing about the social class system and the endemic inequalities that permeated the lives of ordinary working people. He lived during a time when capitalism was beginning to emerge on a global scale. Marx was deeply uncomfortable with what he saw on a daily basis, people whose lives were blighted by poverty and despair, coexisting with those whose lives were characterised by opulent riches and affluence. Marx was very concerned by the conditions of the poor and believed there could be a fairer, more equal form of society.

Marx and social change

Marx was interested in how societies developed and evolved. He noted that in primitive societies members of society coexisted, sharing the production of food and material goods. There was no private property and no one owned the 'means of production'; rather, hunters and gatherers sourced from nature what they needed to sustain life, a truly 'classless society'. As time moved on however, society began to produce more goods than were needed to survive and so people began trading with one another. Production gradually became more specialised and a division of labour began to emerge; rather than families producing everything themselves that they required for survival, they could trade with others to ensure they had everything they needed. This meant that some people were able to achieve a surplus of wealth or a profit.

The ownership of private property gradually began to emerge and there was a need to secure clear lines of heritage through the emergence of the modern family so that property and wealth could be securely passed on. Over time, a class of successful owners of the means of production became economically and socially distinct from ordinary working people.

Famously, Marx wrote: The history of all hitherto existing society is the history of class struggles. *Marx suggested that in order to understand any period in history, it was necessary to understand the antagonism between oppressing and oppressed classes and the ongoing struggle between them. Simply put, Marx believed that inequalities in wealth necessarily generated tensions which ultimately led to conflict, and that this eventually brought about social change. This was true of both ancient society where the struggle was between masters and slaves, and feudal society where the struggle was between lords and serfs. Much of Marx's work, however, was dedicated to analysis of capitalist society, the form of economic and social system that we live in today, where the struggle is between the bourgeoisie and the proletariat.*

Marx argued that capitalist society was an inherently unequal system that was based upon the infrastructure of the economy (the base of society). Like consensus perspectives, Marx also regarded society as comprising interrelated parts, but the key difference was that Marx asserted that it was the base or the economy that strongly shaped all other components. In other words, the ways in which material goods were produced (which are necessary to sustain life) significantly influenced the rest of society. In capitalism, the economy is based around ownership of private property and it is this arrangement that, according to Marx, determines the operation of all other social institutions such as the political system, religion, the media, the family, the education system and so on. Marx referred to these components as the super-structure.

ACTIVITY **1.5**

Sometimes students tell us they find it difficult to understand Marx's concepts. However, if we take some time out to unpack some of his ideas, you will see that they are in many ways relevant to our own lives today. This activity is designed to help you begin to understand for yourself some of the concepts and terms used.

In simple terms, capitalism can be defined as a form of economic system in which there is private ownership of the means of production, or industry.

Try to think of some of the major corporations that exist today that employ workers in return for a wage. (In order to help you compile your list you might want to think about any soft drinks companies that you have bought a can from this week; any fast food place you have been to, the chocolate bars you have eaten; the fashion designers you buy your clothes from; the make of your CD or music player; the designer of your computer system or mobile phone and so on.)

You will often hear on the news when companies announce their profits. Alternatively have a look on the internet. What levels of profits do they make? How do you think they generate their profits?

How are you influenced by capitalism? You may wish to think of the way in which the advertising industry influences us to buy things, or you may wish to have a look through any glossy magazine lying around and see how cars, fashion and music are portrayed. What are the subtle and not so subtle means by which we as consumers contribute to the profits of large corporations?

By doing this exercise you will have hopefully begun to demystify some of Marx's ideas. You will probably have begun to recognise that society today is organised in such a way that some very wealthy people own large, multinational corporations that make significant amounts of money each year, and that they do this by using many persuasive techniques to encourage us to buy their products. Now we will carry on to begin to understand more of Marx's ideas.

Marx identified two main groups in capitalist society; the bourgeoisie, who owned the means of production (in the present day these are wealthy individuals such as the Richard Bransons or Bill Gateses of the world), and the proletariat or workers, who sell their labour to the bourgeoisie in return for a wage. An important point to understand is that the wage paid to the proletariat or workers is far less than the profit generated by them. In other words, although it is the workers that through their own hard effort, blood, sweat and tears physically produce goods such as aeroplanes, cars, CDs, clothes, food, and so on, the wages they are paid in return are relatively low when compared with the amount of money the goods are sold for, thereby generating a healthy profit or 'surplus value' for the capitalist class. Thus, importantly, Marx argued that an exploitative relationship occurs, with the bourgeoisie exploiting the proletariat.

Marx noted however, that the workers accepted this situation unquestioningly most of the time, and that this was due to a number of complex reasons. Essentially, he argued, the proletariat have been socialised to believe that this is the 'way of the world' – that the bourgeoisie are rightfully in their privileged positions because they have worked hard to get there, they are naturally bright, good leaders and deservedly businessmen and -women. Similarly, workers are socialised to believe that they are also in their rightful positions. This may have occurred through the education system where powerful messages are perpetuated around ability, or it may have occurred through religious belief systems which tend to portray inequality as being the will of a supreme being. Some of you will be familiar for example with the words of the well-known hymn 'All things bright and beautiful' which go like this: *The rich man in his castle, the poor man at this gate,* God made them high and lowly *and ordered their estate* [our emphasis]. You can see here how the message is transmitted that God has created some of us privileged and others of us not. Marx refers to this as 'false class consciousness', in other words, that the proletariat are socialised to accept the *status quo* as being normal and are unaware of their true exploited position.

Furthermore, Marx argued that norms and values, which form the backbone of society and are promoted by key institutions in society, are in fact, ruling-class norms and values. Marxists are critical here of functionalist thinking which regards shared norms and values as being applicable to all members of society; by contrast, Marx argues that in fact such values actually serve to maintain and perpetuate the unequal social system. Marxists refers to the set of beliefs and ideas which props up the system as 'ideologies'. In Britain and America, for example, there is an emphasis on material possessions, freedom and working hard. These values are extended to all members of society in subtle ways through the media, the education system, the family and other components of the superstructure. Marx argues that such values contribute to the dominance of the bourgeoisie or ruling class, as they subtly ensure that the proletariat continue to work hard for their wages, to buy as many material goods as they can afford in the belief that they are living free and privileged lives. In reality however, their hard work directly creates profit for the wealthy owners of the means of production, ensuring that they get richer, while the workers buy back the material goods that they in the first place have created. They do this under the belief that they are free, yet in reality they are slaves of the ruling class.

Marx developed the important concept of *alienation* to describe the way in which advanced productive processes in capitalism isolated workers both from their labour and from their true selves. Marx argued that in capitalist society, technology had replaced human beings in most aspects of production, such that workers were effectively machine operatives rather than skilled craftsmen and women. Marx suggested that this changed the very nature of work from being creative and fulfilling to being largely dull and monotonous. Workers on assembly lines were separated entirely from the end product of their labour and were likely to be entirely unfulfilled by their role in the process. Importantly, they were also separated from each other by the noise and speed of the production line. Thus Marx argued that workers would return home dehumanised and alienated from their work, from other workers and from themselves, *physically exhausted and mentally debased* (cited in Bottomore, 1963, p124).

Marx believed, however, that at some point in history the proletariat would ultimately come to see the true nature of their exploitation, and would join together in a state of true class consciousness and revolt. He argued that *The proletarians have nothing to lose but their chains* (Marx and Engels, 1969, p96) and that they would eventually unite to overthrow the system that had always oppressed them and replace it with a fairer communist society in which private property would be abolished and collective ownership would replace capitalism, where no one social group would exploit another.

Marxism has often been criticised for being inaccurate, as most of the regimes set up in Marx's name have been discredited and have collapsed. It is often argued that far from a revolution occurring, any sense of conflict has been weakened by the ideological attacks on the trade union movement and the legislative restraints that were placed on industrial relations in the 1980s. Like functionalism, Marxism is often regarded as being deterministic, as its basic premise is that economic forces differentially determine the social position of members of society. Social action theories reject this presumption, arguing that members of society engage in conscious human action which has the possibility of transcending social arrangements. Finally, Marxism is criticised by for being overly focused upon class, at the expense of other social divisions such as gender or race.

A Marxist perspective of social work

A Marxist analysis of social work begins from the starting point that social work is essentially part of the state apparatus, and as such reflects and reinforces the interests of the ruling class. Marxists dismiss claims that the state in capitalist societies is a neutral entity that reflects the interests of all citizens, making decisions in a neutral, unbiased manner. Rather, the state always acts in the interests of the bourgeoisie, including when it intervenes to provide welfare services. Like all those involved in welfare services, Marxists perceive social work as performing two key functions – a 'legitimation' function and an 'accumulation' function. By legitimation, Marxists mean that social work serves an ideological role, creating the image of a caring capitalism that is interested in the welfare of its citizens. It is the compassionate, civilised face of welfare and is seen by many as an example of society's preparedness to care for and support some of the most vulnerable members of society. Needless to say, Marxists perceive this image of social work to be a myth. Social work also performs an 'accumulation' function in that through discharging some of its 'welfare' functions it serves to enhance profits; for example, social workers are integrally involved in assisting people with 'the problems of living' which might otherwise prevent them from ful-filling roles as members of the workforce. In this sense, it is a component of the welfare state which performs a palliative role in capitalist society, tending to some of the worst excesses of capitalism while simultaneously maintaining the system. Like functionalists, Marxists point to the social control role of social work, but rather than perceiving this as being necessary for the whole of society, they argue that it is predominantly groups that are already excluded and marginalised that find them-selves on the receiving end of harsh and punitive measures of social control. Thus, according to Marxists, much of the social work role is based around surveillance, social control and blaming individuals:

> *For many...social work remains as the last safety net. But is a safety net with many holes, and one that comes at a high price. For many, to call upon the social services – or, more accurately, to be referred to them, since the vast majority of clients do not go willingly but are sent by the courts or other state welfare agencies – it is surrender...often the best that is on offer is friendly advice; at worse a moral condemnation – backed up by extensive powers.*
>
> (Jones and Novak, 1999, p80)

Marxists argue that poverty is a key and defining feature in the lives of many service users, and social workers need to understand this. However, rather than working to address poverty, social workers tend to be ignorant of it and work around and within poverty, rather than empowering service users to take action to bring about change. It is recognised that much (though by no means all) of social work is state sponsored and statutory in nature therefore by definition social workers are constrained in bring-ing about any real change. Utilising Davies's analogy of the motor mechanic, social workers are at best tinkering around the edges of the vehicle, rather than recognising that it is a new vehicle altogether that is needed. Marxist writers call for more con-sciousness-raising approaches that genuinely seek to empower service users to be active in their communities to bring about change. Radical social work in the 1970s began to adopt community approaches but was soon to be constrained by the advent of managerialism in the 1980s and 1990s where state social work became more tightly regulated and proceduralised. More recently, academics in Liverpool have developed a manifesto calling for a new approach to social work. It argues that *the need for a social work committed to social justice and challenging poverty and dis-crimination is greater than ever* (Jones et al., 2004, p1) and suggests that the profession can learn much from the service user movement which has developed innovative approaches to change, such as collective advocacy.

CASE STUDY

Revisiting the case study of Paul

Let us return briefly to the case study of Paul that we considered in the previous section. How would a Marxist analysis of Paul's circumstances differ from a functionalist analysis?

> **CASE STUDY** *continued*
>
> *Marxists would be more likely to see that Paul's depression was influenced by his working conditions. They would argue that the long hours that Paul put in at the packing factory had left him demoralised and alienated. Marxists would point to the bourgeoisie having little or no interest in human suffering; to them Paul is first and foremost a worker and a producer of wealth. Social work would be regarded by Marxists as having a role to play in assisting Paul to return to good health. The social work profession is regarded somewhat cynically as part of the state apparatus which performs various social control functions to ensure that capitalist society continues and functions to generate optimum profit for the ruling classes.*
>
> *Again, this is a somewhat simplistic analysis; however, hopefully you will understand how different perspectives adopt distinct ideological views on individuals who deviate from their social roles and come to the attention of the social work profession.*

Micro approaches

Both functionalism and Marxism are macro, structural theories which are concerned with the way in which society constrains individuals' lives. There are a range of approaches that are critical of the idea that structures influence and shape what individuals do. These are generically referred to as micro, social action perspectives and are concerned with the concept of 'agency' or the capacity of individuals to act upon the environment. The German sociologist Max Weber was significant in contributing to a theory of social action and was influential in the development of many subsequent schools of thought that shared basic assumptions about the primacy of the individual in creating society. Weber argued that in order to understand the social world, sociologists should begin by attempting to understand the subjective meanings that underpin human behaviour. He utilised the German term *verstehen* to emphasise the need to understand the social world from the point of view of those in it. He was critical of suggestions that sociologists could study the social world in the same way that scientists studied the natural world and stressed the need for sociologists to put themselves in the position of those being studied to really appreciate the subjective meanings behind experience. The concept of *verstehen* is consistent with the underpinning ethos of social work, which stresses the need for empathy and understanding of service users. For example, if a social worker visits a service user one day and discovers him or her frantically cleaning the house, the worker would need to understand whether the cleaning was because the service user had important guests coming to stay for the weekend, or as a displacement activity to avoid writing an essay for the college course they were on, or a sign of obsessive compulsive disorder, or something completely different altogether. In this example, you can see how the subjective meaning is key. *Verstehen* then, is a process that social workers use in their practice daily. This concept marks a distinct shift away from the ideas articulated by functionalism and Marxism, and has influenced the subsequent development of other micro theories.

Introducing symbolic interactionism

Symbolic interactionism is a micro, 'agency' theory which is interested in the way that individuals shape their own experiences within society. Symbolic interactionism is concerned with the small-scale interactions that take place between individuals and with the meanings and interpretations that people give to action. Key writers such as George Herbert Mead, Charles Horton Cooley, William Isaac Thomas, Herbert Blumer and Erving Goffman have made a significant contribution to symbolic interactionism.

Symbolic interactionism is critical of structural perspectives that suggest that human beings are passive recipients of the hand that society deals them. It rejects claims that actions are determined by social forces, and by adopting an analogy of a game of cards, symbolic interactionists suggest that although individuals might be dealt a hand of cards by society, the individual *chooses* how to play those cards, *interprets* the meaning of the hand dealt, *decides* what moves to make, how to interpret the rules of the game and indeed, whether to play the hand at all. This differs from structural perspectives that regard individuals' lives as being shaped and determined by the hand that was dealt by society.

Symbolic interactionists begin from the position that human beings differ from animals in one important respect – that they have the ability to think and reflect upon experience. Mead (1934) suggested that thinking was simply *an internalised or implicit conversation of the individual with himself* (p47). This enables individuals to test out situations in their own minds, as well as to interpret symbols in the social world and apply meanings to them. This is the basis of all interaction, and ultimately the basis of all society. We live in a symbolic world, in which symbols and gestures have shared meanings. Common meanings are passed on through the socialisation process, so it is likely that if you see someone waving at you, or sticking their thumb up, or possibly making a rude gesture to you, you will know what is being communicated; you may not know why, but you are able to hypothesise in an internal conversation with yourself about the meaning of the gesture and possibly even the motive. However, meanings of symbols may generate different interpretations to different people. Blumer (1969) sums this up: *A tree will be a different object to a botanist, a lumberman, a poet and a home gardener (p11).* This links with Weber's concept of *verstehen* that we discussed earlier: it is important to be able to understand things from the point of view of the other person. Meanings are context specific. For example, the act of shooting someone dead may command a sense of outrage and revulsion on the streets of Manchester, but may generate feelings of bravery, heroism and duty if carried out in times of war. The act is the same, but the interpretation of the act and the subsequent meaning applied to it are very different. Similarly, it is unlikely that anyone would be too phased by a topless woman on a beach in Greece; however, if the same woman walked topless down a local high street in Britain, it is highly likely she would generate an altogether different reaction. Meanings are also subject to change over time; for example, we may make an initial judgement about someone but later refine our view of them.

Symbolic interactionists note the power of symbols to communicate different messages; for example, someone who drives a Rolls Royce communicates a different image to someone who drives a Metro. As a student on a social work course, it is important that you reflect upon the way that you communicate to people, both in terms of the way you present, the clothes you wear, and the language you use, as we are all communicating things all of the time, even when we don't intend to.

For symbolic interactionists then, it is the interpretation of meanings and the billions of micro interactions that take place every minute of the day that constitute society. Individuals constantly create and re-create 'society', rather than 'society' existing as an objective entity endowed with the ability to act upon its members.

The concept of 'self' holds central importance to symbolic interactionists, who argue that unlike animals, all human beings have a self. Mead (1934) suggests that this is evident when we consider that individuals can undergo experience and be aware of that experience. They have the capability to reflect and be aware of how they present to others. Mead suggests that individuals have what he refers to as an 'I' and a 'Me'. The 'I' is the part of the self which stems from basic impulses; it is the instinctual inner self that is to a large extent unpredictable. You may recall a situation where you appeared to act spontaneously almost on instinct or 'gut feeling'. Mead suggests that it is in the 'I' that our true selves are located, raw, undeveloped and unrefined. The 'Me' however, is the part of the self which receives information from the outer world. It is the more developed and refined part of the self which curbs our basic impulses by receiving feedback from others which allows individuals to live comfortably within society. Mead says that an ongoing internal dialogue takes place between the 'I' and the 'Me', with the result being the *social self*, which is constantly being developed and defined.

Similarly, Cooley (1902) utilises the term 'looking glass self' to describe the ways that we see ourselves based upon or reflecting how we think others see us. The components to this are:

- how individuals are able to imagine how they appear to others;
- how they are able to imagine how others judge the way they appear;
- how individuals develop feelings as a result, often of pride or mortification.

It might help here to give an example. Lucy goes out with her friends one night; she consumes some alcohol and feels sociable and amusing. Lucy is quite 'loud', laughing a lot, telling jokes and generally being the centre of attention. At the time, she is confident that she is coming over as being funny and the life and soul of the party. She imagines that she is popular and vivacious. She goes home to bed, wakes up the next morning with a hangover, and more importantly with utter feelings of horror that she was so loud and brash. She is mortified and feels a great deal of shame and embarrassment. Lucy decides that she is not a good person and that everyone must have been talking about her. She decides to stay in for a while. This example should help you to understand how the 'looking-glass self' contributes to the development of the self concept, or the way that people feel about themselves. You may consider that this is overly psychological in nature. However, importantly, symbolic interactionists are making the point that individuals navigate their way through society by interacting and negotiating with others and that central to this is the way in which individuals' sense of self interacts with and is shaped by others.

Insights for social work

Interactionists are concerned with how actions come to be defined in a certain way and the processes that are involved. This is particularly significant for social workers who are often involved in working with individuals who have labels attached to them, and indeed, they may be involved in assigning labels to individuals. An important consideration is how some individuals come to be defined as delinquent, or mentally ill, or unfit parents for example, whereas others do not. A whole range of factors are important here, including the preconceived ideas, experiences and values of those applying the label. A process of negotiation occurs between the 'actors' or individuals involved in the scenario, who are continually involved in interpreting and then constructing definitions and meanings. The concept of 'labelling' is important; this refers to the process whereby labels are applied to individuals, which evoke certain images and stereotypes. A self-fulfilling prophecy may occur whereby individuals take on the characteristics of the labels assigned to them and start acting accordingly. These ideas are looked at more fully in Chapter 6 in relation to youth crime and asylum, but here we want to use mental health as an example to help you make sense of interactionist thinking and labelling theory.

Thomas Szasz (1972) makes the radical proposition that in fact there is no such thing as mental illness *per se*; rather he suggests that 'mental illness' is more accurately behaviour that others disapprove of, which becomes labelled in a particular way. He argues that:

> *Mental illness is a myth. Psychiatrists are not concerned with mental illness and their treatments. In actual practice, they deal with personal, social and ethical problems of living.*
>
> (1972, p269)

Szasz claims that 'mental illness' must be considered within an understanding of the social context in which it occurs. He rejects any biological basis to mental illness and queries the use of the term 'illness' altogether. He draws attention to the process by which doctors over the years have treated people who act strangely 'as if they were ill', and he claims that over time the 'as if' has been dropped and people are now treated *as ill*, thereby creating the myth of mental illness. In reality then, people who present with 'mental illness' are really showing outward effects of a range of problems that arise throughout life, but they are doing so in ways that generate a social response of disapproval. Szasz draws attention the subtleties of social construction and the ways in which meanings are derived: *If you talk to God, you are praying; if God talks to you, you have schizophrenia. If the dead talk to you, you are a spiritualist, if you talk to the dead, you are a schizophrenic* (1973, p113). He suggests, for example, that the 'mental illness' called 'depression' is in reality a dramatisation of not being happy. In other words, it is about how experience is defined and classified. Szasz attacks the power of psychiatrists to construct *illness* and refers to this role as being one of 'social manipulator' that punishes, coerces, incarcerates and classifies patients.

Szasz's work has been the subject of a great deal of criticism, in particular from medical professionals who argue that there is a medical basis for many forms of mental illness and that denying the existence of such could lead to some patients being untreated.

Although controversial, Szasz's ideas have been supported by others who broadly fall within the interactionist paradigm. Edwin Lemert (1972) for example, writing about paranoia, argued that rather than being a form of illness, paranoia is best understood in relation to the process and relationships that surround it. He discusses the ways in which people who are 'paranoid' or suspicious interact with others. Let us consider an example of Fred, who starts a new job in an office. Fred is uneasy around people, which contributes in turn to other people feeling uneasy around Fred; no one in the office can quite put their finger on it, but they find him slightly 'hard work'. Fred is invited to the office Christmas party but declines because he feels the night would be an ordeal. The others are slightly relieved that Fred does not attend and next time there is a social night out, they do not invite Fred as they assume he will not go anyway. Fred however, is aware of the night out and feels excluded because he was not invited. He reacts against this by becoming even more uncomfortable around his colleagues, and avoiding them by not going to the staff room at all during lunch; he hardly speaks to his colleagues now because he feels so alienated. This new reaction from Fred provides justification for his colleagues to further exclude him as they assume he is a loner at best, or is rude at worst. The colleagues start to discuss Fred's strange behaviour, but they do so covertly, to prevent any further reaction. Fred is aware that others are talking about him and starts to feel paranoid. Far from being a 'mental illness', Lemert would argue that Fred's paranoia is based in reality – he *is* being talked about. This has developed out of the social interactions in his workplace.

Let us stop here and assume that Fred's feelings of paranoia become quite serious and lead him to take time off work and eventually to attend the GP's surgery, where he breaks down and tells the doctor how he feels. The doctor in turn might tell Fred that he is suffering from paranoia. Fred however, decides to take positive action and leave his job to work elsewhere. Largely because of his experiences in the first workplace, Fred begins his new job once again feeling uneasy and worrying about being excluded. His lack of confidence contributes to a similar scenario arising. A vicious circle has developed here for Fred who begins to live up to the label of 'paranoid'.

However, Lemert is keen to stress that rather than having any medical basis, the label 'paranoid' has been constructed out of social processes and relationships. He recognises that individuals can be stigmatised by public labelling and refers to this as secondary deviance; in other words, it is not the original act that was a problem, but the public reaction to it. In Fred's case, it was the interrelated chain of events that led to his paranoia, but the label applied to him classifies him as being 'mentally ill'.

By considering the application of some of the core principles to mental illness, you will hopefully be able to make sense of symbolic interactionism, which is very different to the structural theories that we have so far considered. A symbolic interactionist analysis of social work would be concerned with the individual or micro interactions that take place between social workers and their service users. The principle of *verstehen* is at the centre of practice, emphasising the importance of understanding issues from the viewpoint of the service user. As we have seen, attention to process is important, particularly as social workers hold potentially powerful roles that are capable of assigning labels.

Symbolic interactionism can be criticised for failing to take account of structure when considering human interaction. To deny that social structures impact upon individuals' experiences is regarded by structural sociologists as being naive at best and negligent at worst. Symbolic interactionists have also been criticised for explaining why people act in certain ways in the first place; by overly concentrating upon social reaction, they fail to explain the original act. Ironically, symbolic interactionism has also been criticised for failing to acknowledge more 'microscopic' features such as the 'unconscious', and factors like emotions, motivations and intentions.

Reconciling structure and agency? A way forward for social workers

Although this chapter has broadly separated sociological theories into those which fall under 'structure' and those which fall under 'agency', this dichotomy is to an extent academic for social workers, who may find it more useful to adopt a more eclectically informed approach to their practice. Giddens (1984) uses the concept *structuration* to identify the mutuality of structure and agency; he argues that each is dependent upon and mutually reinforcing of the other. In other words, billions of social actions carried out by billions of individuals create and maintain structures, and simultaneously it is through structures that social actions occur. Although his work has been criticised for lacking an adequate theoretical base, Giddens does offer the possibility of reconciling structure and agency. We began this chapter by arguing that it was essential for social workers to develop a sociological imagination, and by suggesting that they need to be able to locate firstly themselves in the 'bigger picture', but also importantly, be able to locate their service users. Central to this is undoubtedly an understanding of structure. Social workers must have a clear understanding of the unequal nature of society and the way that this impacts upon the lives of service users. However, it is also important for social workers to understand the micro-level issues that are important in service users' lives. Another way of thinking about this is that for some service users, micro level issues are likely to be individual manifestations of inequality. The social work value base is premised upon the fact that social workers should treat people as individuals and respect individual circumstances, and clearly this is extremely important. However, our view is that this should be done within an understanding of the context of the system that people live their lives in.

Both micro and macro perspectives offer valuable insights for social workers who intervene with individuals, but who must do so reflectively and critically, taking into account the impact of structure. However, it would be inappropriate to conclude this chapter without considering more recent developments in sociology. In the final section, we introduce you to some of the key ideas of postmodernism.

Postmodernism

The label 'postmodernism' is one of a number of different terms which have been used to describe the same, or a broadly similar set of processes. Some writers, for example, prefer to use the term post-Fordism, post-industrialism and post-structuralism to refer to the same set of changes and developments, all of which are said by some sociologists to be characteristic of a movement from the 'modernist' era to a new 'postmodern' era.

Clearly, when we talk about post-something or other, we are referring to a later period, a later social order, or a later event. For example, the term 'post-Second World War' is used to refer to the period after the Second World War. In a similar vein, the term postmodernism is used to denote a period, an era, after 'modernism' – hence postmodernism. It might, therefore, be a good idea to begin by looking at the key characteristics of 'modernism', and then we will be in a better position to understand and assess the changes and developments which supposedly led to the development of a 'postmodern' society. It is perhaps worth pointing out that many of the claims made by advocates of postmodernism have not remained uncontested, not least because they challenge the foundations of many key sociological thinkers.

What is modernism?

The modernist period is said to have been characterised by a shift away from explanations of social life that were based on tradition or religion, and movement towards a belief in reason, rationality and the potential of human beings to shape the world and discover universal truths. Hence, the modernist era is said to have been symbolised by a belief in the validity of 'big', overarching political and sociological theories, which purported to be able to explain the world and point the way to a better future. This was, in short, a period when it was assumed that humankind could control the natural world through rational thought and planning, and that it was possible to consciously design a better society. As we have seen, the founding thinkers of sociology sought to provide holistic explanations for how societies work, based upon the notion that it was possible to provide a 'universal' grounding for truth and/or develop a universal strategy that would lead to human emancipation. Although interpretations of the world varied, all were convinced that they could explain past and future patterns of human development. Postmodernists, such as Jean-Francois Lyotard (1984) refer to the theories of those such as Durkheim, Weber and Marx as 'grand narratives', or 'metanarratives'. How then does the new 'postmodern' era that we are said to be living in now differ from the 'modernist' period?

Postmodernist thought

According to postmodernists, the postmodern world is characterised by a loss of faith in 'grand narratives'. As Fiona Williams (1992) explains, with postmodernism there is:

> *an indifference to grand theory – the meta narratives – of either classic Marxism or Parsonian functionalism, or indeed any theory which seeks to establish a total picture or to suggest forms of universalism, determinism, or truth.*

> (p206)

One of the main reasons that postmodernists dismiss the validity of 'grand narratives' is their belief that they are based upon a 'single truth' and that their implementation will often involve the suppression of 'other truths'. At worst, the dogged pursuit of a 'utopia' through a set of universal principles may lead to oppression or totalitarianism, as evidenced in former communist countries, where political freedom and the rights of minorities were sacrificed in the name of the 'common welfare'. At best, the pursuit of an emancipatory strategy, based on a universal grounding for truth (that is, a particular set of ideas and beliefs), may mean that in the quest for the 'common good', particular needs are ignored and not met. Hence, postmodern critiques of welfare and social work have, with some justification, drawn attention to the postwar British welfare state, where a universal 'one size fits all' model of welfare delivery failed to acknowledge or meet the particular needs of particular welfare users, such as women, minority ethnic groups, older people and disabled people.

That this potential for diverse and particular needs to be subsumed by the universalism of grand narratives is a theme that runs throughout postmodernist approaches to welfare and social work. In this sense, as Ferguson (2006) notes, the attractions of postmodernism are obvious. 'Mass', ideologically driven welfare policy failed to acknowledge the voices, desires and needs of some groups of service users, and postmodernist perspectives, with their celebration of fragmentation and particularism, offer us the basis for a new politics. The changes described by postmodernism should, it could be argued, therefore be welcomed and embraced by policy-makers and practitioners. The fragmentation of political life, epitomised by the shift towards self-organisation and self-advocacy among different groups of service users, should be celebrated. Recognition can now be given to those voices that have hitherto been ignored. Commitment to old-style universalism should be abandoned in favour of more specialised, targeted services developed to take account of the diverse needs of 'newly enfranchised' particular groups. In short, the new 'postmodern' world in which we are living should be embraced with enthusiasm.

Discussion

Postmodernism's claims concerning the demise of 'grand narratives' seem to be accurate. Internationally, the ideas of Marx have been discredited with the fall of communism, while domestically, the UK Labour Party appears to have dropped its commitment to socialism in favour of a pragmatic, non-ideological 'what works' approach.

However, the contribution of postmodernism to sociology and social welfare and social work is a matter of dispute. Postmodernism is perceived by some theorists as being premature in its belief in the demise of grand narratives. Marxists, in particular, dispute this latter claim. Alex Callinicos (1989), a prominent Marxist critic of postmodernism, argues that postmodernism's celebration of the 'local' has led it to miss the 'big picture' and hence fail to acknowledge the devastating impact that recent social, economic and political changes have had on huge sections of the population. Postmodernism, he argues, has little to say about what really are the key developments affecting contemporary capitalist societies. In the economic sphere, these include the wholesale transfer of manufacturing industries to developing countries, the end of full employment, and the growth in low-paid, insecure work. In the 'social' sphere, they include the retrenchment of social rights, the infusion of market principles into welfare services, and a more explicit focus on disciplining the poor in social welfare and social work. These developments should, Callinicos insists, be seen precisely for what they are – attempts by capitalists and their political representatives to do what they have always done: maximise profits, cut public expenditure and control the working population. Ruling-class interests are the real driving force behind such changes, and in this sense, postmodernists are naïve and premature to talk of the demise of Marxism's potential. It is, Marxists insist, an odd time to be debating the obsolescence of a class-based explanation for social and economic change, when over the past 30 years economic and social policies in the UK have contributed to, on the one hand, staggering increased incomes for the rich, yet on the other hand, a massive increase in insecurity, and poverty among the working class.

Postmodernism's celebration of political fragmentation that has accompanied the emergence of new social movements and 'issue politics' has also been criticised. Few would dispute that in the past, the claims of such groups have often been ignored by both the labour movement and established political parties. Nor is the recent positive contribution made by new social movements to politics, social policy and social work a matter of contention. However, some theorists have pointed to what they see as the 'dangers' of political fragmentation. The pursuit of sectional interests can, for example, lead particular social groups to fail to acknowledge their shared interests, or their common sites of oppression. Marxists, for instance, argue that there is a common obstacle to the pursuit of effective civil rights for disabled people, black people and women – that is, employers and their pursuit of profit. Organisations representing business such as the Confederation of British Industry and the Institute of Directors have consistently opposed the introduction of anti-discriminatory legislation for these social groups on the grounds of cost. The danger, Marxists argue, is that the fragmented nature of the strategies and demands of new social movements can, firstly, prevent them from acknowledging their 'common enemy', and secondly, dilute their overall political influence and leverage. Political fragmentation can also be used by governments to divide groups whose interests are, in reality, very much the same. As Ferguson (2006) points out, *it can allow governments, whose overriding concern is limiting welfare expenditure, to play one group off against another as they squabble over the limited resources on offer* (p172).

In conclusion, postmodernism is accused by its critics of failing to adequately explain the changes it identifies, having an inadequate grasp of the power relations that underpin those changes, and in doing so acting as an inadvertent 'ideological smokescreen', obscuring the very real political interests that are driving policy.

C H A P T E R   S U M M A R Y

Incorporating a sociological perspective to social work practice enables social workers to locate service users within an understanding of the 'bigger picture'. This is important so that social workers can recognise the structural underpinnings of many of the issues and problems that service users present with. The Structure/Agency debate in sociology analyses the extent to which society constrains the lives of individuals, versus, the extent to which human beings shape and control their own lives. Although there are very many differing sociological perspectives, this chapter has chosen to focus upon Functionalism, Marxism, Symbolic Interactionism and Postmodernism.

FURTHER READING

For students who are new to sociology, there are a range of textbooks available that introduce you to the discipline, including **Haralambos, M, Holborn, M and Heald, R** (2004) *Sociology, themes and perspectives*. 6th edition. London: Collins; and **Giddens, A** (2006) *Sociology*. 5th edition. Cambridge: Polity Press.

For a comprehensive consideration of key debates and theoretical concepts, see **Ritzer, G** (2000) *Sociological theory*. Maidenhead: McGraw-Hill.

Chapter 2
Poverty and social work service users

ACHIEVING A SOCIAL WORK DEGREE

This chapter will help you begin to meet the following National Occupational Standards and General Social Care Council's Code of Practice.

Key Role 1: Prepare for, and work with individuals, families, carers, groups and communities to assess their needs and circumstances
- Work with individuals, families, carers, groups and communities to help them make informed decisions.

Key Role 2: Plan, carry out, review and evaluate social work practice, with individuals, families, carers, groups, communities and other professionals
- Apply and justify social work methods and models used to achieve change and development, and improve life opportunities.

Key Role 6: Demonstrate professional competence in social work practice
- Implement knowledge based social work models and methods to develop and improve your own practice.

General Social Care Council Code of Practice

Code 1.1: Treating each person as an individual.

Code 1.4: Respecting and maintaining the dignity and privacy of service users.

Code 1.5: Promoting equal opportunities for service users and carers.

Code 1.6: Respecting diversity and different cultures and values.

It will also introduce you to the following academic standards as set out in the social work subject benchmark statements.

3.1.1 Social work services and service users
- The social processes (associated with, for example, poverty, unemployment, poor health, disablement, lack of education and other sources of disadvantage) that lead to marginalisation, isolation and exclusion and their impact on the demand for social work services.
- Explanations of the links between definitional processes contributing to social differences (for example, social class, gender and ethnic differences) to the problems of inequality and differential need faced by service users.
- The nature and validity of different definitions of, and explanations for, the characteristics and circumstances of service users and the services required by them.

3.1.4 Social work theory
- The relevance of sociological perspectives to understanding societal and structural influences on human behaviour at individual, group and community levels.

3.1.5 The nature of social work practice
- The characteristics of practice in a range of community-based and organisational settings including group-care, within statutory, voluntary and private sectors, and the factors influencing changes in practice within these contexts.

Introduction

As poverty is a key and defining feature in the lives of many social work service users, this chapter will consider debates about the nature of poverty in modern 'developed' societies, and examine different sociological explanations for the causes of poverty. You will be encouraged to examine your own values and beliefs about poverty and the implications of these for practice. The chapter will discuss the impact of poverty on people's lives and then, drawing upon parallel social work theories, it will consider practical empowering approaches of working with service users who live in poverty.

The relevance of poverty for social workers

Those who use, and are required to use, social work services continue overwhelmingly to be poor and disadvantaged.

(Smale et al., 2000, p18)

Social work service users are among the most impoverished people in Britain and for many, poverty defines their lives. The relationship between poverty and social work is not new, yet it is one that remains understated and implicit in social work training courses and practice. There is an unspoken assumption that poverty is an inherent and integral feature of service users' lives. Certainly, poverty provides the context for other factors that can increase the likelihood of contact with social services. For example, unemployment, social isolation and low incomes can be contributory factors in causing problems such as family break-up, poor health, and difficulties in caring for children and other dependents. Similarly, poverty can increase the likelihood of children being looked after by the care services; of older adults going into residential care; and of admission to a psychiatric ward (Joseph Rowntree Foundation, 1995; Becker 1997; Smale et al., 2000; Social Exclusion Unit, 2004b). Much social work practice therefore takes place within and around poverty. One major criticism of the social work profession is that social work often intervenes without attempting to bring about change in this area of life. However, given the often devastating consequences of poverty, it is not sufficient to work around poverty; later on in this chapter, we will be considering ways of working with service users to challenge the structures which constrain their opportunities and choices. We need to begin, however, by considering what we understand the term poverty to mean and by examining sociological explanations for its existence.

Definitions of poverty

There is no consensus over what constitutes poverty. For some, such as Bartholomew (2006), poverty means a lack of basic necessities, such as food, clothing and shelter. In academic and policy terms, this is often referred to as *absolute poverty*. This takes no account of prevailing living standards. The emphasis is on basic physical needs (rather than cultural or social needs). Absolute definitions, therefore, provide a very meagre view of poverty; for example, a young homeless person who has occasional access to a hostel where she or he can obtain a meal, a bed and charitable clothing, would not be considered poor if a strict absolute definition of poverty was applied. Similarly, a family of five living in damp, overcrowded housing on a deprived estate, in an area of high unemployment, relying upon benefits to survive, would not be considered to be in poverty. In both these cases, individuals have access to the basic requirements to sustain life, and hence they are not considered poor. If we accept this as a legitimate definition of poverty, then very few people are poor in Britain today.

You can perhaps see how absolute definitions of poverty can be attractive to politicians who may want to underestimate levels of poverty, or even deny its existence. For example, in the 1980s and 1990s Conservative ministers used absolute definitions to refute claims that Britain had a significant poverty problem and that their policies had led to increased levels of poverty. The problem of poverty was 'defined away'. Poverty did not exist and in policy-making terms there was no need to do much about it.

Absolute definitions of poverty, however, have been heavily criticised for failing to take into account the prevailing living standards of the day. Most now accept that relative definitions of poverty are more appropriate indicators for measuring poverty in developed countries such as the UK. Peter Townsend provided the classic definition of *relative poverty* in his 1979 book, *Poverty in the United Kingdom*:

> *Individuals, families and groups in the population can be said to be in poverty when they lack the resources to obtain the types of diets, participate in the activities and have the living conditions and amenities* which are customary, *or at least* widely encouraged or approved, *in the societies to which they belong. Their resources are so seriously below those commanded by the average individual or family that they are, in effect,* excluded from ordinary living patterns, customs and activities.
>
> (Townsend; 1979, p31; emphasis added)

As can be seen from the above quote, relative definitions are much broader than absolute ones. The emphasis is on the 'types of diets' that are 'customary' (and not just food needed to secure life), and living standards and conditions which are 'encouraged or approved' (rather than a mere roof over the head, or clothes provided by a charitable organisation). If we adopt a relative definition, therefore, significant numbers of people are in poverty in Britain today. In policy-making terms, poverty becomes a 'problem' and there is more pressure for governments to do something about it.

One of the difficulties with relative definitions of poverty, however, is that when it comes to creating a precise 'poverty line' there is considerable scope for disagreement and controversy. While we may agree it is desirable that poverty lines take into account prevailing standards of living, we might not agree about exactly what living conditions, patterns and amenities should be considered 'customary'. How do we determine who is 'excluded from ordinary living patterns, customs and activities'? For example, should an individual or family that does not have sufficient income to enable them to access a television, a telephone, or presents for their children on special occasions be considered 'poor'? *'Consensual' relative definitions* of poverty seek to overcome such difficulties by seeking to establish what 'most' people think is an acceptable standard of living (hence the term 'consensual'), and then assessing the numbers of people living below that standard. The 1999 Poverty and Social Exclusion Survey was one such study.

The poverty and social exclusion survey

The Poverty and Social Exclusion Survey (PSE Survey) gathered together a representative sample of the population and placed in front of them a series of 52 cards, each of which had written on it a particular good or service – for example, 'television', 'access to the internet', 'holiday once every two years'. People were then asked to place the cards into two piles; in one pile, goods and services they considered to be 'socially perceived necessities' (i.e not necessities needed to sustain life, but goods and services needed for people to participate in what Townsend refers to as 'ordinary living patterns, customs and activities'). In the other pile, they were asked to place those items they did not consider to be 'socially perceived necessities'. If more than half of the people in the survey said a particular good or service (for instance, a television) was a socially perceived necessity, the authors of the survey included it in their basket of goods and services that all families should be able to afford to purchase or access.

The authors of the PSE Survey then used their basket of socially perceived necessities as a yardstick to assess the extent of poverty in Britain. They decided that if an individual or family lacked two or more of their socially perceived necessities because they could not afford them (not because they did not want them – some people might not want a television), then they could be considered to be in poverty. The study found that 28 per cent of the population were lacking two or more socially perceived necessities because they could not afford them. Hence, 28 per cent of the population were in poverty. Poverty, however, was not shared equally across the population. Certain social groups – perhaps not surprisingly, groups that research suggests are the most frequent users of social work services – were more likely to be in poverty than other social groups. For example, 70 per cent of those on Income Support were in poverty, as were 62 per cent of lone parents, 61 per cent of disabled people, 61 per cent of local authority tenants and 57 per cent of housing association tenants. Younger people were also more likely to be poor – 34 per cent of 16–24 year olds and 38 per cent of 25–34 year olds were in poverty. In addition, a much higher rate of poverty was found for non-white ethnic groups, especially among Bangladeshi and black ethnic groups (Gordon et al., 2000, p23).

In this exercise we want you to try replicating the PSE Survey. Listed below are a range of goods and services. Get together with a group of friends or fellow students and as a group try dividing the list into two categories: 'socially perceived necessities' and 'not socially perceived necessities'. Whilst doing so, discuss the relative merits of each. You may wish to think about what you wouldn't want to be without.

- Access to the internet.
- A television.
- A telephone.

- Attending weddings/funerals.
- Washing machine.
- Medicines prescribed by doctor.

ACTIVITY 2.1 *continued*

- Toys for children.
- A fridge.
- Christmas presents for children.
- Birthday presents for children.
- A warm coat.
- Attending a place of worship.
- Dictionary.
- Roast joint or vegetarian equivalent.
- Going to the pub once a fortnight.
- Two pairs of all-weather shoes.

- Fresh fruit and vegetables daily.
- Holiday away from home once a year without relatives.
- Car.
- Regular savings of £10 per month (for rainy days or retirement).
- Dressing gown.
- CD player.
- Carpets in living room and bedrooms.

At the end of this exercise, you will probably have become aware of the contentious nature of establishing a precise relative poverty line!

It is partly a result of the controversy over establishing a precise relative definition of poverty that some have advocated the use of *income-based relative definitions*. With income-based relative definitions, an assessment is made as to what percentage of average income is needed to secure a decent 'socially acceptable' standard of living, and people living on incomes below that standard are considered to be in poverty. It is a 'relative' definition because it tracks average income and hence takes into account general improved standards of living. For example, let us say (hypothetically) that in 2006 average income was £400 per week, and that it was determined that an income of at least 60 per cent of average income was necessary to secure a decent 'socially acceptable' standard of living. Here, the poverty line would be £240 per week. If, however, in 2007, average income increased to £800 per week, the poverty line for that year would increase to £480 (because this is 60 per cent of 800). The advantage of this kind of definition of poverty is that it ensures that the poverty line keeps track with average standards of living – as the living standards of those on average incomes improve, so too do the living standards of those on poverty-line incomes. Another advantage is that this definition sidesteps debates about what goods and services are 'appropriate', one of the main drawbacks of consensual, relative definitions of poverty.

The Child Poverty Action Group (CPAG), and other groups that campaign on behalf of people on low incomes, have long called for poverty to be measured using income-based relative definitions. Significantly, Labour governments since 1997 have chosen to adopt such an approach, defining poverty (as our example did above) as the numbers of individuals living on incomes that are below 60 per cent of the average after housing costs. To give you some idea as to the monetary equivalent of this measurement, in 2004/05 a lone parent with two children aged 5 and 11 was in poverty if his or her income was below £186 per week (£9,672 per year) after housing costs. The poverty line for a couple with two children aged 5 and 11 was £282 per week (£13,936 per year) (CPAG, 2006, p4).

Using this definition of poverty, we can estimate the extent of poverty and assess how poverty levels have changed over the past 25 or so years.

- In 1979, 13 per cent of people in the UK were living on below 60 per cent of average income after housing costs.

- By 2003/04, 21 per cent of people (12.3 million) were living on below 60 per cent of average income after housing costs.

These statistics suggest that a huge increase in poverty occurred in Britain between 1979 and 2004/05. Once again, though, the indicators suggest that the risk of poverty is not shared equally. Economic status (whether a person is employed or not), ethnicity, age and household structure all influence the experience of poverty. As the Child Poverty Action Group (2005) point out:

- 78 per cent of people in households where the head or spouse was unemployed were in poverty; by contrast, in households where all adults are in full time work, only 4 per cent are in poverty.

- 19 per cent of white people are in poverty, whereas 58 per cent of Pakistani and Bangladeshi and 40 per cent of black or black British people are in poverty.

- 47 per cent of lone-parent households are in poverty, compared with 20 per cent of two-parent households with children.

(CPAG, 2005, p4)

These different levels of poverty are a reflection of the wider structural disadvantage and sometimes discrimination that these groups face.

Hopefully, you will now have some understanding of the significance of the 'definitions' debate. Ultimately, the answer to the question 'how many poor people are there in the UK today' depends on the definition of poverty adopted. If poverty is defined in 'absolute' terms, as it was in the 1980s and the 1990s by Conservative ministers, then very few people are poor. By contrast, relative definitions are much broader and uncover much higher levels of poverty. The 'definitions debate' is therefore important, and its relevance for helping us to understand levels of poverty and policy responses should not be underestimated. That said, we do need to be aware that the overwhelming focus placed on the question of definitions, both within academic literature and policy debates, can act as a 'smokescreen', diverting attention away from the devastating consequences of poverty. Hence, while books, academic journals and government consultation exercises deliberate the relative merits of competing definitions, the experiences of the millions of people living through the hardships that poverty generates can remain largely unnoticed. It is to the experiences of those living in poverty that our discussion now turns.

The impact of poverty on people's lives

Susie is a 29-year-old woman who lives with her three children in rented accommodation. Her home is damp and cold and in a poor state of repair. Susie claims benefits and cannot afford to adequately heat her home. She would like to move out of the flat as she is really unhappy there; she finds it gloomy and depressing, and doesn't know where to start to try and improve it. The job just seems too big to take on. Susie's children are two, three, and five years of age. They frequently have bad coughs and colds and have recently been diagnosed as being asthmatic. The family have to go to the doctor's surgery often, which is a long walk in the cold as they cannot afford the bus fare. Susie has very poor self-esteem, and believes she has failed her children. She has no contact with her family, who live many miles away. She often feels weepy and depressed – that life is not worth living. She has no idea what she can do to make her life any different. Susie owes money to a local firm who give loans with high interest rates. She borrowed the money to buy Christmas presents, but is now worried sick about paying it back. She's had various letters through the door and last week she was paid a visit by the debt collector who frightened her so much she contemplated ending it all. On top of all of this, Susie's fridge has broken down.

The father of two of the children works on the fairground and is away many months of the year. He calls round occasionally, without warning, and stays for a few days at a time. Susie is very fond of him, as are the children, but he is prone to mood swings, and gets sick of Susie asking for money for the children.

Susie feels that she needs some help, but she's scared of approaching social services in case they take the children off her. She doesn't know which way to turn.

The impact of poverty

Spend some time thinking about the Susie's life with her three children. If you were a social worker assessing this family's needs, how would you describe the impact of poverty upon Susie's life? You may wish to think about this emotionally, physically, practically and socially.

Having completed this activity, you might have recognised the hopelessness and despair that people can sometimes feel when they live in poverty. It is often the cumulative effects of deprivation that can lead to high stress levels, feelings of strain, and utter desolation. Constant worry is common, whether this is about debt or paying bills, or whether it is about health, housing or other problems. Worrying consumes a great deal of emotional energy and can sap people's spirits and contribute to stress, anxiety and in some cases depression or other mental health problems. It is not uncommon for people to feel that they have failed in some way, which contributes to poor self-esteem and feelings of worthlessness. Relationships may also deteriorate under strain, which can exacerbate stress and feelings of failure. In addition to the emotional impact of poverty on people's lives, you may also have noted the lack of choices or options available to Susie, and the fact that she felt unable to bring about any change in her circumstances.

Despite acknowledging the potential impact of poverty upon people's lives, it is important not to stereotype or pathologise people who are poor and to recognise that poverty affects people differently. Many people who experience poverty are able to manage their situation by showing immense strength and resourcefulness, despite extreme hardship. They are able to live their lives with dignity and pride. However, the impact of poverty on the lives of individuals and families is frequently so extreme that the brutal consequences of poverty can take their toll even on the most resilient.

Images of 'the poor': a moral judgement

Individuals in poverty are frequently talked about and treated without dignity or respect, which according to Novak (1997) generates irreparable psychological damage, which far outweighs the level of material poverty endured. As this quote below from a woman in poverty indicates, being poor is hard work:

> *You're more tired. I mean just the thing that being poor is so much work, your whole life. You see people going into a shop they buy what they want and they leave. But you're there, you're having to calculate how much money you've got as you go around, you're having to look at one brand then another, and meanwhile the store detective is looking over your shoulder which is also work having to cope with that kind of scrutiny, because you're poor they expect you to take something ... There's that pressure all the time.*
> (Woman talking to Beresford et al., 1999, p94)

Poverty then, is much more than a lack of money. It is also about how people are treated, how they see themselves, and about loss of dignity and feelings of power-lessness. Linked to this, is the notion that poverty also involves moral judgements.

ACTIVITY **2.3**

Think about the messages you have heard about 'poor people' from family, peers, the media, or in popular culture; list adjectives that have been used to describe people in poverty throughout history.

Collect newspaper articles which describe people who live in poverty. What messages emerge from these?

What purposes do these images and messages serve?

When doing the first part of the above exercise, you have probably come up with a range of terms such as 'idlers', 'rogues', 'vagabonds', 'scroungers', 'dross', 'under-class', 'wasters', 'rough', and so on. Words like these still permeate the popular press today and in doing so they seep into the self-image of people who are rendered as being 'different' from the rest of society.

Compare this quote from a national newspaper with the one below it. What differences are there?

> *We are turning into a nation of chavs and spivs. And many of our children are now being brought up to know no other way. The feckless, the workshy, the scroungers, the loafers are all laughing all the way to the next Giro cheque.*
>
> (The *Sun* 10 June 1995)

> *How can you want to live on benefits? If you analyse what people really get on benefits you can't buy nothing much. You can't buy proper shoes, you can't buy these fancy things that children would like, so why would you really want to live on benefits if that's the only thing? And you're having to go down to the DSS and talk to these people and people looking down on you. I assure you nobody in their right sense would want to be on these benefits, it's degrading.*
>
> Contributor to women's discussion group (cited in Beresford et al. 1999, p109)

Popular discriminatory images of 'the poor' have shared a common theme throughout history, that poor people are somehow to blame for their state of affairs. Stereotypical images of poverty encompass a moral judgement, that shifts emphasis away from anything to do with a lack of cash, and becomes a statement on the moral character of those involved. Sociologically, this is interesting as this process serves two important purposes.

- Firstly, if poverty is reconstructed in terms of the failures and weaknesses of those who are in it, it enables attention to be shifted away from structural causes of poverty, and away from government policies which may be responsible.
- Secondly, the moral judgement of poverty creates something of a self-fulfilling prophecy for people, who begin to internalise their 'otherness' and thus become emotionally marginalised as well as structurally excluded.

The concept of the 'looking-glass self' is useful here. Symbolic interactionist, Charles Horton Cooley (1902) utilised this term to describe how individuals see themselves through the eyes of others, who give them feedback, which in turn is internalised and enables individuals to develop feelings about themselves, often of pride or mortification. For people in our society who live in dire poverty, the prevailing message to emerge from popular culture is that they are lazy, irresponsible, weak and entirely culpable for their plight. Such messages are likely to be internalised, which may lead to feelings of shame and embarrassment, psychologically excluding them from mainstream society. Dominelli (2004) utilises the concept of 'othering' to explain the processes that occur when comparisons are made that evaluate some people as being superior to others. This creates a group who become constructed as being inferior and outside prevailing social norms, who are distinguished as being 'undeserving' and in need of being policed. When applied to people in poverty, it can clearly be seen how labels and popular images contribute to the construction of a deviant group who can be blamed for their situation. This is important to understand within social work because as a group, 'the poor' are highly visible and are therefore vulnerable to surveillance from health and social care professionals. As agents of social control, social workers can potentially contribute to this process. Such visibility is also felt by those who live in poverty as is illustrated in the quote below:

> *I am frightened of going to Social Services. Poverty is when you need help, but you are too scared of being judged as an unfit mother to ask for it. Asking for support shouldn't mean you are investigated, it shouldn't mean you lose your dignity.*
>
> (Service user talking to ATD Fourth World, 2006)

It is imperative that social workers are aware of the power of stigmatising and discriminatory messages that seep into popular culture and ensure that they are practising from within an anti-oppressive framework. The social work value base is an attempt to ground social work practice within a set of values and principles which counter unfair and inequitable beliefs.

ACTIVITY 2.5

Social work values

You may have noted that each time we refer to 'the poor' in this chapter, we have used inverted commas to denote the fact that this is an artificial and socially constructed grouping. Look at your GSCC Code of Practice (if you do not have one, you can download this from www.gscc.org.uk), and consider how you can uphold Standard 1, in relation to service users who are in poverty. You may wish to think about:

- *ways in which you can treat people as individuals rather than as a stereotype;*

- *how you can respect and maintain the dignity of service users;*

- *how you can promote equal opportunities for service users and carers;*

- *how you can guard against 'povertyism' or treating people in oppressive or discriminatory ways, because they are in poverty.*

The point of this exercise is to translate the GSCC Code of Practice, from mere words alone, into practical ways of working. You may wish to refer to the National Occupational Standards Statement of Expectations to help you with this. This can be downloaded from www.skillsforcare.org.uk

---

It is essential that social work students develop the ability to be reflective and develop critical practice (Adams et al., 2005) to guard against discriminatory practices. As part of this it is important to adopt a sociological approach to your practice. As we have outlined in Chapter 1, this attempts to move beyond individualised responses to situations faced by service users, to adopting a position which locates individuals within wider underpinning structures. This is reflected in the subject benchmark statements for social work which set out the knowledge, understanding and skills required to become a social worker:

> *The relevance of sociological perspectives to understanding societal and structural influences on human behaviour at individual, group and community levels.*

This emphasises the importance of understanding human behaviour from within a sociological perspective.

ACTIVITY *2.6*

Let us return to Susie, who we considered in Activity 2.2 above. If you adopt a sociologically informed approach to working with Susie, how might your assessment of her and subsequent intervention be different from if you adopted an individualised approach? You may wish to undertake this activity with a group of other students.

By doing this exercise, you will have hopefully recognised the importance of implementing a sociologically informed assessment to your work with Susie, in order to plan intervention which recognises the structural basis of some of the difficulties she is facing. This would be different from an individualised approach which would tend to focus upon individual 'failings' or inadequacies of service users.

Sociological explanations of poverty

Competing explanations for the causes of poverty are well documented. In this section, we provide a summary of some of the most influential. These fall into three categories: functionalist theories; individualistic explanations; and structural (Marxist) explanations.

ACTIVITY *2.7*

Recapping key sociological theories
In Chapter 1, we outlined the key tenets of the core sociological theories to be considered in this book. As the discipline of sociology will be new to many of you, it is important that you recap and refresh the central components of each theory each time you approach a new topic in sociology. This will enable you to become comfortable with the theory base as you go along, and importantly, to situate each new topic within an understanding of underpinning theory.

Complete a 'crib list' for Marxism and symbolic interactionism. We have done functionalism for you to assist you with this process.

Crib list: functionalism

- *Structural theory.*
- *Macro level of explanation.*
- *Society is the 'whole', which has various component parts.*
- *Each part contributes a function which ensures the survival of the whole.*
- *The notion of 'consensus' (or shared norms and values) is fundamental.*
- *Social order is significant.*
- *Socialisation by family, education, wider culture.*
- *Key sociologists: Comte, Durkheim, Parsons, Davis and Moore.*

The functions of poverty

Functionalist explanations of poverty are based around the belief that poverty serves a positive function for society. This may sound strange, as at first sight it is hard to think of any benefit at all to being in poverty. However, you should remember that functionalism is interested in large-scale structural explanations of social life. Therefore, poverty is regarded on a macro scale in terms of the benefits it provides for society as a whole, rather than for the individuals in poverty. The most influential writer from within this perspective is Herbert J Gans (1971), who argues that poverty survives in part because it is useful to a number of groups in society. He suggests that poverty benefits the non-poor and also the rich and powerful, who therefore have a vested interest in maintaining poverty. According to Gans, the functions of poverty can be summarised as follows.

1. Poverty ensures that society's 'dirty work' is done

In other words, the existence of poverty ensures that there is always someone available to do physically dangerous, temporary, undignified and underpaid work; as the low wage they gain for doing it is better than destitution.

2. Poverty subsidises the rich

Linked to the above point, Gans further points out that without the very low-paid in society, many industries would be unable to function as they presently do; they rely upon low-paid workers to ensure their profit and survival. Furthermore, because the poor pay a higher proportion of their income in taxes they further subsidise more affluent groups.

3. Poverty directly creates jobs

Gans identifies a number of occupations that 'service' the poor:

> *Penology would be miniscule without the poor, as would the police. Other activities and groups that flourish because of the existence of the poor are ... the sale of heroin and cheap wines and liquors, Pentecostal ministers, faith healers, prostitutes, pawn shops and the peacetime army which recruits its enlisted men mainly from among the poor.*
>
> (Gans, 1971, p21)

ACTIVITY 2.8

Critiquing sociological theory
There are many assumptions contained in the above quote that are rather judgemental. Can you spot them? If so, you can weave this into a critique of Gans's work. This should help you to develop skills of analysis which are vital both to the discipline of sociology and for developing professional practice in social work.

In addition to the occupations cited above, Gans also identifies what he calls jobs for 'poverty warriors'. Here he is referring to the likes of social workers, social scientists and journalists, for example.

4. The social functions of poverty

Significantly, Gans suggests that the existence of poverty provides reassurance and support for the rest of society. The existence of poverty and of poor people in society provides a yardstick against which the rest of society can measure themselves. This reassures those who are not poor of their worth and reminds them that their life is worth living. In simple terms, there is always somebody else worse off, and this serves as a useful reminder to the majority of society.

5. The scapegoat function

Gans (1971) suggests that the existence of poor people in society also provides a scapegoat for the non-poor. He maintains that the defenders of the desirability of hard work, thrift, honesty and monogamy need people who can be accused of being lazy, spendthrift, dishonest and promiscuous to justify those norms (p22).

He goes on to suggest that the poor function to reinforce mainstream norms; even though there is evidence to suggest that the poor are as law abiding and moral as anyone else, they are more likely than their middle-class counterparts to be caught and punished when they participate in deviant acts. They also lack the cultural power to correct the stereotypes other people have of them. This explanation links with the 'othering' argument that was made earlier in this section.

It should be noted that Gans offers a functional analysis to explain the continued existence of poverty. He is not advocating that it should exist, rather that poverty serves a number of functions for society, and that affluent groups in particular benefit from its continued existence. Gans is, therefore, arriving at a similar conclusion to that of conflict theorists. He concludes that:

> ... phenomena like poverty can be eliminated only when they become dysfunctional for the affluent or powerful, or when the powerless can obtain enough power to change society.

(Gans, 1971, p24)

Individualistic explanations of poverty: the focus on 'problem families'

These are theories that attempt to explain the existence of poverty by focusing upon the moral failings and ineptitude of those who are in it. Such explanations tend to adopt a blaming approach. We have chosen to focus upon three such explanations here. Together they contribute to the ideology of the 'problem family', a highly discriminatory concept that was popular in the 1960s and 1970s which largely shaped policy and social work intervention at the time.

1. Culture of poverty

This explanation for poverty was developed by Oscar Lewis in 1966, when he based his work on observations of Mexican and Puerto Rican families. Although this research is clearly dated and may seem divorced from life in Britain today, the underpinning ideas behind Lewis's work remain influential. Lewis was interested in the lifestyle of the poor and suggested that people are in poverty due to a set of values, which they internalise and then pass on over the generations. He referred to this as a 'design for living' and argued that people learn to accept poverty because they can't do anything about it. According to Lewis, the poor adopted self-defeating attitudes, by becoming fatalistic and resigned to the situation, which prevented them from breaking out of it. Lewis identified feelings of dependency and helplessness, with little sense of the future. He also found that family life was characterised by high levels of illegitimacy, divorce, and the predominance of women, due to high levels of male desertion. Children grew up to internalise behaviours and values, thereby perpetuating the norms and values of a 'culture of poverty'.

This theory is criticised for failing to explain the existence of poverty in the first place. Critics suggest that people in poverty are in fact no different in terms of their moral outlook from other members of society; rather it is their lack of income, and poverty, that prevents them from achieving mainstream values. The culture of poverty then, is regarded as a response by the poor to the realities of their situation. Despite the obvious weaknesses of this theory, the ideas have been influential in Britain among commentators who perceive different cultural values to exist among the poor.

2. Cycle of deprivation theory

The idea of a cycle of deprivation is associated with Sir Keith Joseph, who was the Conservative Party Secretary of State for Social Services in the early 1970s. Sir Keith believed that it wasn't merely lack of income that caused poverty and that some 'problem families' had interrelated difficulties which were to a greater or lesser extent inflicted from within (cited in Denham and Garnett, 2002). Here he was referring to factors such as low intelligence, temperament and poor health. The cycle of deprivation theory holds that such chronic problems recur in the next generation, as children from poor families tend to marry into families with similar difficulties, thereby reproducing a cycle of deprivation. Such families live in inner-city areas, have poor housing, inadequate diets, poor health, do badly at school, leave without qualifications, enter poorly-paid work, bring children up in an unsatisfactory manner, are more likely to fall into delinquency and are unable or unwilling to find work. The theory is similar to the culture of poverty above as it assumes that people perpetuate their own deprivation.

The cycle of deprivation theory has also been widely criticised. Extensive research has found that children of 'the poor' frequently break out of the so-called cycle of deprivation, which is supposed to determine and constrain their life chances. Further, the difficulties noted do not cause poverty; such problems, if in fact they exist, are likely to be a response to an unequal society which offers little chance of success. The theory falls short of addressing the root causes of poverty and fails to explain why some people get into poverty in the first place.

3. Underclass theory

This concept emerged more recently and, according to Jones and Novak (1999), constitutes the return of a victim-blaming ideology of poverty with a vengeance. The most vociferous proponent of the underclass theory was Charles Murray who, in an article in the *Sunday Times* in 1989, warned of the dangers of an underclass developing in Britain, characterised by high levels of illegitimacy, crime and dropping out of the labour market. Murray argues that poverty essentially results from the behaviour of individuals:

> When I use the term underclass, I am indeed focussing on a certain type of person defined not by his condition e.g. long term unemployed, but by his deplorable behaviour in response to that condition, e.g. unwillingness to take jobs that are available to him.
>
> (Murray, 1990, p68)

Murray also pointed to communities in which he claimed the family had effectively collapsed, degenerating into a 'new rabble' who would become increasingly chaotic and violent. The key danger, for Murray, was long-term dependency upon benefits and social disintegration. Lone parents were of particular concern to him in this respect, as were their children, who he believed were learning 'faulty' values.

The underclass theory was extremely influential on the Conservative Party at the time, which along with a rampant media, contributed to the development of a moral panic around lone parents.

Criticisms of Murray's work are well rehearsed, in particular the complete disregard for structural causes of poverty and the flimsy and inaccurate nature of his 'evidence' for the existence of such a class.

Are individualistic theories of poverty relevant to social work practice today?

Despite the obvious criticisms of individualistic explanations of poverty, they have been extremely influential. Politicians and the media have perpetuated the underpinning ideas persuasively; and there is a clear residual effect in present-day policy and practice. New Labour's Sure Start programme that was launched in 2000 followed the government's first annual report on poverty, which stated that *we need to break the cycle of deprivation, to stop it being transmitted through generations* (DSS, 1999, p5). Again, more recently, Tony Blair said:

> This cycle of deprivation is bad for everyone. But it is particularly unfair for children who miss out on opportunities because they inherit the disadvantage faced by their parents, so their life chances are determined by where they come from rather than who they are.
>
> (Social Exclusion Unit, 2004a, p5)

So, governments are still talking about a cycle of deprivation as causing poverty, but still failing to explain why it exists in the first place. This does not mean that policies designed to improve the lives of those living in poverty are not valid. The Sure Start programme, for instance, has provided valuable input to the lives of many families who have used it.

Structural explanations for poverty

Structural explanations of poverty focus upon the structure of society and associated political or economic factors, such as low pay, unemployment, economic recession, the demise of industry; the widening gap between rich and poor; and the withdrawal of welfare services. The causes of poverty then, are located within structural forces, not the individual.

Marxist/conflict view

This perspective critiques all individualistic arguments and maintains that poverty, like wealth, is an inevitable consequence of a capitalist society. Like Gans, Marxists argue that poverty benefits the ruling class, as it ensures that there is always a workforce willing to accept low wages. Similarly, the existence of unemployment and job insecurity means that there is always a 'reserve army of labour' able and willing (or, unable to be unwilling!) to take their place if they are not happy. Capitalism and the bourgeoisie therefore benefit from the existence of poverty. As Kincaid (1973) has stated, it is not simply that there are rich and poor, rather some are rich because others are poor.

For Marxists then, poverty is an intrinsic and integral feature of capitalist society, which is a direct consequence of the inequality inherent in the class system. They argue that until the bourgeoisie are overthrown by the proletariat and the capitalist system is replaced by an egalitarian socialist system, there will always be poverty, irrespective of any half-hearted attempts to alleviate it by the welfare state. How then, do Marxists explain the existence of welfare institutions including social services departments, that appear ostensibly designed to assist the poor and eradicate poverty? Jones and Novak (1999) note that it is essential for capitalism that poverty is maintained and managed, hence welfare benefits, like the rest of the welfare state, are not designed to assist people out of poverty. Rather, the welfare state has a palliative role, as it offers a partial cure for the worst effects of capitalism, ensuring at the same time that social harmony and the *status quo* are maintained. Social work is regarded as an instrument of the state, which further exists to maintain the *status quo*. Social workers help people to adjust to their difficulties, by providing services, or a listening ear; and in doing so, ensure structural problems become individualised with attention shifted away from the real underpinning cause. In this sense, poverty is maintained as poor people internalise their own failings, are partially soothed by the help being provided, and any revolutionary threat arising out of discontentment is negated. Becker (1997) is critical of social workers and the state regulation they implement. He scathingly suggests:

Social workers have become ideologically incorporated into their employing organisation; they owe their existence and power to the power of the state, and their function is largely to maintain institutional ends. For many tens of thousands of poor families with children, contact with social services, and with social workers in particular, continues to be fraught with danger.

(Becker, 1997, p118)

Marxists, then, clearly locate the source of poverty in the structural nature of society; they identify the welfare system as an instrument of the state, which acts to maintain gross inequalities of wealth that see some people living in dire destitution with little chance of ever really escaping from it.

The role of social work in relation to poverty

It is now important to examine the role of social work in relation to poverty. As a profession, social work intervenes with some of the most impoverished and disadvantaged people in Britain. This is not new; social work has been linked with poverty since it began, and the profession largely emerged out of charitable attempts to address the plight of the poor. It could be argued, however, that as time has gone on social work has perhaps lost sight of its role in relation to poverty. Becker (1997) is scathing of the profession for its lack of what he calls 'poverty awareness' and suggests that social workers lack insight of the issues.

Social workers have little understanding of the complex processes that generate and maintain poverty; they have limited insight into how their political and welfare ideologies and attitudes to poverty affect their daily practice with poor people; they have failed to place poverty on the agenda for social work theorising, education, policy and practice .

(Becker, 1997, p114)

He goes on to argue that social workers are no different to others, in making distinctions and judgements between different groups of the poor, between the 'deserving' and 'undeserving', between 'copers' and 'non-copers', and so on (Becker, 1997, p116). He suggests that most social workers believe they can have little strategic impact on poverty itself and believe therefore that they should intervene with individuals rather than on a structural level. These ideas are interesting. Years of teaching social work students has led us to recognise that many do still want to intervene to bring about change. However, when students commence their placements (often those in statutory social services) they often report that their initial ideas are constrained by cultures in organisations which are mostly based upon an ideological premise that change is not possible at a structural level. Students tell us that it feels like they have a 'mountain to climb', and that they come up against barriers imposed by managerial regimes of working and a culture of defeatism. Research by other academics backs this up (see for example, Jones, 2001), but it is our view that bringing about change in social work is always possible, however small and however insignificant it may at first seem.

So, what methods could be employed by social workers to address the impact of poverty on service users' lives? *Task-centred practice* could be used to work with service users who are in poverty, in very practical ways (see for example, Marsh and Doel 2005; Reid and Shyne, 1969). Service users have often been critical of social workers for failing to help them with practical problems, such as those of debt, housing difficulties and other 'problems of living'. Task-centred practice offers a very practical model which is potentially very empowering to service users as it is they who choose which areas they wish to work on. Task-centred practice is based on the premise that the service user will work in partnership with the social worker and learn new methods of problem solving which will equip them in the future. In this sense, workers could adopt a very practical way to address some aspects of poverty. However, perhaps this still doesn't go far enough, as this method of practice is based upon an individualised approach and doesn't address the bigger picture. Possibly combining task-centred working with other more radical methods of working might address this.

The work of Bob Holman is useful when considering what role (if any) social work has in alleviating poverty. Holman suggested as far back as 1973 that a casework approach to social work only served to mask the social and political forces operating in people's lives and maintained their depriving situation. He purported that a casework approach denied the collective problems of those in poverty, and in common with other radical approaches to social work, Holman promoted methods in social work which were aimed at reducing inequality and combating poverty and oppression.

In 1993, Holman suggested social workers adopt an approach of 'mutuality'. This recognises mutual obligations and stems from the acceptance of common kinship, expressed in joint action, towards a more equitable sharing of resources and responsibilities. He argues that the role of the social services should be to support families and individuals exposed to poverty, and to prevent them reaching the point where intervention and control are placed upon them. He claims that the aim should be *to modify the devastating effects of social inequalities which now ruin the lives of so many* (Holman, 1993, p71). To do this, *community social work* should be at the core of social services. He suggests that neighbourhood-based family centres are more valuable than approaches which aim to monitor and control families. Community-based social work has partnership, respect and empowerment at its heart and is committed to achieving change in people's lives.

Indeed, community work has been around for a number of years and emerged from a more radical base that was premised upon shared experiences and collective action, as vehicles to bring about change.

More recently, a *new manifesto for social work* has emerged from academics concerned about the direction of the social work profession (Jones et al., 2004). In it, the authors identify a crisis in social work which has resulted from years of managerialism, a paucity of resources, and the domination of care management approaches. They highlight the fact that social workers are frustrated by 'surface' responses to deep-seated problems and note that there is a need for a new, engaged social work, committed to social justice and to challenging poverty and discrimination. They stress the importance of collective approaches, and a redefinition of the profession in terms of its value base, rather than the functions it serves for the state. They use examples of how service user-led collective advocacy in the mental health field has both met individual needs of service users while also contributing to structural changes in relation to service provision for mental health. They conclude by emphasising that most people enter the social work profession to pursue an ethical career that could contribute even in small ways to social change. They argue that the:

> *potential for social change has all but been squeezed out of social work by the drives towards marketisation and managerialism ... yet overwhelmingly it is still the case that people can enter social work not to be care managers or rationers of services or dispensers of community punishment, but rather to make a positive contribution to the lives of poor and oppressed people.*
>
> (Jones et al., 2004, p4)

The very *role* of the social work profession is at the heart of this debate and many social workers struggle to balance their own ideological beliefs with those of their employing agency. Social workers may consider themselves to have a moral responsibility to work in partnership with service users, to at least raise the profile of those in poverty and work in an empowering way to bring about as much alleviation as possible. Whether this goes far enough, however, is an issue individual social workers must grapple with in terms of their own practice and choice of employing agency.

ACTIVITY 2.10

Where do you stand?

In small groups, discuss the Manifesto for Social Justice *and identify the key points. You can download this from www.liv.ac.uk/sspsw/*

What do you think about the manifesto? With reference to your placement setting, how are the principles in here applicable in your agency and how can the suggestions for an alternative social work be translated into practice?

What are the potential problems and benefits of adopting such an approach?

Having read this chapter about poverty and social work, what do you think your role will be? In other words, where do you stand?

C H A P T E R   S U M M A R Y

Poverty continues to be an enduring feature of the lives of many social work service users. It is therefore extremely important that social workers possess a sociological understanding of key debates and issues. These debates are not purely academic. Policy-makers tend to gravitate towards either behavioural or structural explanations, with those from the right traditionally veering towards behavioural interpretations and those from the left towards more structural interpretations. Hence sociological debates about the causes of poverty shape official responses to it and structure the framework within which social workers respond to it. In addition, the impact of poverty upon service users should not be underestimated. Social workers need to develop an understanding, not only of the material and practical consequences of poverty, but also its emotional impact upon the ability of individuals and families to cope with the associated stresses.

FURTHER READING

For up-to-date statistics and policy developments relating to poverty, see **Flaherty, J, Veit Wilson, J and Dornan, P** (2004) *Poverty: the facts*. 5th edition. London: CPAG. More generally, we would recommend that you utilise the Child Poverty Action Group website **www.cpag.org.uk** and the Joseph Rowntree Foundation website, **www.jrf.org.uk**.

For a perspective on the experiences of those who live in poverty in Britain today, see **Beresford, P, Green, D, Lister, R and Woodward, K** (1999) *Poverty first hand: poor people speak for themselves*. London: CPAG.

For a discussion of poverty related to social work, see **Jones, C and Novak, T** (1999) *Poverty, welfare and the disciplinary state*. Abingdon: Routledge.

Peter Townsend's (1979) *Poverty in the United Kingdom*. London: Allen Lane is a classic study of poverty in which he makes a powerful case for the adoption of relative definitions. For a contrasting perspective which advocates the use of absolute definitions, see **Bartholomew, J** (2006) *The welfare state we're in*, London: Politico Publishing.

Chapter 3
Social exclusion, sociology and social work

Introduction

Following on from the discussion on poverty in Chapter 2, this chapter examines the concept of social exclusion, assessing its sociological origins and its relevance to social work. In terms of the importance of the concept to you as a social work student, its relevance may seem fairly obvious, since the social work profession is responsible for delivering services to a range of 'excluded' individuals and groups. A cursory glance at the extracts from the GSCC's *Code of Practice* and *National Occupational Standards,* and the *Subject Benchmarking Statements for Social Work* listed above will serve to reinforce its significance. As the *Subject Benchmarks* state, there is a need for social work students to have an understanding of the *poverty, unemployment, poor health, disablement, lack of education (and other sources of disadvantage) that lead to marginalisation, isolation and exclusion and their impact on the demand for social work services.* In this sense, the relevance of social exclusion to you as a social worker could not be made more explicit. The concept of social exclusion is, however, also interesting sociologically, because explanations as to its causes vary, as do the potential 'solutions' that have been recommended by different academics and politicians. Hence, as with many of the concepts examined in this book, 'social exclusion' has been the subject of much heated debate and disagreement, and there is no consensus as to what measures should be taken in order to tackle it. In this chapter we examine the competing interpretations of social exclusion and their implications for policy and practice. We also look at the direction of social exclusion policy in the UK, examining both the assumptions that underpin it, and its sociological 'ancestry'.

Origins of the concept

The concept, social exclusion, emerged out of developments at a European Union level, but since the election of Tony Blair's first Labour administration in May 1997, it has come to permeate social policy documents and guidance across a range of UK government departments. The integration of the term 'social exclusion' into the UK social policy agenda occurred almost immediately after the 1997 general election, when the government announced it was creating a Social Exclusion Unit (SEU). Riding upon a wave of optimism following its landslide election victory, the government declared that it would put the priority of tackling social exclusion at the forefront of its strategy to create a more fair society. The Unit, we were told, would help find joined-up solutions to joined-up problems. The Social Exclusion Taskforce (SET) has superseded the SEU, but its location at the heart of government in the Cabinet Office is seen as a reaffirmation of the government's commitment to combating social exclusion. A number of social work textbooks have sought to provide social work students with practical, 'hands-on' guides for tackling social exclusion (see, for example, Pierson, 2002). While we certainly intend to direct you to relevant skills and knowledge, our main aim as sociologists is to facilitate an adequate understanding of the concept itself, and an awareness of the different purposes its usage may be said to perform. This is an important and worthwhile task, for as Barry (1998) argues, social work responses to social exclusion are ultimately shaped by the legislative and policy responses that are themselves influenced by wider ideological and conceptual debates over its causes.

We need to begin by examining how social exclusion differs from the concept of poverty that we examined in the last chapter. The concept is essentially based on the notion that low income alone is not the only, or indeed the prime, cause of social ills such as poverty, crime, teenage pregnancy, homelessness, substance misuse and unemployment. There is, advocates of the concept argue, a need to acknowledge other causes of 'exclusion'. To quote the SET:

> Social exclusion is about more than income poverty. It is a short-hand term for what can happen when people or areas have a combination of linked problems, such as unemployment, discrimination, poor skills, low incomes, poor housing, high crime and family breakdown.
>
> (SET, 2007a)

ACTIVITY 3.1

As we saw in the previous chapter, lack of income is a key factor which prevents people from fully participating in social life. However, there are other factors which contribute to the marginalisation of people socially, economically and politically.

(a) Take a look at the data below, which relates to rates of unemployment among different ethnic groups across Great Britain. How might you explain the different levels of unemployment?

Ethnic group	Unemployment rates (%)	
	Males (2004)	**Females (2004)**
White British	4	3.5
Other white	6.5	6.5
Indian	7	8
Chinese	9.5	7
Black African	13	12
Pakistani	11.5	19.5
Bangladeshi	13	Not available
Black Caribbean	14	9

(Source: National Statistics, 2007)

(b) In small groups, discuss the circumstances which can lead to some people being excluded. You may wish to think about factors which:

- *prevent some people from being successful in the job market;*
- *prevent people from being involved in their community;*
- *prevent people from accessing services;*
- *lead to some children being excluded from school;*

ACTIVITY **3.1** *continued*

• *contribute to some people not exercising their right to vote;*

• *lead to some people facing harassment and being victims of hate crime.*

Try to think as widely as possible and consider a wide range of people. If you have been on a practice placement and encountered service users who were socially excluded, you may wish to focus upon the service user group you worked with and consider some of the factors that contributed to their social exclusion.

The above exercise will have helped you to think about some of the non-income-based factors which can cause social exclusion. In relation to Activity 3.1 (a) above, your discussion of differential rates of unemployment may have touched upon issues relating to prejudice and discrimination. There can, in fact, be little doubt that prejudice and discrimination do impact upon the unemployment rates of people from minority ethnic group backgrounds. By way of example, a 2004 BBC survey sought to assess levels of discrimination at 'application form level'. CVs from six fictitious candidates, each of whom were given traditionally white, black African or Muslim names, were sent to 50 firms. All the candidates were applying for the same jobs, which had been advertised in the press or on recruitment websites, and all candidates were given the same standard of qualifications and levels of experience. The only differences between the candidates lay in the presentation of their CVs and their inferred ethnic origin. As the table below shows, white candidates were far more likely to be offered interviews than those with black- or Asian-sounding names, despite their identical qualifications and experience. The authors of the survey concluded that the only possible explanation for the differential levels of success of the 'candidates' was racism.

Name of candidate	% of interview offers
Jenny Hughes/John Andrews	25
Fatima Khan/Nasser Hanif	9
Abu Lolasemi/Yinka Olatunde	13

(Source: BBC, 2004)

In your discussion of the factors outlined in question Activity 3.1 (b), above, you will hopefully have discussed the impact this kind of prejudice and discrimination can have on other groups, including service users. As we explained in Chapter 2, a key role of social work is to assist service users to overcome the disadvantages they experience, and one of the main advantages of the concept of social exclusion to you as a social worker is that it can help you in understanding the complex, multi-faceted factors that contribute to patterns of exclusion.

In its most common usage, therefore, with the concept of social exclusion the emphasis moves away from material resources, particularly income, to other potential causes of exclusion. Hence, in John Pierson's (2002) summary of the main features of social exclusion, poverty/low income is just one of five key components, the others being:

- barriers to the jobs market (including discrimination);
- lack of support networks;
- the effects of living in extremely deprived communities;
- lack of access to good quality services.

Social exclusion, therefore, is not necessarily linked to financial hardship, and although 'poverty' is clearly an important 'excluder', it is not the only one that individuals and groups face. In this sense, there is potential for a greater acknowledgement of the way other forms of exclusion – for example, racism, gender, ageism and disability discrimination – can structure and shape disadvantage. When we think of social exclusion like this, as sociologists we can see its explanatory potential. For example, the discriminatory barriers that people who are disabled, black, lone parents or mental health service users face often arise irrespective of income. The societal 'inclusion' of these social groups may ultimately be impeded more by these factors than low incomes *per se*. Certainly, as Activity 3.1 demonstrated, there can be little doubt that racism, disability discrimination and gender discrimination shape opportunities and life chances and can act as barriers to inclusion.

Despite the apparent usefulness of social exclusion as a concept, its emergence into the political mainstream has not occurred without contention. This is because there is no consensus as to what the causes of social exclusion are, or what the solutions to it should be. In the brief summary above, we referred to a range of structural problems that can contribute to exclusion. However, social exclusion is a slippery concept and there are widely different interpretations as to its causes, some which point to structural factors and others behavioural causes. Ruth Levitas (2005), a leading writer on social exclusion, has offered three dominant interpretations of the concept, each of which we outline briefly below.

Three interpretations of social exclusion

Redistributionist discourse

In explaining social exclusion, redistributionist (or redistribution) discourse places a primacy on causal factors such as low income, prejudice, discrimination, lack of opportunity to a decent education or to work, and other 'barriers' that prevent individuals and groups from participating fully in society. From this perspective, the 'socially excluded' (or certainly the bulk of the 'socially excluded') are not held responsible for their situation. Their exclusion results less from their own moral culpability or failings, and more from structural constraints that are largely beyond their control. In this respect, the concept is seen to provide an effective and more progressive alternative to the pejorative term 'underclass' that tended to dominate and shape debates about poverty and disadvantage in the 1980s and 1990s. Instead of focusing on the behaviour of disadvantaged groups, the social component of the term 'social exclusion' draws attention to the wider societal factors that create barriers to inclusion. Indeed, for some it goes much further, highlighting the relationship between the excluded and those who do the excluding. Exclusion, David Byrne argues, is *something that is done by some people to other people* (Byrne, 1999, p1). When viewed in this way, not only does social exclusion offer the potential for shifting attention away from excluded people's so-called behavioural or 'handicapping characteristics', it can also lead us to focus instead on the culpability of those who are doing the excluding, whether this be employers (as in our racism example above), welfare agencies or governments.

In its most common manifestations, analyses of social exclusion written from within a redistributionist discourse stop short of calling for a radical transformation of capitalist society. It is generally believed that social exclusion can be tackled 'from within' by the removal of discriminatory barriers, by improved educational opportunity and moderate levels of income redistribution. In terms of its ideological origins, the philosophy underpinning redistributionist discourse contains elements of a concern for social justice and fairness, combined with a belief that exclusion is harmful to the social and economic fabric of society. Social exclusion, therefore, is seen as morally wrong, and as posing a threat to cohesion, efficiency and stability. Solutions focus on the need to introduce social reform to tackle the structural constraints that inhibit inclusion – for instance, economic and social inequality, prejudice and discrimination.

One of the major criticisms of redistributive discourse stems from politicians and academics on the right of the political spectrum; they argue that by overly concentrating on the supposed social and economic barriers that inhibit inclusion, the culpability of many 'problematic' individuals and families remains unacknowledged. Put simply, they argue that redistributive discourse fails to appreciate that many individuals simply choose to live a lifestyle which itself is responsible for their exclusion – some choose not to take up employment opportunities that are available; some choose to take addictive, illegal drugs; some choose to have children outside wedlock and remain dependent on welfare; and some choose to engage in disruptive anti-social behaviour. Critics, therefore, accuse redistributive discourse of misguided sentimentality, and of being too reluctant to apportion blame. This kind of criticism is linked to the Levitas's second interpretation for social exclusion, moral underclass discourse.

Moral underclass discourse

Advocates of individualistic, behavioural interpretations for social problems have not relinquished their influence on debates about poverty and disadvantage without a fight, and they too have sought to shape social exclusion debates. Levitas refers to this as the 'moral underclass discourse'. With this interpretation, blame for exclusion is placed upon the socially excluded themselves. It is their behaviour – their lack of moral fibre, their drug addiction, their criminal behaviour, their poor parenting skills, their laziness, their unwillingness to work or to take up other opportunities offered – that determines their marginal position in society. Clearly, moral underclass discourse has much in common with the individualistic, behavioural explanations for poverty that were examined in Chapter 2. A small but significant number of 'dysfunctional' individuals and families are, it is argued, choosing to engage in anti-social, problematic modes of behaviour and in doing so are destroying their own life chances as well as the fabric of the communities within which they reside. For advocates of moral underclass discourse, the solution to social exclusion lies in coercive, targeted interventions designed to deter and control the inappropriate, 'deviant' patterns of behaviour that lie at its heart. The focus of attention (and intervention) is on a relatively small group of recalcitrant individuals, rather than wider economic and social structures.

Advocates of the moral underclass discourse also bemoan the 'morally corrupting' affects of state welfare, believing that it serves to encourage and inculcate the 'dysfunctional' patterns of behaviour that lead to social exclusion. They argue that well-meaning, but misguided welfare provision saps motivation and initiative, turning naïve, easily led sections of society into a dependent, 'cowed' clientele. The 'lure' of a council house encourages teenage girls to get pregnant; the 'promise' of a benefit income encourages idleness; and the 'coddling' of vulnerable individuals by social workers has led to a denial of the socially excluded's own agency in contributing to their circumstances. This approach is vulnerable to the same kind of criticisms marshalled against 'behavioural' interpretations for poverty in Chapter 2. In short, it stands accused of ignoring wider structural determinants of social exclusion, which are beyond the individual's control.

Social integration discourse

With this interpretation, the primary focus is on paid work and its importance as a means of ensuring effective inclusion. Although it shares some aspects of redistributionist discourse, this explanation pays far less attention to non-labour-market based causes of exclusion, such as low income and low levels of social participation, and much more emphasis is placed on the primacy of work as a means of securing 'inclusion'. Within this discourse, the terms 'social exclusion' and 'exclusion from paid work' are used interchangeably, and the panacea to exclusion is integration, or re-integration into the workplace. While there is an acknowledgement of some of the barriers that prevent access to the labour market (for instance, prejudice and discrimination), it is generally assumed that work opportunities are available and, with 'encouragement', those who are socially excluded can be enticed into taking these up.

Social exclusion, therefore, is principally construed as non-participation in the labour market and solutions are aimed at increasing work participation, through both incentives, and, crucially, in some cases, coercion. On this latter point, it is worth noting that social integration discourse, like moral underclass discourse, is concerned about the potentially dependency-inducing effects of welfare. Hence, the creation of a more 'active' welfare system, which provides greater encouragement for those who are 'inactive' to take up employment opportunities, forms an important part of any inclusion strategy. Reforming welfare, by placing more emphasis on the fulfilment of duties and obligations, will, it is hoped, help to tackle the 'culture of aspiration' that is said to contribute to exclusion. The resultant increase in employment activity will, social integrationist discourse assumes, ultimately contribute to a reduction in social exclusion.

Importantly, for advocates of social integrationist discourse, it is not only the economic status that work confers that is at the heart of its attraction. As well as providing obvious financial benefits, it also boosts self-esteem, provides participants with the opportunity to develop, socialise, build social networks, imparting a sense of dignity, self-worth and purpose. With work comes a moral and social status – a sense that one is part of and making a contribution the economic and social well-being of everybody. Work, then, provides an 'integrative' function and is beneficial for all – individuals and society.

Social integrationist discourse has been criticised for failing to fully appreciate the structural barriers that prevent people from accessing work, such as a lack of employment opportunities and/or deeply embedded prejudice and discrimination. The notion that 'inclusion' can be reduced to employment activity has also been challenged:

> *Such an analysis ignores the possibility that paid employment per se may not, in any case, be the most appropriate answer to the problems encountered by many marginalised groups, such as people who cannot work because of, for example, disabilities, or people who have left the labour market, such as retired people.*

(Barry, 1998, p7)

The suggestion that 'inclusion' can only be achieved through paid work effectively denies or negates the claim that social exclusion can or should be tackled through mechanisms other than the labour market. It can serve to legitimise the notion that being out of work and on benefits inevitably leads to poverty and social exclusion, making 'inclusion' a status to be earned through work, rather than, for example, as a potential right to be entitled to via state provision.

The three social exclusion discourses are summarised in Table 3.1.

Table 3.1 Summary of Levitas's social exclusion discourses

	Causes of social exclusion	Solutions to social exclusion
Redistributionist discourse	• Low income • Poor educational opportunity • Lack of decent work opportunities • Prejudice and discrimination • Other economic and social barriers that inhibit inclusion.	• Moderate levels of income redistribution within the existing system • Higher wages • Improved welfare benefits • Improved educational opportunities • Anti-discriminatory legislation
Moral underclass discourse	• Lack of moral fibre • 'Dysfunctional', irresponsible patterns of behaviour (for example, illegitimacy, bad parenting, criminality, and substance misuse) • Over-generous levels of welfare, which reward or encourage dependency and 'deviancy'.	• Punitive, coercive interventions designed to deter irresponsible behaviour • Reductions in levels of welfare support, aimed at reducing dependency and forcing people to take responsibility for their own lives and situations • Stigmatisation of deviancy and reinforcement of 'appropriate' behaviour and moral values

| Social integrationist discourse | • Non-participation in the labour market
• Low levels of motivation and aspiration
• An outdated welfare system that expects far too little in return for the rights that it confers
• Prejudice and discrimination. | • Encourage greater participation in the labour market
• Tackle the 'culture of aspiration' that is said to contribute to exclusion
• Reform welfare, so that more emphasis is placed on duties, in particular the responsibility to participate in the labour market
• Anti-discriminatory legislation. |

ACTIVITY 3.2

Read the case study below relating to John. Using Levitas's three interpretations of social exclusion above, identify how a social work approach might be different if a moral underclass, redistribution or social integrationist approach were adopted.

CASE STUDY

John is an Afro-Caribbean man who is 20 years of age; he grew up in a severely deprived area with his mother, Kelly, a lone parent reliant upon benefits, and his sister, until he was 13. John was then placed in the care system as Kelly, who experienced poor mental health, felt unable to cope and expressed real concerns about her son's welfare. At the time she described John as being 'out of control', not attending school, staying out all night and getting involved in petty crime.

John spent the next five years of his life initially with many different foster carers, and eventually in a residential home. He sometimes returned home for short periods but remained 'looked after' until he was 18. He was excluded from school on numerous occasions and consequently his education was badly disrupted; he regularly smoked cannabis and became withdrawn.

When John left the care system at 18, he initially went home but felt he was a worry to his mother, Kelly, so he left and lived on various friends' sofas, sometimes sleeping rough and occasionally returning home.

John is IT literate and hoped to work in this field. After school, with the help of one of the social workers in the residential home where he lived, he applied for several jobs, but had little success. Each time he applied and was turned down, John's confidence sank further and he has never been in employment.

John is bored through the day and watches daytime TV, occasionally smoking dope. He has indicated that he is lonely and depressed and Kelly sometimes worries that he will harm himself.

There are a range of factors that moral underclass discourse might point to in interpreting John's situation. His involvement in petty crime and other forms of problematic behaviour could be put down to the lack of a positive influence and discipline of a father figure. It might also be seen in the context of the proliferation of 'liberal' criminal justice policies, which have removed the threat of deterrence and effectively absolved young criminals of responsibility for their actions. In interpreting John's unemployment, moral underclass discourse might point to the dependency-inducing affects of his mother's reliance on welfare. John, it would argue, has grown up without any work ethic, thinking he has a right to be maintained at the state's expense. Solutions would focus on the need for tough, punitive action to ensure that levels of illegitimacy and dependency, and the problems said to be associated with them, do not spiral out of control. Welfare provision must be severely curtailed and those who choose not to follow mainstream values (through, for example, having children outside wedlock, or choosing not to support themselves independently) must be made aware of the consequences of their actions.

While advocates of social integrationist discourse would not see John's mother's lone parenthood as a major issue, they too would focus on the problems associated with both Kelly and John's lack of participation in the labour market. With this perspective, work is seen to impart a sense of worth and value, acting as an integrative force, contributing to cohesion, binding people together with a shared sense of responsibility and duty. The solution to John and Kelly's 'inclusion', therefore, may lie in the introduction of a combination of supportive and coercive mechanisms, which enable and encourage them to participate in the labour market. This may involve improved childcare provision, better training opportunities (such as the New Deals for Lone Parents and Young People), and welfare reforms, designed to create a more proactive social security system which has more appropriate balance between rights and responsibilities.

Redistributionist discourse might point to the impact low benefit income had on Kelly's ability to cope with the stresses of everyday life. It may also emphasise the discrimination John possibly faced as both a young Afro-Caribbean male and a child in the care system, and how this affected his educational and employment opportunities. Redistributionist discourse would also draw attention to the unemployment that blights the neighbourhood where John was brought up and lives. In this sense, John's disruptive behaviour and, more recently, his depression and fatalistic attitude towards life, can be interpreted as an understandable response to the structural barriers that have contributed and continue to contribute to his exclusion. From this perspective, any solution must address low levels of benefit, the absence of genuine work opportunities and the prejudice and discrimination that shapes the lives of people like John.

Sociology and social exclusion

You should by now have gained an understanding of the key elements of each if the three major different interpretations of social exclusion. Before further assessing the relative influence of each of these approaches on policy, it is important to consider the sociological origins of some of the ideas they contain. At first they seem to have little in common, in that they differ in their explanations for social exclusion and the solutions they advance. However, as we show below, when looked at 'sociologically' there is one key area of similarity.

Functionalism and social exclusion

While moral underclass, social integrationist and redistributionist discourses appear mutually exclusive, they do, in fact, share a common intellectual heritage, in that all three, to varying degrees, accept the *status quo* as essentially sound, and at the same time see social exclusion as posing a threat to the stability of society. In this sense, they are influenced by the functionalist tradition of sociology, and in particular the ideas of Emile Durkheim, which see society as being held together by the integrative institutions of, for example, the labour market, the community and family. Participation in all three spheres of life is considered to be of primary importance by functionalists, with those who do not participate for whatever reason being perceived as 'dysfunctional' in some way. As outlined in Chapter 1, the central themes within Durkheimian functionalism are social order, social cohesion and solidarity, and functionalists are concerned with how these are affected by the particular conditions and pressures of modern industrial societies.

Functionalists accept that moral and social breakdown can occur within society, but they see this as being the result of temporary disturbances to the social equilibrium, which can be quickly corrected, rather than a major fault with the system itself. While differences of interest exist, and order, cohesion and solidarity are sometimes threatened, the bigger picture is one of shared values and a belief that all groups benefit if society runs smoothly. If the social order breaks down, and people or groups are perceived to present a threat to social cohesion, society needs to have adequate means of ensuring that anti-social behaviour is dealt with and conformity re-established.

In relation to our different interpretations of social exclusion above, it is clear that all three, like functionalism, are concerned with the 'disintegrative' impact of what they see as 'dysfunctional' social and economic trends. Moral underclass discourse warns of the dangers posed to society by moral failure, deviant behaviour and family breakdown, whereas social integrationist discourse focuses upon the 'disintegrative' affects of detachment from the labour market. Redistributionist discourse appears more radical than either of the other two interpretations, in that it places a much greater emphasis placed on wider, structural determinants of exclusion. However, as with the other two, the basic structure of society is seen as sound, fundamental reform is deemed unnecessary, and it is important for the 'greater good' for the equilibrium in society to be restored and maintained. Of course, the solutions advocated by these three discourses vary, but the main point here is that all three see social exclusion in terms of the negative impact it has upon what is seen to be an essentially 'sound', well-functioning social system. Levitas has thus described all three as conservative theories of social exclusion, in that they view current social and economic arrangements as given. Neither, for example, contemplates the solution to social exclusion as lying with a fundamental redistribution of income from rich to poor.

Marxism and social exclusion

You may have already noticed that one key sociological tradition – Marxism – is not represented in any of the three dominant interpretations of social exclusion we have discussed. As we have already seen, functionalist claims that capitalist societies are characterised by solidarity, cohesion and integration are dismissed as an illusion by Marxists, who see such societies as being defined by gross inequalities in power, wealth and privilege. For Marxists, the real world is shaped by injustice and exploitation and this inevitably generates endemic poverty, social dislocation, opposition and conflict. It is, Marxists argue, in the interest of the bourgeoisie to present this poverty, and the conflict it generates, as 'abnormal' and 'pathological', rather than an inevitable outcome of an unjust system. Herein lie the 'functions' of the social exclusion debate. According to Marxists, social exclusion discourses understate division, portray society as well functioning and cohesive, and imply that poverty and other social problems are 'aberrations', only experienced by an excluded 'minority', and are capable of 'cure':

> *It [social exclusion] detracts attention from the essentially class divided character of society, and allows a view of society as basically benign to co-exist with the visible reality of poverty. It does this by discursively placing the unwanted characteristics outside society.*
>
> (Levitas, 2005, p188)

Hence, Marxists are deeply suspicious about the ascendance of the concept of social exclusion in academic and political debates. They argue that, at best, 'social exclusion' (in the form of redistributionist discourse) offers us little more by way of explanatory potential than traditional structural interpretations of poverty, which have always drawn attention to the social causes of structural disadvantage. More fundamentally, they insist that the universal embrace of the concept among political elites owes much to attempts to politically 'sanitise' debates about poverty and serve 'closure' on solutions that are based on demands for much greater income redistribution and a radical transformation of society. Thus, Piccone has described social exclusion as the *liberal snake oil prescribed for all social ills by those who uncritically assume the existing system to be fundamentally sound* (cited in Barry, 1998, p5). Levitas has also argued that the operationalisation of the concept in the UK has served a wider 'political' function in that it has detracted attention from the fundamental reforms – in particular, a wider degree of income redistribution of income from rich to poor – that are needed to tackle social exclusion:

> *The overall thrust of both policy and rhetoric has been to reduce poverty and exclusion without tackling overall inequalities in income and wealth, and without increasing either income tax or corporation tax.*
>
> (Levitas, 2001, p456)

In conclusion, Marxists argue that debates over social exclusion serve to obscure the unacceptable inequalities in wealth that are a feature of many advanced capitalist nations. Society is portrayed as comprising an 'included' majority and an 'excluded' majority. On the one hand, this serves to marginalise the vulnerable, often justifying coercive interventions, while on the other hand, attention is diverted away from the gross inequalities in wealth, opportunities and advantage that exist among those who are 'included'. As Levitas (2005, p7) argues, the excluded are conceptually placed 'outside' society and held morally culpable, while *the very rich are discursively absorbed into the included majority, their power and privilege slipping out of focus if not totally out of sight*. We are left with a rosy, overly homogenous view of society, one where poverty, deprivation, conflict and division are seen as marginal and patho-logical conditions, rather than endemic features of a fundamentally unjust system.

How can social work contribute to the demise of social exclusion?

For Marxists, social work cannot make any serious inroads into the endemic poverty that dominates the lives of service users. At best they can mitigate its impact, by providing palliative advice and services. At worst, they become agents of the state, implementing policies designed to re-moralise the poor and reintegrate them into a non-existent, harmonious Durkheimian utopia. Jones and Novak (1999) feel that, historically, this has been a key function of social work:

> *For all their psycho-social rhetoric, social workers diagnosed the problems presented by clients as being rooted not in their poverty but in their flawed personalities. In many respects, their incursions into the underbelly of British society were similar to those of the missionaries of colonial Britain. There was nothing to learn from the 'natives'; social workers were the carriers of 'truth' and bringers of civilisation.*

> (p83)

Ultimately, Marxists argue that the solution to the social and economic problems that are a feature of capitalist societies lies in the creation of a radically different social and economic order, based upon the principles of equality and social justice. In short, poverty, discrimination and urban decay are all key features of capitalism, and their solution requires more fundamental social change than social workers have the power to affect. That is, of course, not to say that social workers have no role to play in working with service users to bring about positive change in their lives, or in exposing the injustices of current economic arrangements.

Nor do adherents to moral underclass discourse see the solution to social exclusion as lying with social work. Indeed, social workers and state welfare are seen as part of the problem. Their 'liberal' values and cosseting of vulnerable individuals has exacerbated the problems service users face, creating a dependent social service clientele. Irrespective of moral culpability, social workers, according to moral underclass discourse propo-nents, treat their service users as 'victims', provide excuses for their dysfunctional behaviour, and aid their attempts to eke out a livelihood on welfare. For example, Charles Murray (1994), a leading proponent of this discourse, argues that when it comes to explanations for so-called 'disadvantage', there is *no shortage of social workers and academics prepared to make excuses to try to shield them from the consequences of their behaviour* (p86). Moral underclass discourse influenced social policy reforms intro-duced during the 1980s and 1990s by successive Conservative governments, which sought to curtail state responsibility for welfare, and reinforce individual responsibility.

Advocates of redistributive discourse would, however, see a far more positive role for social workers in tacking social exclusion, acknowledging the potentially progressive role social workers can play in transforming the lives of service users. Social workers, for example, can help to maximise the incomes of the poor by guiding them through the intricacies of the benefit system, advising them of their rights and ensuring they receive support to which they are entitled. They can also help service users develop social networks, supporting them to access agencies and organisations that provide opportunities for further inclusion. Social workers can also act as advocates for service users, assisting them to overcome discriminatory barriers and prejudice that prevent them from accessing services and opportunities. In addition, social workers can campaign on behalf of service users, drawing the attention of policy-makers to the exclusionary impact of regressive economic and social policies. Social workers are, in short, in a position to empower service users; they can act as progressive agents of change and help reduce levels of social exclusion.

Likewise, advocates of social integrationist discourse would welcome the impact social workers can make in tackling social exclusion, though they would place much greater emphasis on the role they can play in encouraging or enabling people who are excluded to engage or re-engage with the labour market.

What direction social exclusion policy?

Within the academic literature on social exclusion in the UK, much attention has been given to analysing the trajectory of the Labour government's response to the issue. Perhaps not surprisingly, the government itself claims to have achieved much. It points out that the number of people in employment has increased by 2.5 million since 1997. Since 1998, 700,000 children and 1 million pensioners have been lifted out of poverty, and, overall, there are now 2.4 million fewer people living below the poverty line. In addition, the number of people experiencing homelessness has declined and rough sleeping is down by 73 per cent since 1998. The government also draws attention to the increased investment it has made in education and health, all of which have contributed to improved levels of inclusion. For example, the government estimates that the number of young people leaving school with no qualifications has halved since 1997, while the proportion gaining five good GCSEs has risen from 45 per cent to 58 per cent (SET, 2007b).

However, critics argue that the potential and flexibility of the concept of social exclusion is not being realised in the government's inclusion strategy. Hopes among some that Labour would embrace redistributionist discourse have, they argue, been dashed, and Labour's responses to social exclusion owe much more to the ideological influence of social integration and moral underclass discourses than redistributive concerns. The government, Fiona Williams argues, has *managed to combine the integrationist emphasis of ... social exclusion discourse with the 'underclass notion' of neo-liberal poverty discourse, whilst moving away from the focus on inequality and redistribution* (Williams, 1998, p17).

Levitas (2001) also detects the influence of moral underclass and social integration discourse in the government's policies. Labour, she claims, has sought to 'marginalise' and 'individualise' social exclusion, by creating the impression that it affects only a small section of society, who are failing to take up the 'opportunities' offered to them. She notes that the SEU's (and latterly the SET's) initiatives have been aimed at relatively small groups, whose behaviour is deemed to deviate from the prescribed norm, and who are seen to pose a threat to social and moral order. The 'poor parenting skills' of teenage mothers and lone parents are blamed for community breakdown, while young people not in education, employment or training (often referred to as NEETs) are portrayed as lazy, feckless youths who laze around all day, engaging in idle games and petty crime. At the same time, the unemployed and disabled people are accused of failing to take up work opportunities and are held responsible for burgeoning welfare bills. Thus, interventions influenced by moral underclass discourse have been implemented to tackle the supposed inappropriate, 'dysfunctional' patterns of behaviour among the poor, while a 'works first' approach, influenced by social integrationist strategies, has been introduced to drive people into employment, whatever the cost. Meanwhile, the structural causes of social exclusion – economic decline, lack of work opportunities, inadequate benefits, prejudice and discrimination – remain unresolved. Critics of the government, therefore, argue that the redistributive rhetoric that surrounds its social exclusion strategy has not been matched by its interventions, the effects of which have been to pathologise the excluded and blame them for their own fate and also wider social and economic problems. How justified is this criticism of the government's social exclusion strategy? We begin with an analysis of its response to social exclusion among disabled people. Following this, we look at the government's proposals for combating the endemic problems experienced by a section of the population that it considers to be among the most severely socially excluded.

Disability and social exclusion

It is widely acknowledged that people with disabilities are far more likely to be experiencing social exclusion than non-disabled people and that they fair less well than non-disabled people across a whole range of social and economic indicators. For example, 26 per cent of long-term disabled people have no educational qualifications, compared with 11 per cent of non-disabled people, and disabled people are only half as likely as their non-disabled counterparts to be educated to degree level. Disabled people are more likely to experience difficulties accessing decent housing. According to one recent survey, 181,000 households in England contain people with a serious medical condition or disability whose accommodation is not suitable for them (Prime Minister's Strategy Unit, 2005, p50). Difficulties accessing public transport also contribute to the wider social exclusion of disabled people, affecting not only work opportunities, but also their ability to maintain social networks. Remarkably, as late as 2003, only around 30 per cent of buses across the UK could be described as 'accessible' (Prime Minister's Strategy Unit, 2005, p50). Disabled people are also more likely to be victims of race or hate crime, and many cite fear of this as a key contributory factor when explaining their feelings of isolation and exclusion. Disturbingly, a quarter of all disabled people and 47 per cent of disabled people with mental health conditions report that they have been victims of race or hate crime.

Disabled people also fair less well in the labour market and data show that they are less likely to be economically active than their non-disabled counterparts. In Autumn 2004, the overall employment rate for disabled people in Britain was 51 per cent, compared with 81 per cent for non-disabled people. For people with learning difficulties, the employment rate is an even lower 26 per cent (DRC, 2005). This exclusion from the labour market is a consistent feature throughout the life cycle and young disabled people are more likely to be not in education or training than their non-disabled counterparts – 27 per cent of disabled 19-year-olds, compared with 10 per cent of their non-disabled counterparts (Prime Minister's Strategy Unit, 2005, p44). In the light of these findings, we should not be too surprised to find that disabled people's incomes are on average half those of non-disabled people, and that they are more likely to be in poverty.

RESEARCH SUMMARY

The exclusion of disabled people from the labour market

Explanations for the exclusion of disabled people from the labour market do vary, but for organisations representing disabled people, the prime cause is discrimination and prejudice. The extent of this was highlighted by the mental health service users' charity Scope's 2003 survey, Ready, willing and disabled, which examined employers' views on employing disabled people.

- *Employers stereotypically assumed that disabled people would be a 'burden'. Forty-five per cent said they would not be able to employ a disabled person because they could not afford it.*

- *Nineteen per cent said that the fact that they had never worked with a disabled person before, and so did not know what to expect, would prevent them employing a disabled person.*

- *Eleven per cent said that they would not employ disabled people because their clients/ customers would not want to be served by them, while 45 per cent said they did not know if this would prevent them employing someone.*

A 2004 Disability Rights Commission survey of small-employer attitudes to disabled people confirmed these findings. Thirty-seven per cent believed disabled people would be a drain on their finances, 33 per cent believed they would be a drain on their colleagues, and 44 per cent believed they would take to take too much sick leave (DRC, 2005).

This research seems to confirm the potential of social exclusion as a concept in helping us to understand the causes of disadvantage. Like the BBC study on racial discrimination we discussed earlier, it can assist us to appreciate the role discrimination and prejudice play in shaping the disadvantage faced by disabled people. It acknowledges the non-income based, structural, discriminatory barriers that prevent, or 'exclude', disabled people from accessing the same opportunities as non-disabled people, and shares much in common with the 'social model' of disability that has emerged as an explanation for the marginalisation of disabled people over the past three decades.

The social model of disability

The social model of disability emerged in the 1970s. It represented a reaction against 'individualised' or 'medicalised' explanations for disabled people's social exclusion (often referred to as the medical model) that located the blame for exclusion with their own impairments or motivation. With the medical model, disabled people are seen primarily as passive users of services, which are aimed at 'curing' or 'managing' their disabilities through 'special' targeted interventions from doctors, specialists, surgeons, educational psychologists and social workers. Solutions based on the medical model focus on the development of sheltered workshops, training centres and 'special schools', which are created to help 'manage' those who, because of their disability, are deemed ill-equipped to participate in mainstream society. By contrast, the social model *directs the analytical focus away from individual functional limitations to the barriers to social inclusion created by disabling environments, attitudes, and cultures* (Barnes and Mercer, 2005, p527). It focuses on the exclusionary barriers that intersect disabled peoples' lives, *such as inaccessible education, information and communication systems, working environments, inadequate disability benefits, discriminatory health and social support services, inaccessible transport, houses and public buildings and amenities, and negative cultural and media representations*. While not dismissing the potential of specific interventions into the lives of disabled people, whether these be medical, rehabilitative, educational or employment related, there is an insistence that these are in themselves insufficient to achieve 'inclusion'. It is societies that impair disabled people and it societies that are in need of 'rehabilitation' and reform, not disabled people themselves. In terms of its relation to our models of social exclusion outlined earlier, the social model of disability approximates most closely to redistributive discourse.

Government policies to address disabled people's social exclusion: A redistributionist, social integration or moral underclass approach?

There can be little doubt that since 1997 Labour governments have acknowledged the structural determinants of the social exclusion experienced by disabled people. In the introduction to the government's 2005 report, *Improving the life chances of disabled people*, the Prime Minister, Tony Blair, stated that disabled people *are still experiencing disadvantage and discrimination. Barriers – in attitudes, the design of buildings and policies, for example – still have to be overcome by disabled people, reducing their opportunities and preventing them fulfilling their potential* (Prime Minister's Strategy Unit, 2005, p5). In addition, policies targeted at tackling the discriminatory barriers disabled people face, particularly those relating to employment, have been introduced. The 1995 Disability Discrimination Act, the main piece of legislation designed to combat disability discrimination, has been strengthened. In addition, a Disability Rights Commission was formed, giving disabled people for the first time a statutory body with similar powers to the Equal Opportunities Commission and the Commission for Racial Equality (these three bodies have now come together to form the Equality and Human Rights Commission). The introduction of personal job advisers via the New Deal for Disabled People, and the removal of some of the inflexibilities in the benefits and tax credits systems, which previously acted as disincentives to re-engage with the labour market, have arguably made returning to work somewhat easier and less of a risk for disabled people. Consequently, the employment rate among disabled people, though still low, has improved since 1997, when it was only 47 per cent (Finn, 2005). Other policies have been introduced, ostensibly designed to enable and empower disabled people, giving them more control over their lives. For example, *Valuing People*, the government's strategy for transforming the way people with learning disabilities are supported, is intended to enable them to overcome some of the exclusion and disadvantages they have experienced. *Valuing People* identified a number of issues to be addressed, including the need for greater choice and control over service delivery, geographical inconsistency in provision, and, more generally, the social isolation experienced by people with learning disabilities (Burton and Kagan, 2006).

These initiatives seem to hint at a redistributive discourse influence, and certainly it is possible to detect elements of this in the rhetoric used to justify policies, much of which seems to be radical, ambitious and optimistic in tone. However, for some the government's 'inclusion' initiatives for disabled people owe less to social justice and redistributive concerns and more to a desire to get disabled people off benefits and into employment. While few deny the value of employment as a route to greater 'inclusion' for disabled people, some have questioned the overarching emphasis that has been placed on employment, and the tone of the rhetoric that has been used to justify the government's welfare-to-work strategy. The government's critics point to the emphasis placed on the social and economic 'costs' of 'dependency', which serves to reinforce the notion that disabled people are a 'burden'.

Roulstone (2000) is one of those who detect a contradiction in the government's approach to tackling disabled people's social exclusion. He notes that alongside 'progressive' rhetoric and policies – seemingly shaped by redistributionist and social integrationist discourse – we have also seen the influence of the moral underclass approach to social exclusion, where emphasis continues to be placed on individualistic, behavioural interpretations for the problems faced by disabled people. For instance, the government has made much of the supposed dependency-inducing and morale-sapping effects of state welfare. Many disabled people, we are told, are failing to take up the 'opportunities' provided by the government because they have come to see a benefit income as a 'way of life'; they are 'trapped' on welfare, their confidence is low and they need to be 'incentivised' to enable them to lead a more independent lifestyle. Certainly, it is possible to detect evidence of such thinking in government documents relating to the social exclusion of disabled people. *Instead of being empowered to work, earn, spend and pay taxes*, one such report argued, *too many disabled people are left to depend on benefits and government support*. It is time, the report states, *to end the culture of dependency and low expectation* (Prime Minister's Strategy Unit, 2005, pp10–11). The solution to exclusion, from this perspective, lies not in the extension of civil rights (as groups representing disabled people would argue), but in the development of a range of employment initiatives designed to 'motivate' disabled people, 'weaning' them off benefits and into work. To a certain extent, this is the philosophy that underlies much of the current government's 'inclusion strategy' for disabled people, the New Deal for Disabled People, and in some cases the 'stimulus' for motivation is the threat of withdrawal of benefits.

Such strategies have not been without their critics. There is a danger, some argue, that such solutions serve to 'pathologise' disabled people, and at the same time obscure the government's failure to address the wider structural barriers to inclusion, including prejudice and discrimination which, as we saw earlier, disabled people still face. Although the rhetoric underpinning the government's welfare-to-work strategy for disabled people may be progressive and inclusive, some argue that its underlying philosophy is that it is disabled people and not society that is in need of 'cure', 'care' or 'rehabilitation'. The problems disabled people face are thus individualised and the focus of intervention is disabled people themselves – it is their dependency, their lack of motivation and their fatalism that needs addressing, and not the societal barriers they often face in accessing services and employment. Hence, Roulstone (2000, pp428–9) argues that *Similarities can be observed between the victim blaming representation of the 'underclass' and the imagery created of a dependent disabled population.*

As hinted at above, similar criticisms have been made on a more general level of the government's social exclusion strategy. Levitas argues that the SEU's reports have concentrated on issues relating to moral and social order, focusing on particular groups that are perceived to be a 'problem', and who, to varying degrees, are considered responsible for their own situation. In the next section we will look at one of the government's more recent reports on social exclusion and assess the validity of these criticisms. Before doing so, we would like you to explore the shape and direction of the government's social exclusion strategy yourselves.

ACTIVITY 3.3

Take a look at the now archived SEU website http://archive.cabinetoffice.gov.uk/seu/ and have a look at a sample of SEU reports such as:

- *Bridging the gap – New opportunities for 16–18 year olds not in education, employment or training (1999);*
- *Teenage pregnancy (1999).*

How were the issues in these and other SEU reports presented? What 'threats' were the problems discussed said to pose?

What explanations are advanced for the problems discussed in the reports?

Is the emphasis more on structural or behavioural interpretations, or a combination of the two?

What solutions are proposed?

Reaching out

In September 2006, the government published what it described as a key document on social exclusion, *Reaching out: an action plan on social exclusion* (SET, 2007b). In the Preface to *Reaching out*, Tony Blair reaffirmed the government's commitment to tackling social exclusion, insisting that a commitment *to ensuring everyone should have the opportunity to achieve their potential in life* remained *at the heart of this government's mission* (p3). However, since the report's publication, the underlying philosophy of the government's social exclusion strategy has been questioned. While some welcomed the report and its recommendations, for others it seemed to signal a further shift away from a redistributive approach and a movement towards behavioural, 'moral underclass' strategy.

Reaching out began by outlining the successes of the government's social exclusion strategy. Since 1997, 2.5 million more people had found work, one million fewer people were on benefits, and levels of income poverty, particularly among families with children, had fallen. Child poverty rates had dropped at a faster rate in the UK than in any other European country and educational attainment rates had improved, especially in disadvantaged areas. In explaining these positive indicators, *Reaching out* drew attention to the increased 'opportunities' the government had provided, which had encouraged and enabled people to climb out of their previous precarious, insecure predicaments and become fully active, 'inclusive' members of society. However, the overarching focus of *Reaching out* was on those who, despite the government's best efforts, seemed, to be *stuck in a lifetime of disadvantage* (p3). Against this background of success, the government argued, *the relative lack of progress of a small minority stands out* (p19). The 'minority' was said to consist of 2.5–3 per cent of the population, roughly 1.3 million people, though this was not made explicit in either the document itself, or in subsequent media coverage of the report's recommendations.

How did the government explain this relative lack of progress among certain sections of the community? *Reaching out* sought to draw a stark contrast between, on the one hand, the achievements of those who had embraced the 'opportunities' provided, and on the other hand, the continued deep-seated exclusion of those who had not. The message was simple: the opportunities were now there, and if individuals or families were failing to grasp them, then some more targeted, focused and coercive levels of intervention were necessary. Hence, responsibility for the chronic social exclusion experienced by the bottom 2.5–3 per cent of the population was seen to lie largely with the socially excluded themselves. According to the report, it was a consequence of their *problematic lifestyles,* which resulted from *chaotic lives – such as anti-social behaviour, criminality and poor parenting* (p74).

In language reminiscent of Keith Joseph's 'transmitted deprivation' theory (see Chapter 2), *Reaching out* suggests that dysfunctional 'cultural' characteristics are passed down from one generation to the next via a *cycle of deprivation* (p19). In this sense, the intellectual origins of the analysis and policy prescriptions contained in *Reaching out* did seem to have much more in common with the moral underclass discourse than they did with the redistributive discourse. Even the rationale for intervention –

that is, the reason for wanting to tackle exclusion – focused more on the 'problems' caused by sections of community to society, as it did the need to tackle the wider societal barriers that inhibit inclusion, such as low incomes, discrimination and barriers to the job market. The *behaviour of some people*, the report argued, *particularly some of the most challenging families – causes real disruption and distress to the community around them.* The government also outlined the financial cost of 'problem families', estimating this to be around £250,000 per year, per family (Campbell and Temko, 2006).

Reaching out's recommendations generated a good degree of controversy when the report was published. In short, the report outlined a plan for the early identification of future 'chaotic' and 'problematic' individuals and families, backed up by a series of sanctions designed to force people to change their behaviour. Some of the criticism the government faced focused on the case it made for using sanctions, such as benefit withdrawal or even the removal of children from parents, as a means of ensuring co-operation, and the possible dangers of removing financial support from already vulnerable families. However, the major area of contention and controversy centred on the age at which attempts to identify risk ought to begin. Basically, *Reaching out* suggested that this process should start *before individuals are born*.

ACTIVITY 3.4

When Reaching out *was published, the proposals were greeted by a flurry of sensationalist, but largely supportive, headlines in the tabloid press. Below are a representative selection of headlines:*

Blair's Attack on Unborn Thugs – Daily Star (1/9/06).
ASBOs in the Womb: Blair Aims to Spot Problem Kids Before They Are Born – Mirror (1/9/06).
£250,000 a Time: The Cost of Problem Families – Express (4/9/06).

What impact do you think the above headlines would have in shaping public opinion about people who are socially excluded?

Reaching out identified a range of 'pre-birth' and 'post-birth' 'risk factors' which, it announced, community midwives and health visitors will use to 'diagnose' an unborn child's potential for future misbehaviour and exclusion (p28). Below are the pre-birth risk factors highlighted in the report.

'Pre-birth' risk factors

- Genetic predisposition.
- Obstetric difficulties.
- Prematurity/birth factors.
- Stress in pregnancy.
- Teenage pregnancy.
- Smoking in pregnancy.
- Neglected neighbourhood.
- Low income.
- Poor housing.

The existence of any or a combination of these pre-birth 'risk factors' could be sufficient to trigger an initial two-year period of interventions with families. The precise nature of these interventions is not yet clear, but based upon the experience of similar schemes in the United States, the government seem to be envisaging regular checks by social workers and health professionals and compulsory involvement in pro-grammes (again, under the threat of sanctions) designed to improve parenting, conduct and behaviour. The rationale, to cite one recent government-funded report, is that it is possible to identify factors that place unborn children *at risk for life-course persistent criminal involvement, antisocial behaviour and social exclusion* (Utting, Monteiro and Ghate, 2007, p80), and the aim is to alter what is perceived to be the families' predetermined, 'dysfunctional' life course.

ACTIVITY **3.5**

Consider the pre-birth factors cited above that have been identified as being linked to potential future problematic behaviour. Put yourself in the position of a practitioner who is asked to use these indicators to predict future behaviour.

- *What value issues arise?*

- *How might this kind of intervention affect the already low take-up rates of pre-maternity services among disadvantaged families?*

- *In various chapters in the book we have discussed labelling theory. What would labelling theorists have to say about the recommendations for the 'early identification' of future problematic individuals?*

Criticisms/discussion of *Reaching out*

Genetic predisposition

You may have noticed that 'genetic predisposition' featured among the risk factors to be used to identify future problematic behaviour. *Reaching out* did not elaborate upon how a genetic predisposition to social exclusion might be identified or defined, but the notion that 'exclusion' can be seen as a hereditary condition is deeply con-troversial and cannot be allowed to pass without comment. Social policies based on claims of genetic predisposition have a justifiably unfavourable reputation. Pseudo-scientific claims that certain groups, or races, are 'genetically inferior' than those within the 'mainstream' have been used to justify a range of injustices, from compul-sory sterilisation programmes for 'undesirables' in some countries, to Hitler's programmes of mass murder of millions in the 1930s and 1940s. More recently, Charles Murray has claimed that the entrenched poverty that is a feature of some Black and Hispanic communities in the United States is a result of genetic, rather than structural, factors. The higher levels of poverty in these ethnic groups is, he argues, a result of genetic failings – for instance, lower levels of intelligence – rather than the structural environment which surrounds them. On publication, Murray's ideas were immediately condemned, and much of the IQ 'evidence' cited in support of his ana-lysis has subsequently been discredited, with some of it being linked to white supremacist organisations in the United States. We discuss Murray's ideas on IQ and intelligence in Chapter 7.

Labelling

There is also the question of the potentially detrimental impact that labelling a baby, or a family, as potentially dysfunctional might have. As Vicki Harman (2006) argues, rather than acting as an inclusionary mechanism, it may actually contribute to their exclusion:

> *These measures are aimed at the 'difficult to reach' – but it is this kind of stigma, scrutiny and labelling that leads people to avoid engaging with services. The challenge of how to support families in need without labelling them problematic, and further isolating them through stigma and blame, remains unexplored.*

Indeed, the government's own commissioned research seems to reinforce the dangers of labelling that are associated with the sort of interventions contemplated in *Reaching out*:

> *The task of developing robust instruments is fraught with difficulties; not least those associated with the important issue of 'false positives' and stigmatising children with labels that unintentionally damage their life chances.*
>
> (Utting et al., 2007, p86)

Here then, we must consider the impact that being labelled might have on a young child and/or its family. For example, a certain amount of stigma is bound to be associated with the label 'potential deviant', and it is through this label that this child's future behaviour will be viewed by midwives, social workers, the police and others whose role it will be to monitor him or her. It may be that an incident, or pattern of behaviour that otherwise might have remained unnoticed or dismissed (had it manifested itself with a child in a different family), will be picked upon and seen as evidence to support the original diagnosis. This may lead to further intervention and the creation of a 'self-fulfilling prophecy'.

Ineffectiveness of the proposed intervention

Research funded by the government itself suggests that those suffering from the most deeply rooted forms of social exclusion – that is, those targeted by *Reaching out* – are the least likely to benefit from its proposals. After evaluating evidence from US evaluations into similar initiatives, Utting *et al.* (2007) found that:

> *What little evidence exists suggests that within a 'treated' population it is generally the most needy, most challenging families and young people who are least helped by these programmes. In families where parents have mental health problems, where there is substance misuse, or where there is a background of serious abuse and neglect the outcomes are often least positive.*
>
> (p84)

Furthermore, the government's focus on modifying 'dysfunctional' behaviour seems to exclude the influence 'structural' problems can have on a family's ability to fulfil its parental obligations. As one evaluation of a UK initiative for combating social exclusion in disadvantaged families noted, *factors that make good parenting difficult require action at a political level, for example developing better housing stock, improving schools and providing more income support* (Scott, O'Connor and Futh, 2006, p3). In this sense, interventions targeted at social and parenting skills may sound laudable, but they can never inoculate children from the impact of being brought up in severe poverty.

Earlier in the discussion, we posed the question 'what direction social exclusion policy?' If we take *Reaching out* as a representative strategy, then the trajectory is certainly imbued with a moral underclass slant. It would, however, be a mistake to assume that the whole of the government's social exclusion strategy is imbued with the influence of moral underclass discourse. In fact, it often contains elements of all three interpretations of social exclusion. As we saw earlier, its response to social exclusion among people with disabilities is a case in point, with all three discourses shaping the different elements of the government's strategy. For some, this 'elasticity' of the concept of social exclusion is one of its major problems, allowing it to be used to suit different political purposes. Others, though, point to this being one of its advantages, particularly for social workers. Pierson (2002), for example, argues that *The fact that social exclusion means different things to different people allows for greater flexibility in practice than you might have thought* (p7). Citing society's response to juvenile crime, he points out that government legislation, influenced by moral underclass discourse, has focused on punitive and retributive methods of preventing crime, but in their practice social workers have succeeded in achieving the same objectives through continuing to pursue redistributionist and social integrationist strategies. The point here is that although the legislative framework within which social workers operate may at times contradict and mitigate against redistributionist responses to exclusion, in practice social workers are able to reconcile these contradictions, pursuing essentially progressive strategies within what is sometimes a regressive ideological and legislative climate. We end the chapter with a discussion of the role social workers can play in combating social exclusion.

Tackling social exclusion

We began this chapter by recognising that social workers are centrally involved in providing services and support to individuals and groups who are often socially excluded. In order to be able to do this effectively, it is of fundamental importance that social workers hold values that are based on a commitment to social justice; in other words, commitment to fair and equal treatment of all individuals and a fair distribution of resources.

The teaching of social work values permeates social work training courses, however, for social workers who are committed to tackling social exclusion, values must be translated into daily practice. This involves a passionate commitment to helping to make a difference in the lives of the people we work with and this begins with the way in which we interact on an interpersonal level with service users. In order to intervene sensitively and professionally with individuals who are socially excluded, social workers need to be able to actively demonstrate respect and the ability to value people from all walks of life. Actively demonstrating respect involves the social worker being warm and open, supportive and facilitative, listening carefully and allowing service users to talk freely, while facilitating a relationship that is based on honesty and trust. It further involves a commitment to perceiving and valuing service users' qualities and strengths, their uniqueness and individuality, and working in ways which validate the worth of every individual that receives social work services. Assisting service users at a micro level to recognise how the dominant forces in their lives have impacted upon their personal experiences is an important task for social workers. In this sense, moral underclass discourse offers us as social workers the least in terms of helping us comprehend and respond to social exclusion. Its overtly moralistic, 'blaming' explanations for exclusion, and its insistence that state welfare agencies and welfare professionals are themselves major contributory factors, affords us with little opportunity to understand the complex causes of the difficulties faced by service users, or develop positive, progressive solutions.

Clearly, tackling social exclusion cannot be achieved solely by intervention that occurs on an interpersonal level. A commitment is needed for social workers to work in partnership with service users to intervene to make a difference at a community and structural level. This is not easy, and here the warnings advanced by critics of the social exclusion debate should not be ignored.

As Dominelli (2004) states, *Social workers ... have difficulty addressing the structural problems that bedevil communities because they have become enmeshed in a web of competence based approaches to social work advanced under new managerialism* (p224). The proceduralisation of modern social work and the advent of numerous administrative procedures has meant that much state-sponsored social work at least, is significantly reined in, such that social workers have time only to fulfil prescribed requirements of procedural systems and paperwork, leaving little time to go out and really engage with the structural causes of social exclusion. Dominelli mounts a forceful argument which suggests that the social work profession must become independent from the state, if it is to truly advocate for and on behalf of socially excluded individuals and groups:

> *Social workers have to free themselves from the shackles of a government imposed bureau-rationality that has turned them into bureau-technocrats unable to rise to the challenges of twenty-first century practice.*
>
> (2004, p253)

Whether or not this position will ever be realised is a matter of debate. However, in the meantime, Dominelli does advocate an approach in which social workers must exercise what she refers to as their *moral and ethical responsibility* to promote social change at both individual and structural levels. She calls for needs-led universal services, rather than 'stigmatised residual services' and for an approach that works to undermine the forces of oppression.

Social workers often feel constrained by their role and their organisation; however, it is vital for social workers to move beyond these constraints to retain a commitment to change that is done in a spirit of hope and enthusiasm. Pierson's (2002) work is extremely helpful in identifying achievable and practical ways of working to tackle social exclusion. He recognises that; *It is tempting to think that you and your colleagues can wait until someone fires the 'time to start tackling social exclusion' gun before taking forward elements of practice outlined in this book* [Tackling Social Exclusion]. *But that is not a luxury you have. On the contrary, your role should be one of catalyst and change agent regardless* (p232). Pierson identifies core strategies for tackling social exclusion. These are:

- maximising income and welfare rights; knowing the benefits system and working to maximise the income of service users;

- working to strengthen networks, to provide emotional support and to facilitate inclusion in the community;

- building partnerships to strengthen ways of tackling exclusion, by joined-up solutions, sharing expertise and using collective muscle;

- promoting participation of service users in discussing, planning and arranging services and programmes that will affect them;

- working in the neighbourhood to help facilitate joint action and community development.

Pierson's book is a worthy and useful read for all social work students as it addresses strategies for working with different excluded groups. In terms of the three interpretations of social exclusion we outlined earlier, this kind of approach would share most in common with redistribution discourse.

C H A P T E R   S U M M A R Y

As we have seen, debates about the causes of 'social exclusion' now permeate the social policy agenda. Even Conservative politicians, many of whom have traditionally shown a reluctance to embrace any concept which hints at 'social' causes of social problems, now seem as comfortable with the concept as their counterparts of the political Left. However, popular acceptance and usage of the concept should not be allowed to disguise the real differences that exist between the explanations that have been advanced to account for social exclusion. Throughout this chapter we have drawn attention to the fact that there is no consensus as to what the causes of social exclusion are, or about what the solutions should be. It is, we have argued, a 'slippery' concept, meaning different things to different people. It is this that largely explains its popular appeal. For example, those on the Right can 'cash in' on the current 'vogue' for social exclusion discourse, while at the same time remaining wedded to moral underclass interpretations of social problems. By contrast, those on the Left seize on the opportunity that the 'social' component of social exclusion seems to provide them to reinforce redistributive, structural explanations for social problems. Meanwhile, government ministers seem happy to continue to bask in the glow of 'social exclusion', while charting a pragmatic 'what works' approach. As we have illustrated, the Labour government's social inclusion strategies draw from social integrationist, moral underclass and redistributive discourses, prompting inevitable debates in academic circles about the respective influence of each. We will leave you to make your own mind up as to the merits of the different discourses, but in doing so we would implore you to bear in mind the practice implications of the three. At the same time, we would ask you to consider the compatibility of the competing discourses with the social work value base and their potential impact on different groups of service users. Finally, think about the reasons why you made the decision to become a social worker and consider the extent to which each of the three explanations for social exclusion 'fit' with your own perceptions about what the causes of social exclusion might be.

Levitas, R (2005) *The inclusive society? Social exclusion and new labour.* Basingstoke: Palgrave Macmillan. It is in this influential book that Levitas sets out her explanations for the three different social exclusion discourses.

Jones, C and Novak, C (1999) *Poverty and the disciplinary state.* Abingdon: Routledge. This book provides a Marxist analysis of poverty, social exclusion and welfare.

Marsland, D (1996) *Welfare or welfare state? Contradictions and dilemmas in social policy.* Basingstoke: Macmillan. This book is written by a UK sociologist who offers a similar slant to Charles Murray's. Like Murray's work, it should not be read uncritically.

Pierson, J (2002) *Tackling social exclusion.* Abingdon: Routledge. This book offers an excellent read for social workers as it combines theory with clear practical approaches for tackling social exclusion.

Chapter 4
Families

This chapter will help you begin to meet the following National Occupational Standards and General Social Care Council's Code of Practice.

Key Role 1: Prepare for, and work with individuals, families, carers, groups and communities to assess their needs and circumstances
* Work with individuals, families, carers, groups and communities to help them make informed decisions.

Key Role 2: Plan, carry out, review and evaluate social work practice, with individuals, families, carers, groups, communities and other professionals
* Develop and maintain relationships with individuals, families, carers, groups, communities and others.
* Apply and justify social work methods and models used to achieve change and development, and improve life opportunities.
* Examine with individuals, families, carers, groups, communities and others support networks which can be accessed and developed.
* Work with individuals, families, carers, groups, communities and others to initiate and sustain support networks.

Key Role 3: Support individuals to represent their needs, views and circumstances
* Advocate with, and on behalf of, individuals, families, carers, groups and communities.

Key Role 4: Manage risk to individuals, families, carers, groups, communities, self and colleagues
* Assess and manage risks to individuals, families, carers, groups and communities.

Key Role 5: Manage and be accountable, with supervision and support, for your own social work practice within your organisation
* Carry out duties using accountable professional judgment and knowledge based social work practice.
* Use professional and managerial supervision and support to improve your practice.

Key Role 6: Demonstrate professional competence in social work practice
* Work within agreed standards of social work practice and ensure own professional development.
* Implement knowledge based social work models and methods to develop and improve your own practice.
* Use professional assertiveness to justify decisions and uphold professional social work practice, values and ethics.
* Work within the principles and values underpinning social work practice.
* Critically reflect upon your own practice and performance using supervision and support systems.
* Use supervision and support to take action to meet continuing professional development needs.
* Manage complex ethical issues, dilemmas and conflicts.

General Social Care Council Code of Practice

Code 1.5: Promoting equal opportunities for service users and carers.

Code 1.6: Respecting diversity and different cultures and values.

Code 3.8: Recognising and using responsibly the power that comes from your work with service users and carers.

Code 5.5: Must not discriminate unlawfully or unjustifiably against service users, carers or colleagues.

Code 6.3: Informing your employer or the appropriate authority about any personal difficulties that might affect your ability to do your job competently and safely.

Code 6.4: Seeking assistance from your employer or the appropriate authority if you do not feel able or adequately prepared to carry out any aspect of your work, or you are not sure about how to proceed in a work matter.

It will also introduce you to the following academic standards as set out in the social work subject benchmark statements.

3.1.1 Social work services and service users
- Explanations of the links between definitional processes contributing to social differences (for example, social class, gender and ethnic differences) to the problems of inequality and differential need faced by service users.

3.1.2 The service delivery context
- The issues and trends in modern public and social policy and their relationship to contemporary practice and service delivery in social work.

3.1.3 Values and ethics
- The complex relationships between justice, care and control in social welfare and the practical and ethical implications of these, including roles as statutory agents and in upholding the law in respect of discrimination.

3.1.4 Social work theory
- The relevance of sociological perspectives to understanding societal and structural influences on human behaviour at individual, group and community levels.

3.1.5 The nature of social work practice
- The place of theoretical perspectives and evidence from international research in assessment and decision-making processes in social work practice.
- The integration of theoretical perspectives and evidence from international research into the design and implementation of effective social work intervention with a wide range of service users, carers and others.

Introduction

Given the centrality of the family in social work practice, it is helpful for social workers to have an understanding of the nature of family life from within a sociological framework. This chapter depicts the variety of family forms in modern society and encourages you to think about how social work intervention may help or sometimes hinder the experiences of family members. It challenges you to reflect upon your own values and to critically consider these in light of the social work value base. Consideration of sociological theories and different feminist approaches to the family will draw upon relevant policy initiatives and the intersection with practice.

The family is one of the core social institutions in our society. The social work profession intervenes with families both in a supportive capacity and to exercise social control functions. The extent to which the family has rights to privacy from intrusion, versus the right of the state to intervene in families to protect vulnerable citizens, is a core area of debate in social work. Sociological insights are helpful for social workers to enable them to think critically about family life; this is important so that taken-for-granted assumptions about families can be challenged and the complexities of family life understood. It is necessary to give serious thought to the nature of social work intervention in family life; to ask what gives social workers the *right* to intervene. Certainly, this is a fundamental question and social workers need to have thought it through carefully, so that they are ultimately comfortable with their role. Moreover, this is important if practice is to be grounded, legitimate and ethical.

ACTIVITY **4.1**

Why do you think social workers have the right to intervene in family life?

You may have identified reasons such as the duty of the state to protect vulnerable citizens; children's rights to be safe and protected from harm; the existence of legislation and policy. However, it is important to balance these factors with an acknowledgement of the damage that intervention can sometimes incur. As Thompson and Bates (1998) note:

> *It would be naive in the extreme to fail to recognise that social work intervention is capable not only of making a positive difference to people's lives, but also doing considerable harm. The social worker has a great deal of power and such power can result in successful or unsuccessful outcomes ... intervention can have an extremely detrimental effect on individuals, families and groups. This can include: breaking up families, reducing self esteem, creating dependency, reinforcing stigma, discrimination, and oppression.*

(p6)

It is also worth pointing out at this stage that social workers intervene with some families and not with others. Certain families are more visible to the gaze of the state whereas others are able to establish boundaries that keep professionals at bay. It is fair to say that social work surveillance tends to be directed at families from poorer, disadvantaged backgrounds. The disparity of state involvement with particular families and the fact that intervention can sometimes bring about more harm than good, are uncomfortable truths that social workers should be aware of and reflect upon throughout their careers. As social work intervention is premised upon decision-making of professionals, a critical approach to practice is necessary, as well as an ongoing inner dialogue regarding the values that underpin decisions.

Before we proceed further with looking sociologically at the family, we want you to think more about the family and about your own experiences within families.

ACTIVITY 4.2

Make a list of the common characteristics of families. To help you do this, you might wish to reflect for a few moments on your own experiences of family life.
How did your personal experiences of family life influence what appeared in your list?
Working with someone you trust, share and compare your lists; what were the similarities and differences?

In this exercise, you may have come up with a list of positive characteristics such as:

- warm;
- loving;
- providing security;
- acceptable conflict;
- unconditional love;
- durable ties.

Alternatively, you may have come up with more negative characteristics, such as:

- arguments;
- violence;
- abuse;
- loss;
- bullying;
- conflict.

Or more likely, you will have identified a combination of positive and negative characteristics. For some of you, this exercise in itself will have been a painful experience as family life can often leave scars on people that go with them into their future lives. You may wish to reflect upon whether you drew up your list from experiences in your family of origin, or where applicable, from your own adult family life. Students often talk with us about their experiences of family life, some good and others not so good; one thing is clear – their experiences are incredibly diverse and varied, and they bring these into social work training with them. It is important that as trainee social workers you are able to think carefully about and reflect upon your personal experiences of family life, to enable you to enter the territory of family life as a professional. Failure to do so can lead to social workers being unable to separate out their own experiences and feelings from those of their service users. In the first chapter, we asked you to debunk your own life sociologically to enable you to locate yourself within society. In this chapter we will be asking you to do more of this, but specifically in relation to family life. Firstly, we want you to begin to think about the boundaries around personal and professional life.

ACTIVITY **4.3**

Discussion exercise
Why is it important for social workers to be able to separate out their own experiences of family life from those of their service users?
To what extent are social workers' own experiences a help or a hindrance in their professional practice?

We will return to this issue later on in this chapter, but you are encouraged to give this issue some thought.

Different forms of family life

The question 'what is the family?' is frequently posed by sociologists and underlies the point that although in generic terms we talk about 'the family', in reality this can mean very many things to different people. The much-quoted popular image of 'the family' is of a typical nuclear family which consists of two married, heterosexual parents and their two children, who live together in their own home, often depicted with roses growing around the door, with their car in the drive. This is often referred to by sociologists as the 'cereal packet family', as it reflects the ideal image traditionally portrayed on TV adverts. However, the reality for a large proportion of the population is a very different form of family life and the sweeping assumptions that frequently permeate popular culture are not helpful to people whose lives are so very different from the 'ideal' quoted above.

One classic definition of the family came from George Peter Murdock back in 1949:

> *The family is a social group characterised by common residence, economic cooperation and reproduction. It includes adults of both sexes, at least two of whom maintain a socially approved, sexual relationship, and one or more children, own or adopted, of the sexually cohabiting adults.*

(p1)

Murdock's formative work emerged from careful examination of 'the family' in 250 societies; he concluded that the family existed in some form in all known societies and was therefore a universal institution. Although some sociologists have refuted this claim, Murdock's work has remained influential and his definition has been widely quoted. Notwithstanding the fact that the definition is now dated, the essence of it remains very much part of common assumptions about the average nuclear family in contemporary society. The typical nuclear 'cereal packet' family cited above reflects this norm.

ACTIVITY 4.4

Looking carefully at Murdock's classic definition of the nuclear family, in what ways could it be critiqued for failing to reflect the reality of family life for significant numbers of the population?

In completing this exercise, you have probably identified factors that reflect trends in social life, including the following.

- Increased number of divorces – In 1958, there were 24,400 divorces in Great Britain, compared with 155,000 in 2005.

- Cohabitation rather than marriage – The proportion of non-married adults who were cohabiting in Great Britain more than doubled between 1986 and 2005.

- More births outside of marriage – In 2005, these accounted for 42 per cent of all births.

- Increased numbers of lone-parent families – Between 1972 and 2006, the proportion of children living in lone-parent families rose from 7 per cent to 24 per cent.

- Increased recognition of gay or lesbian couples – Between December 2005 and September 2006, 15,700 same-sex civil partnerships were formed.

- Gay or lesbian parents – more gay and lesbian adults are increasingly choosing to become parents, through donor insemination, surrogacy or fostering and adoption.

- Growth in single-person households – In 1971, there were 3 million one-person households. By 2005 this had increased to 7 million.

- Adults who live together but who choose not to have children – Since 1971, the proportion of people living in couple families with no children increased from 19 per cent to 25 per cent.

- Adults who live together but cannot have children – Infertility affects one in seven couples (Human Fertilisation and Embryology Authority, 2007).

- The growth of step-families – More than 10 per cent of all families with dependent children in Great Britain were step-families in 2005.

- Children who live in a shared care/co-parenting capacity with their parents and sometimes step-parents.

- Families who live together with other families.

- Extended families living under one roof.

- Foster families – There were approximately 50,000 children living in foster families in 2005.

- Households that contain single adults who either live alone or share with friends.

(Source of data unless otherwise stated: ONS, 2007)

This exercise reveals that despite the prevalence of 'familism', (an ideology which suggests that *there is one type of family, one correct way in which individuals should live and interact together*, Gittins, 1985, p167), in actuality, there is huge diversity in Britain today in terms of how people live. Indeed, taking into account all the trends outlined above, the proportion of people living in the 'traditional' family household of a couple with dependent children now constitutes a minority of the population (37 per cent today, compared with 52 per cent in 1971) (ONS, 2007).

For social workers who work with families, it is of course essential that they are able to transcend familial ideology, which situates the typical nuclear family as being both the norm, and as being the institution that members of society aspire to. Social workers need to have a commitment to both recognising and valuing diversity if they are to practise in ways that are not oppressive. This is particularly pertinent if you think for a moment about the types of decisions social workers are involved in making. These potentially life-changing and sometimes devastating decisions, such as removing children from their birth families, placing children for adoption, making recommendations concerning residence and contact, for example, must be made on the basis of fair and equitable practice centred on the best needs of the child, not based on prejudiced views concerning particular family forms and lifestyles.

ACTIVITY *4.5*

You may wish to complete this exercise on your own or with others in a small group. Either way, it involves a critical consideration of your value base and therefore requires complete honesty.

ACTIVITY *4.5 continued*

Taking some of the trends in family formations that you (and we) identified above, assess the potential positives and negatives of each.

Critically examine your values in relation to each of the social trends. Where have your values come from? Think about how values are influenced by the media, our families, religion and other factors.
How can social workers ensure that their practice is ethically sound?

By completing this exercise you will hopefully have considered the importance of reflecting upon your own values and practice, and the value of using others to challenge perceptions, within team discussions and supervision. It may be more helpful to think about *households* rather than families, to more accurately reflect diversity in the way that people live today. The term 'family' tends to carry with it emotional connotations which perpetuate powerful ideological ideals to aspire to, but that may not accurately reflect the reality of how people live.

Sociological approaches to the family

We will now consider a range of key sociological approaches to the family. What follows are summary explanations of some of the key writers; however, this is not intended to be exhaustive and further reading will be indicated at the end of the chapter to further assist you.

Functionalist theory of the family

As we discovered in Chapter 1, functionalism is premised on the assumption that all social institutions perform an important role, both for society and its individuals. The family is regarded positively by functionalists who identify important functions that are carried out for the benefit of society as a whole.

ACTIVITY *4.6*

If you have become familiar with the functionalist perspective, you should now be comfortable with the key tenets of the theory. You may wish to revisit Chapter 1 to refresh yourself with some of the core ideas.
Once you have done this, write down what you think are the functions of the family, firstly for society and secondly for the individuals within it.

Murdock's (1949) work on the family identified four positive functions that he suggested were performed by the family. These were:

- reproduction;
- sexual gratification;
- economic well-being;
- education.

Murdock's first function of *reproduction* may seem rather obvious as society needs to ensure the continuation of the population; however, there is an important point here. Implicit in the assumption that reproduction is most effectively carried out within the institution of the family, is the notion that children are afforded the stability of being raised within the family unit. Furthermore, kinship rights and obligations of families are protected if reproduction is predominantly carried out within families and there are clear lines of heredity. Linked to this is Murdock's second function, that of the *sexual gratification* of adults. The nuclear family provides a socially approved structure around the fulfilment of adult sexual urges, which mitigates against adults fulfilling their desires freely and which might have a negative impact such as the spread of sexually transmitted diseases, emotional turbulence, and confusion regarding lines of heredity. Additionally, by restricting sexual activity to spouses, there is an effective barrier against the likelihood of emotional difficulties associated with incest.

Murdock's next function of *economic well-being* is also linked to the previous two functions, as he contends that providing for family members is the most effective means of 'cementing the union' between husband and wife. For Murdock, writing in 1949, there was a clear division of labour within families, whereby husbands performed the traditional hunter-gatherer role (albeit in the workplace as opposed to in the wild), and wives predominantly stayed at home to bear and nurture children and transform the product of their husbands' labour into nourishing meals. For Murdock, this is functional both for family members, and for society, as the family effectively keeps the economy strong by being a consistent unit of consumption.

Finally, Murdock identifies the function of *education* or *socialisation* as being essential for society. The family is the primary institution that teaches its members to internalise prevailing norms and values which enable them to fit into society. This point is taken up by Talcott Parsons (1951), who identifies two 'basic and irreducible functions of the family', the first being primary socialisation of children. He argues that the *human* personality is not born, but *made*; children effectively come into the world as blank slates, and it is through the socialisation process that they gradually acquire the values of society. Parsons graphically refers to the family as *'factories' which produce human personalities ... so that they [children] can truly become members of society into which they have been born* (p16). Families socialise children from the moment they are born, both formally, by explicitly teaching the rules of social life, such as manners and customs, and informally, by setting examples to children and by modelling socially desired behaviours. Parsons, however, argues that *it cannot be assumed that the human personality would remain stable in the respects which are vital to social functioning* (p16). He therefore suggests that the second irreducible function of the family is the *stabilisation of the adult personalities of the population*. By this, Parsons is referring the role the family, and specifically the role the married couple, performs in supporting each other through daily life. Couples are expected to form durable, emotional bonds which ensure that they care for one another emotionally, which contributes to the psychological well-being of each individual. This is important in modern society in which the pressures of working life, the strain to engage in constant consumerism and competition can all have an impact upon adults. The family therefore and, in particular, the marital couple act as a buffer against such stresses by providing emotional support. This is perhaps more important in modern society, since many nuclear families live away from relatives who once traditionally fulfilled aspects of this role.

Murdock and Parsons both provide core functions that they argue the family fulfils for the well-being of society first and foremost, but also for individuals. Of course, as we have seen, the nuclear family form is not compulsory within our society. However, it is very much regarded as the norm and as we outline below, effective pressures exist to try to support compliance to the norm. For example, historical taboos have existed around cohabitation, having children outside of marriage, bringing up children alone, and, of course, around incest. Although, with the exception of incest, these taboos have to a greater or lesser extent broken down as society has evolved, it is clear to see how such norms permeate individual consciousness and importantly, how they form the ideas upon which social policies are crafted.

Lone parenthood and the dysfunctional family?

In recent years some politicians and sociologists have suggested that certain family formations – in particular lone parents – are incapable of performing key socialisation functions. Of course, the notion that lone-parent families are in some way 'inferior' to two-parent families, and are incapable of socialising their children effectively, is not new. Indeed, throughout the 1980s and 1990s, Conservative governments, backed by sympathetic newspapers such as the *Daily Mail*, condemned lone-parent families as 'dysfunctional', linking the increased incidence of lone parenthood to a range of social and economic problems. However, over the past few years such claims have re-emerged with renewed vigour, and lone parenthood – whether it be the result of divorce, relationship breakdown, or births out of wedlock – now appears to be 'under attack' from all sides. Whereas in the past senior Labour politicians criticised Conservatives' preoccupation with 'the family', and celebrated family diversity and difference, now Labour ministers seem equally obsessed with the family, and, in particular, with the potentially destructive impact of 'disintegration' of the traditional family. The following comments are taken from a speech made by Labour's then Work and Pensions Secretary, John Hutton.

> *The family is the bedrock of the welfare state. It is the family which cares for the newborn, raises children, instills a sense values, coaxes and encourages children to learn and thrive ... But alongside this, we cannot ignore the increasing evidence that points to the benefits for children of a stable family life with two parents living together ... For example, children from separated families are more likely to have no qualifications than those from families with two parents living together ... And not only are children in lone-parent families more likely to be living in poverty at any one point in time – but they have a consistently lower probability of moving out of poverty.*
>
> (Hutton, 2006)

Labour's change of stance dates back to at least 1998, when its Green Paper, *Supporting families*, celebrated the benefits of marriage over other family forms, and set out a series of proposals for strengthening it. Indeed, Beatrix Campbell referred to the Green

Paper as *The government's make 'em marry crusade* (Campbell, 1998, p5). According to Barlow and Duncan (2000), the Green Paper represented a retreat from the moral high ground, and a capitulation to a reactionary, conservative critique of non-traditional families, which portrays them as a social threat and a social problem. Like previous Conservative government policy, it seemed almost *entirely premised upon the essential superiority of the married family form* (pp31–2).

There does indeed now seem to be a functionalist-influenced political consensus over the central role the 'traditional' family plays in securing social order and stability. The following extract, taken from one of the Conservative Party's Social Justice Policy Group's (2006) reports, serves to illustrate the similarity in the stances of the UK's two major parties:

> *The family is where the vast majority of us learn the fundamental skills for life; physically, emotionally and socially it is the context from which the rest of life flows. However family life in Britain is changing such that adults and children today are increasingly faced with the challenges of dysfunctional, fractured, or fatherless families ... Family breakdown, whether by dissolution, dysfunction or 'dad-lessness', has many and varied effects and few of them are beneficial to the individuals, their wider family, or society at large.*
>
> (2006, pp9–10)

ACTIVITY 4.7

While space prohibits us from devoting too much attention to the media's reinforcement of familial values, it is important you are aware of its opinion-shaping potential. We discuss the pervasive influence of the media in relation to asylum policy in Chapter 6, and what we say there is equally applicable here. In our research for this chapter, we undertook a national newspaper database search of articles with 'lone parent' in the headline, and virtually all of the hundred or so articles we found were negative in their portrayal of non-traditional families. The following headlines were fairly typical:

> *Children's Single Risk; Half of all Reported Abuse Cases Involve Youngsters Brought up by Lone Parents,* Daily Mail, 14 August, 2007.
>
> *Cot Death link to Lone Parents,* Express, 31 August, 2006.
>
> *Lone Parents in Tax Credits 'Fraud',* Times, 13 March, 2006.
>
> *Young Prosper in Stable Family, says Hutton. Children of Lone Parents Fare Worse, says MP,* Daily Telegraph, 16 September, 2006.
>
> *Lone-parent Children More Prone to Illness; Broken Home Can Double Risk of Mental Health Problems,* Daily Mail, 24 January, 2003.
>
> *Children Face Double Risk of Suicide Bid: Hell of Lone Parent Kids,* Express, 24 January, 2003.

ACTIVITY *4.7 continued*

In this task, we want you to scan newspapers for a period of perhaps one month, saving all the articles on lone parenthood. You can either buy the newspapers yourselves or use online newspaper search engines.

Place the articles you have collected into two categories, positive and negative (reflecting their portrayal of 'non-traditional' families). Our powers of prediction tell us that your 'negative' category will be the larger of the two!

- *What social problems were lone parenthood, divorce and family breakdown equated to? Did you detect a functionalist influence in the language used in the articles?*

- *Do you think the attention placed upon lone parenthood as a potential cause of the problems it is linked to disproportionate? Did you find any examples of 'distortion' or exaggerated emphasis in the articles you read? Might Stanley Cohen's moral panic theory (outlined in Chapter 6) be useful in helping us to understand how non-traditional families are popularly portrayed?*

- *What other explanations might account for the economic and social problems commonly linked to lone parenthood?*

Hopefully, the above exercise will have encouraged you to think about how your views of 'the family' may have been shaped by media representations. As future social workers you will be working with many types of families, and as we have already intimated, it is essential that you are able to move beyond pejorative, derogatory perceptions of certain family formations.

Criticisms of functionalist views of the family

Both Murdock and Parsons have been criticised for idealising family life, with feminist writers among others suggesting that families can in fact be dysfunctional for some family members. This argument will be considered more fully later in this chapter, but in short they point to the abuse and violence that some women and children experience daily as being more realistic than the happy, harmonious haven where adult personalities are stabilised and children nurtured. Other criticisms are based on the fact that the functions identified by Murdock and Parsons could in fact be performed outside of the institution of the family. One example of this is that children may be successfully raised in a kibbutz, a hippy commune or within residential settings (though of course each of these settings potentially brings its own challenges).

Functionalist claims that family breakdown necessarily contributes to a range of social and economic ills, threatening the well-being of society, can also be criticised with reference to other countries' experiences. For example, levels of lone parenthood, divorce and cohabitation are as high, or in some instances higher, in Scandinavian countries than they are in the UK. In Sweden in 2005, 55 per cent of births were outside marriage, compared with 42 per cent for the UK. The respective figures for Denmark and Finland were 45 per cent and 41 per cent (ONS, 2007, p22) The levels of single-parent families and step-families in Scandinavian countries are also remarkably similar to those in the UK (UNICEF, 2007, pp26–7). Scandinavian countries, however, are not characterised by the sort of social problems that in the UK are said to be linked to the growth in non-traditional families. Child poverty rates in each of these nations are strikingly low, educational well-being is regarded as excellent, and children are far less likely to be engaging in risk-taking and disruptive behaviour than in the UK (UNICEF, 2007). Nor is there talk in these countries of lone parents being guilty of raising generations of 'dysfunctional' children. In fact a recent UNICEF report concluded that these countries were characterised by the highest levels of childhood well-being in the developed world. The UK, by contrast, came bottom in UNICEF's league table of child well-being.

The experiences of Scandinavian countries, therefore, provide us with evidence to counter the notion that the 'traditional' two-parent family is a crucial prerequisite for the social and economic stability of society. Although space precludes us from discussing in detail the reasons why this is the case, one of the key features shared by each of these countries is their commitment to gender equality. Extensive, subsidised in-work support (for instance, childcare, parental leave and paternity leave) is provided, enabling all parents, married and single, male and female, to balance work and family life responsibilities. Hence, Scandinavian nations have very high levels of female employment (including among lone parents), strong levels of female representation in public life, and high degrees of male participation in children's upbringing. Alongside this, there is a more general commitment to ensuring a fair, equal distribution of resources, ensuring that levels of poverty for all families remain low.

Social work, functionalism and the family

For social work, it is clear to see that the functionalist perspective holds a resonance. The family is regarded as being perhaps the most important institution in society and every effort is made to support and uphold this. A great deal of social workers' time is devoted to working in supportive ways with families to help them survive and flourish, to function effectively, and to meet the needs of different family members. Indeed, if we consider some of the core pieces of legislation that underpin social work practice, you will see that the Children Act 1989, for example, is premised upon the overriding principle that in most cases children are best brought up within their family of origin. Similarly, in the NHS and Community Care Act, there is a core principle that vulnerable adults are best cared for by their own families, wherever possible within their own homes. The centrality of the family in social work is clear to see, which is not surprising when one considers that ideologically, economically and politically families are deemed by all political parties to be the cornerstone of society. When things go wrong, however, and families cannot care for their own children or are unable to perform the nurturing functions to a standard deemed satisfactory by the state, social workers seek alternatives to perform the required functions of the family on behalf of the state. Two good examples of this which already mirror the birth family are of course adoptive and foster homes.

Marxist theory of the family

Marxists are concerned with the relationship between the family and private property. Frederich Engels' seminal work provides an important starting point for understanding Marxist views on the family. In *The origins of the family, private property and the state* (1968), Engels, influenced by the work of anthropologist Henry Morgan, adopted an evolutionary approach and suggested that the prevailing family form of any particular period was inextricably linked with the mode of production at that time. Engels cites Morgan:

> *The family ... represents an active principle. It is never stationary, but advances from a lower to a higher form as society advances from a lower to a higher condition.*

(cited in Engels, p31)

In primitive society where property ownership did not exist, Engels suggests that there was no identifiable family as such; rather a form of group marriage existed where sexually active individuals had a number of sexual partners. At this time, women were more powerful than men and society was matriarchal. Economic relations in society were based around subsistence, in other words people hunted and gathered what they needed to survive and regularly shared this among members of the local group. Over time, society became more advanced and gradually cattle- and land-ownership emerged. According to the division of labour at the time, it was men who were in charge of the cattle and the instruments of labour. It follows that once property (in this case, herds of cattle and land) is seen to be owned privately, men needed to secure legitimate heirs to pass their property on to. At this stage Engels identifies a gradual shift to patriarchy and the implications for women.

> *The overthrow of mother-right was the world historical defeat of the female sex. The man seized the reins in the house also; the woman was degraded, enthralled, the slave of the man's lust, a mere instrument for breeding children.*

(p57)

Thus Engels suggests that the oppression of women is directly linked to the ownership of private property. Men needed to be absolutely sure of the legitimacy of their sons, and therefore they needed to control women's sexuality. In Engels' words:

> *In order to make certain of the wife's fidelity and therefore of the paternity of the children, she is delivered over unconditionally into the power of the husband.*

(p58)

Consequently, the monogamous family was born. Engels is clear that this family form was not based on love or sex, but rested entirely on economic foundations: *It is based on the supremacy of the man, the express purpose being to produce children of undisputed paternity; such paternity is demanded because these children are later to come into their father's property as his natural heirs* (p62).

In this way then, women effectively became the economic and sexual property of men, a direct result of the emergence of private property. With the development of capitalism, the nuclear family came to be a central component of both its success and survival. A Marxist analysis of the family draws attention to the functions that the monogamous nuclear family performs for capitalism. In short:

- the family reflects inequalities in wider society; some family members are privileged, while others, women and children in particular, are not;

- the family passes on ideological messages to children about obedience and hard work, which prepares them for their future role as workers;

- women in particular play an important role in reproducing workers, by performing for free tasks such as cooking, cleaning, shopping, housework tasks and emotional tasks such as comforting and supporting tired workers that directly enables capitalism to continue;

- furthermore, families are the primary unit of consumption that supports capitalism commercially.

In the Communist Manifesto, Marx and Engels (1969) famously called for the abolition of the family, as they contended that family members were simply *articles of commerce and instruments of labour* (p70). They decry the 'bourgeois clap trap' about the family and point out that in reality, women are regarded as mere instruments of production. They suggest, however, that as capitalism and private property are abolished, so too will the family vanish as a matter of course.

Criticisms of Marxist theories of the family

Marxist theories of the family can be criticised for focusing exclusively upon the economic basis of family life and ignoring the powerful emotional ties that define many families. Engels' work has been refuted for being based on unreliable anthropological evidence (Haralambos et al., 2004, p109), however, as Rosalind Delmar (1977) suggests, at the very least Engels' work is pivotal in defining women's oppression *as a problem of history, rather than of biology* (cited in O'Donnell, 1992, p48). For more criticisms of Marxism, see our comments in the later section on Marxist feminism.

Social action approaches

Many of the sociological approaches to the family that we consider in this chapter are concerned with either the positive or negative side to family life. Social action perspectives, however, are less interested in the relative merits of the family and more interested in observing the smaller-scale interactions between family members. This type of approach is useful to social work because it focuses upon the meanings that underpin family activity and the processes by which relationships are negotiated in families.

As we outlined in Chapter 1, social action perspectives concentrate on the micro aspects of social life. Symbolic interactionism, for example, is interested in how individuals make sense of the social world and how they shape their own paths through life. In relation to families, interactionists focus their attention on the minutiae of family life in order to learn about how it is experienced subjectively. As we have seen, both functionalism and Marxism place attention on the functions the family fulfils for society as a whole (functionalism) or for capitalism (Marxism). Interactionists however, are more interested in individual experiences within families. While both of the structural theories focus upon the macro role of families in socialising children for the benefit of society, interactionists are interested in different ways of socialising children. Through the application of qualitative research, sociologists who are informed by this approach are able to elicit rich information about the micro cultures that exist within families and how these shape individual experiences of family life. Gillies *et al.* (2001), for example, carried out an in-depth study into families that had a child between 16 and 18 at home to learn more about the family lives of young people. They found that a variety of experiences existed in the families they studied, but that the majority described the supportive and emotionally meaningful nature of their family lives. This contrasted with headline messages in common culture that teenage years and parent–child relationships were characterised by turbulence and stress. Many of the young people in the study emphasised agency and responsibility, negotiating their independence over time. Their parents perceived their role as continuing to steer and advise teenagers into adulthood. The authors describe the range of different approaches adopted across different families:

> *Some parents emphasised their respect for the teenager's autonomy, while others felt a responsibility to ensure that appropriate decisions were made. Other parents assumed a more subtle role, seeing dictating to teenagers as counterproductive.*

> (Gillies et al., 2001, p3)

Importantly, from a micro perspective, this study identifies the fact that although there are similar experiences shared across families, a range of different meaning systems exist with families that are more useful to understand when attempting to learn about the social world. For social workers of course, this is an important principle to inform practice; looking at the minutiae of family life helps us to gain an understanding of how individual families work and to think about the process of interaction within families. Reder *et al.* (1993), in *Beyond blame*, review cases where children have died within families due to abuse or neglect. They identify the need for social workers to assess the 'meaning' of children within families, where there is a concern about risk to the child. This is based upon findings that repeatedly, children who have been murdered by their parents have held specific meaning or significance; for example, the child might have symbolised a previous marriage or emotional bond, if the child wasn't the biological child of both caregivers. So, for social workers, a micro perspective can be useful to help us learn about the intimate functioning of families. However, as Macionis and Plummer (1998) point out, care should be taken not to miss the bigger picture in doing so. For social workers, it is helpful to understand families from a micro perspective while locating this within an understanding of wider structural issues such as those we have considered earlier in the chapter.

Feminist theory of the family

Feminist writing has in many ways revolutionised thinking about the family by drawing attention to the more harmful aspects of family life. It is important to point out that there is no single 'feminist theory of the family'; rather, feminism is an umbrella term to describe a collection of approaches which are concerned with the oppression of women. Beyond that, the similarities end. We have chosen to focus upon some of the classic contributors to different strands of feminist thought. This is by no means exhaustive as space prevents a more detailed examination. However, we hope that you will at least be able to identify the key points of each by the end of this section and consider our suggestions for further reading.

Marxist feminism

Marxist or socialist feminism builds upon the work of Engels described previously, and should be read in conjunction with that section. For Marxist feminists, women's oppression is a by-product of capitalism. Barrett and McIntosh (1982) argue that the nuclear family performs key functions for capitalism. In particular, it produces future workers who keep the system going and, at the same time, it acts as an important unit of consumption. They note that as society became more industrialised and there was a separation of the workplace and the home, women became identified with child-bearing and -rearing, and importantly, the home became a much more privatised and personal realm.

However, Barrett and McIntosh also draw attention to the anti-social side of the family, which is significant for social workers. They argue that for women who are confined to the home as mothers, housewives or carers, the insular nature of families can become a prison rather than a haven. This is especially so, of course, for those who experience violence within the family. In explaining domestic violence, Marxist feminists acknowledge that it is predominantly perpetrated by men on women. They see the principal cause as being the stress caused by poverty, exclusion and the pressure to make ends meet that is the characteristic feature of many families' lives under capitalism. Furthermore, the state-engineered dependence of women on men (institutionalised by the absence of affordable childcare, labour market discrimination, and low levels of income maintenance) ensures that women who do experience domestic violence find it extremely difficult to escape from abusive relationships.

Regarding women's paid employment, Barrett and McIntosh note that when women do return to work, many do a 'double shift', by retaining their prime responsibilities within the home in addition to their working life. This is because their position in the labour force is not taken seriously; it is secondary to their mother–housewife role. Women are often found in low-paid, low-status jobs which are regarded as an extension of their 'natural' female roles; they tend not to get promotions at the same rate as men and tend to be found lower down in the hierarchy.

Barrett and McIntosh note that the family ideal is so pervasive that others who live outside this are seen as 'pale and unsatisfactory' in comparison, living in a 'cold and friendless world'. They suggest that societal norms are so engrained that many customs and practices are based around families, which is exclusionary for those outside:

> *The cosy image of the family makes all other settings where people can mix and live together seem second best. Nurseries, children's homes, student residences, nursing homes, old people's homes, all in their different ways conjure up pictures of bleakness, deprivation ... to be resorted to only if normal family life cannot be provided.*

(p77)

Using Barrett and McIntosh's concept of the 'anti-social family', think about how this might this have relevance for some users of social work services.

You might wish to think about the emotional impact on individuals and consider how this may bring them to the attention of social work agencies.

So, what do Barrett and McIntosh suggest should be done to counter the damage they perceive to be invested in the anti-social family? Essentially, they argue for changes that will displace the family as being *the sole and privileged provider of moral and material support* (p133) and argue that these things should be more available throughout the community. In doing so, they envisage an end to women's dependence and aim for more choice around living arrangements and, importantly, for a more collective approach to caring and domesticity. They believe that a cultural and political shift should take place which cuts across the ideology of the family as the cornerstone of society, to encompass a broader range of alternatives. These would include more opportunities in the workplace for women on a more equal footing, better social security provision and a more collective approach to care, rather than seeing it as a natural (biological) duty borne by women.

Although Barrett and McIntosh's work is now dated, it has become a classic text which builds upon Engels' work and sets out a Marxist feminist position on the family. Now some 25 years on, it is worth analysing to what extent women's position has changed.

RESEARCH SUMMARY

Women in Britain today
Formed in 1975 and given a remit to monitor and combat gender discrimination, the Equal Opportunities Commission (EOC) is an excellent source of information on trends in gender equality (in 2007 the EOC merged with the Commission for Racial Equality and the Disability Rights Commission to form one broad Equalities and Human Rights Commission). Here we summarise some of the key findings of a number of its publications.

The EOC's findings show that although women are more fairly represented in the workforce and in public life than they were in the past, they do still occupy a subordinate position to men. In relation to the workplace, they are less likely to be employed than men (67 per cent of women compared with 90 per cent of men in 2005), and when they are employed they tend to occupy lower-status, lower-paid positions. They also continue to often work part-time, combining work with family caring responsibilities. In 2005, 58 per cent of women worked part time, compared with only 4 per cent of men. In addition, women tend to be employed in the 'caring' services, a reflection perhaps of familial assumptions about what are 'appropriate' roles for women to perform. Thus, women comprise 79 per cent of those employed in health and social work professions, and 73 per cent of those employed in education. They

RESEARCH SUMMARY *continued*

constitute 84 per cent of those employed in personal services and 81 per cent of those engaged in administrative and secretarial work. This bias towards caring professions looks set to continue in the future. For example, despite the fact that girls now outperform boys at GCSE level across all subjects, they are still being directed towards the personal service and 'caring' professions. Thus, girls constituted 97 per cent apprenticeship starts in early years care and education in 2004, 91 per cent in hairdressing and 87 per cent in health and social care (EOC, 2006).

Regarding public life, despite some improvements, women remain grossly underrepresented across a whole range of public appointments, services and elected positions. In 2006, for example, women only constituted 19.5 per cent of all MPs in the House of Commons; 18.9 per cent of members of the House of Lords; 13.8 per cent of local authority council leaders; 20.6 per cent of local authority chief executives; 9.8 per cent of the senior judiciary; 12.3 per cent of senior police officers; and 13.2 per cent of university vice chancellors (EOC, 2007).

For Marxist feminists, the outcomes we have outlined above are not a result of physiological or biological factors, nor are they a product of rational choice on the part of women. On the contrary, these differential outcomes are socially engineered. In short, for the reasons outlined above, capitalism benefits from gender segregation and hence key institutions – for instance, the education and social security systems – seek to reinforce women's domesticity. While this may sound conspiratorial, Marxist feminists are right to point out that social policy has traditionally sought to encourage and strengthen gender-specific roles. The UK's social security system has been based around the male-breadwinner model, the assumption being that women would remain in the home and be financially dependent on their husband's earnings and National Insurance contributions. In addition, as we will see in Chapter 5, community care legislation has been based upon the notion that families are willing and able to bear the responsibility of caring for dependent relatives.

Marxist feminism has been criticised for being overly sceptical about the possibility of initiating progressive change for women without the need for revolutionary upheaval. Critics would point to the substantial gains made by the feminist movement over the past hundred years or so, which have led to a significant improvement in women's representation in political, economic and social life within capitalist nations. Arguably, the experience of Scandinavian countries which are characterised by a high degree of gender equality, shows us that women's opportunities and status can be substantially improved without the abolition of capitalism. Marxism, therefore, has been criticised for paying too little attention to the 'here and now', and how the key tenets of familial ideology can be challenged in the present to improve women's status and material well-being now. In short, Marxism has faced the charge that it has subordinated women's demands and the fight for gender equality to what it has seen as the 'real struggle' (that is, wider revolutionary change).

Radical feminism

Unlike Marxist feminism which is based upon the premise that women's oppression stems first and foremost from capitalism, radical feminists stress the patriarchal nature of society, and argue that women's oppression is a direct result of patriarchy which is a universal system of male power and domination. They argue that:

> *Male supremacy is the oldest, most basic form of domination. All other forms of exploitation and oppression (racism, capitalism, imperialism etc) are extensions of male supremacy; men dominate women, a few men dominate the rest.*

> (Redstockings Manifesto, 1969, p1)

The slogan 'The personal is political' is at the heart of this perspective, denoting the idea that what happens to individual women in the home is also political because it involves wider relations of power and exploitation. The argument is that women's individual battles at home, their personal experiences of oppression and violence, in fact have an inherently political base and therefore can only be resolved through collective action.

For radical feminists such as Shulamith Firestone (1970), women's inferiority is linked to their biological sex. In *The dialectic of sex* Firestone argues that the origins of the sex class system lie in the biologically determined reproductive roles of men and women. She argues that men and women are not equally privileged, with women at the continual mercy of their biology. The natural reproductive difference between the sexes led directly to the first division of labour which renders women dependent upon men for their physical survival. This in turn leads to the domination of women by men.

However, although women's oppression has its origins in biology, Firestone argues that this does not mean it is unchangeable. Technological developments such as birth control and artificial reproduction have the potential to free women from the tyranny of their reproductive biology, so that child-rearing becomes the responsibility of society as a whole. However, she argues that oppression will not cease just because its biological determinants are overcome, as the supporting structures, such as the nuclear family, are still functioning. Thus a feminist revolution is needed. There must be total integration of women and children into all aspects of larger society, with full sexual freedom guaranteed. The implications of this would effectively mean the destruction of the nuclear family.

Not all radical feminists subscribe to Firestone's biological explanation, but all agree that past and present societies are patriarchies, in which men have institutionalised their domination over women via social structures such as love, romance, marriage, motherhood, sexual intercourse, religion and the family. Radical feminists claim that violence and importantly, the threat of violence, play a crucial role in male systems of domination.

As noted, the belief is that revolution, not reform, is needed and that institutions which foster sexist ideology must be destroyed. Men too will benefit, by being freed from the masculine binds which tie them (although radical feminists suggest, they cannot be expected to realise this as they have been warped by power psychology and the very real benefits of the current system). They argue that women need to construct alternative selves that are healthy, independent and assertive, and value themselves, rather than awaiting judgement from men.

Radical feminists have been influential in challenging established thinking about a range of social problems social workers deal with. In the sphere of child sexual abuse, for example, radical feminists have led the challenge against the 'family dysfunction' analysis of abuse, which sees sexual abuse resulting from unsatisfactory relationships within the family. This interpretation, radical feminists argue, has a strong tendency to hold the mother responsible for abuse, ignoring the culpability of the actual perpetrators – invariably men. McLeod and Saraga (1988, p40) were foremost among those who sought to locate child sex abuse within a patriarchal framework, as *one part of a spectrum of male violence against women*. In terms of its wider influence on practice, radical feminism has also played a key part in development of a range of women-only services such as women's refuges, rape crisis centres and survivor groups.

Liberal feminism

Liberal feminists hold the view that there should be equality of opportunity for women and men. Writing in the 1960s, Betty Friedan (1963) in *The feminist mystique* identifies what she refers to as *the problem that has no name* that had blighted the lives of American women for many years:

> It was a strange stirring, a sense of dissatisfaction ... Each suburban wife struggled with it alone. As she made the beds, shopped for groceries, matched slipcover material, ate peanut butter sandwiches with her children, chauffeured Cub Scouts and Brownies, lay beside her husband at night – she was afraid to ask even of herself the silent question – 'Is this all?'
>
> (p4)

Friedan's work recognised that the family in its present form is oppressive to women. She argues that as long as women are relegated to being mothers and mothers only, women would remain largely unfulfilled. Her view was that women must cut through their own psychological chains that bound them to the powerful feminine mystique, an ideology which is perpetuated by the media and popular culture, and be free to be full, equal human beings. When this is realised and women can see the binds of housework and marriage in more realistic terms, they can achieve a new life plan in which they will find creative ways to achieve their own fulfilment. Only then will the family no longer be oppressive and women can be who they want to be.

Like Marxist feminists, liberal feminists agree that women's subordination owes little to their biological or physiological differences to men. However, they do not believe that capitalism itself is the principal cause of women's oppression. For liberal feminists, the roots of women's oppression lie with the irrational prejudice, stereotyping and outdated attitudes and practices that lead to sex discrimination occurring in all spheres of life. Like Marxists, they would point to the gender bias in education, social security and community care policies, but unlike Marxists they believe that the prejudice and stereotypical attitudes inherent in these institutions and policies can be 'reformed away' through the introduction of anti-discriminatory legislation. Liberal feminists, therefore, would welcome the removal of overtly gendered children's textbooks (of the Janet and John variety!) from schools and the shift towards a non-gendered curriculum. They would also applaud the introduction of equal pay and anti-discriminatory employment law which, theoretically at least, prohibits discrimination and allows women to compete in the labour market on an equal basis to men. Likewise, liberal feminists would welcome the introduction of women-only shortlists as a means of circumventing the traditional hostility to women's involvement in politics and increasing women's representation in representative assemblies. Finally, liberal feminists are insistent that nobody benefits from gender segregation and discrimination. Women lose out on the ability to develop their talents, business loses out because it fails to harness the potential and ability of 50 per cent of the population, and men lose out because they are denied the opportunity to develop close ties with their children.

Postmodernist feminism

As we explained in Chapter 1, postmodernism rejects explanations of society that are based upon holistic theories. For postmodernism, there is no 'one truth', or 'correct' explanation for social phenomena. We saw earlier how this leads postmodernism to reject 'universal' grand narratives, such as Marxism, but postmodernism's distrust of holistic explanations also extends to what are seen as overarching strands of feminist thought. Each woman's experience is seen as unique and in interpreting each woman's situation attention needs to paid to their own diverse identities and biographies. For example, the variables that shape the oppression experienced by a white, middle-class, married woman who is experiencing domestic violence, may be very different from those that shape the oppression of a poverty-stricken Black parent. In the case of the former, patriarchy may be the most important variable, whereas with the latter, class or race (and their interaction with possibly even more variables) may be more pertinent. The fact is, though, that without a detailed knowledge of the individual circumstances of each of these two women, it is impossible to tell which variables or identities have structured their experiences. The point, for postmodernist feminists, is that we should not 'assume' one way or the other, without detailed interrogation. With postmodernist feminism, therefore, no one source of identity – whether it be class position, gender, race or disability – is privileged, and emphasis is placed on the need to understand the way different identities determine women's experiences.

As social workers, we can see how postmodernism's emphasis on what are sometimes referred to as 'local narratives' can perhaps be the basis for a truly emancipatory practice. However, as we pointed out in Chapter 1, losing sight of the wider origins of oppression, negating shared experiences and undermining the potential for collective action can result in unwittingly disempowering women.

Possibilities for a feminist approach in social work

Although feminists do not agree on the origins of women's oppression, they all recognise, albeit in different ways, that the family has been an important vehicle in perpetuating the subordination of women over the years. But what possibilities does feminism offer social workers in terms of practice with families?

Firstly, feminist contributions to sociology and social work have enabled social workers to have a grounded awareness of gender issues. This might involve defining or even redefining the difficulties experienced by service users from a feminist perspective. The following detailed case study gives an example of how this might be done.

CASE STUDY

Ellie, a social work student was on placement with MIND in her local area. She was allocated the case of Doreen, 45-year-old single woman who had been described by her GP as being depressed. Doreen has a 12-year-old son, Billy. The purpose of Ellie's intervention was to assess Doreen's needs and to recommend a support plan.
Ellie visited Doreen on two occasions and discussed her visits with her practice assessor.

Ellie's assessment of Doreen
Ellie described Doreen as weepy, depressive and fragile and as having health problems that Ellie assessed to be 'psychosomatic'.

She described how Doreen had a male visitor to the house, Tom, who initially had been very flattering of Doreen but who now came for sex. Doreen was quite frightened of Tom. Ellie felt Doreen was being weak and couldn't understand why she didn't just tell him he wasn't welcome any more. Ellie's view was that this situation wasn't good for Billy and was not consistent with acceptable mothering. Furthermore, Doreen had no control over her son, who was cheeky and stayed out too late. Ellie's view was that this was another sign of her weakness and Doreen should be reported to Social Services.

Ellie's recommendations
Ellie felt that Doreen was depressed and should go back to the GP for antidepressants and should get out more. Ellie decided to contact Social Services regarding Billy, who she felt was not being cared for properly.

Work in supervision
Ellie's practice assessor spent time with Ellie talking about gender issues and asked her to revisit her assessment of Doreen following the discussion and to unpack some of the assumptions she had made. Ellie worked hard on this and returned to supervision the following week with some further thoughts.

1. *On what basis had both she and the GP used the term 'depressed?' Ellie had read that the term is regularly misused and could be assigned to women more than to men. Ellie wondered if perhaps Doreen was struggling with aspects of her life and needed help to address them, but that she might not be 'depressed'. Ellie changed her recommendation regarding Doreen seeking out antidepressants.*

> ### CASE STUDY *continued*
>
> 2. Ellie thought back to her visits with Doreen – she remembered that Doreen had in fact become upset on one occasion and that was when she was confiding in Ellie about Tom and how he was quite forceful. Ellie changed her assessment report where she had written that Doreen was 'weepy' and recognised that she had in fact assigned gendered characteristics quite unfairly.
>
> 3. Ellie thought about Doreen's interaction with her son one day she had visited; she recalled they had been laughing together about something on TV. Doreen had mentioned that the previous night Billy had stayed out past his usual time, but Billy had replied that he had lost his watch. Ellie questioned her haste to portray Doreen as a bad mother and recognised that she had been quick to pathologise her.
>
> 4. Ellie reconsidered Doreen's position in relation to Tom. She recognised that Doreen was lonely and had initially been pleased that Tom had shown her some affection. She also thought about how upset and fearful Doreen had been when discussing Tom. Ellie realised on reflection, that perhaps it wasn't easy for Doreen to simply tell Tom to stop coming, as she was genuinely frightened of him. Doreen needed some support with this situation.
>
> With her assessor, Ellie was able to revisit some her gendered assumptions about Doreen, and question why she was assigning gendered labels to her service user. From the above scenario it is possible to see how with supportive challenging from her practice assessor, Ellie was able to reframe her initial assessment of Doreen and begin to work in more positive ways.

An important contribution made by feminist literature has been to recognise how social work has sometimes reinforced traditional gender roles within families and contributed in some cases to women's oppression. Hanmer and Statham (1999) note the importance of social workers accepting women service users as women first and foremost, rather than as occupants of social roles such as wife, mother and carer. This involves valuing women and recognising their strengths and abilities as women, rather than consigning them to traditional roles and seeing them only in those terms. Linked to this is the need of social workers to understand the role that men play in family life. The complexities which underpin relationships in the home should not be oversimplified and it seems important for workers to take time to understand individual dynamics and guard against making assumptions.

Social work can be criticised for contributing to 'mother blaming', by traditionally intervening primarily with women. Indeed it could be argued that social work has largely institutionalised mother blaming since the inception of the profession. For the most part, this stems from stubbornly pervasive notions that women, as bearers of children, are also primarily responsible for their safety and well-being. Social work intervention has traditionally been premised upon notions of good enough parenting, but in reality this has often meant good-enough mothering.

As women are seen as responsible for the care and control of their children, when something goes wrong the mother is blamed for inadequacy and negligence.

(Hanmer and Statham, 1999, p52)

This has resulted in social workers focusing their intervention towards women, with fathers sometimes engaging in what Milner (1993; 1996) refers to as a 'disappearing act'. She suggests that men in these instances have been able to 'disappear', by fading into the background, leaving women to answer for the well-being of their children. Milner (1996) further comments that men can be adept at using a range of strategies to resist social workers. Strategies include the intimidation of social workers, expressions of remorse, and portraying mitigating factors to effectively negate their actions. As we explained earlier when discussing radical feminism, McLeod and Saraga (1988) point out that even in cases of sexual abuse, where the perpetrator is male, women have on occasions been blamed for this too by being regarded as somehow failing in their wifely duties in relation to the sexual fulfilment of their partners, as well as in their primary duty to protect their child.

Since the recognition of the institutionalised tendency of social work to intervene primarily with mothers and to regularly hold them responsible for a whole range of family failings, advocates of feminist practice have identified principles to underpin more empowering forms of intervention (see for example, Hanmer and Statham,1999; Dominelli, 2002). Such principles include the need to recognise the political nature of many personal troubles. In short, feminist social work reconfigures many of the difficulties experienced by female service users – abuse, sexual assault, domestic violence, low self-esteem, isolation, to name but a few – as being inherently political issues. The emphasis of intervention, therefore, shifts from pathologising individual women to assisting them to perceive and understand their particular challenges in light of wider oppressive social conditions. The aim is to empower women to be able to gradually transcend psychological factors such as the guilt and responsibility that women often feel, which in turn prevents them from moving on. We have already addressed the danger of applying stereotypical labels, and feminist social work guards against making assumptions both about women and about men. As with all good practice, it is important that social workers check things out, rather than making assumptions. This involves moving beyond powerful unconscious ideologies about the family and about gender roles, which is not always easy. Hence, it is important for workers to reflect upon practice, be open to challenge from their colleagues and managers and be prepared to challenge back where they perceive sexist practice. Social workers need to be able to recognise that, for some service users, experience of family life is at best difficult, and for some, is downright unbearable. Where this is the case, it is simply not helpful for social workers to constantly reinforce the family, supporting damaging families to stay together come what may. As we hinted earlier, despite legislation and policy to the contrary, there is life outside the nuclear family and sometimes work with individuals which assists them to make choices will ultimately lead to a better life.

An important principle in feminist social work is to provide women with the space to talk about their lives, if they want to. This recognises the need to work in non-hierarchical ways with women to value individual experiences. Through positive communication it is possible to find positive solutions. Women are able to feel validated by sharing their experiences with others; being heard and being valued are powerful components of empowering practice. Featherstone (1999) makes an important point when she identifies the complex emotional dynamics that potentially underlie some encounters between social workers and women service users. She asks:

> *Many social workers are women, some of whom are mothers. Are they able to* hear *a range of stories about mothering?*
>
> (p50; emphasis added)

She acknowledges that social workers may sometimes find women's positions difficult to bear or hear and may themselves need support to intervene.

Women should be supported to find their own solutions and encouraged to be involved in wider decision-making of agencies. Linking women with other women has long been a strategy of feminist groups, as this can collectively assist women to recognise the shared nature of many experiences and find collective solutions to problems that are social in nature rather than individual. By seeing women as a resource for each other, social workers can empower women to use their strengths. 'Consciousness raising' is a term associated with radical feminists, but should form part of all social workers' repertoire of skills. Often the mere process of spending time listening and gently challenging can be positive in itself, allowing women the space to make sense of their lives and value their own achievements.

However, feminist social work is not solely confined to women. Dominelli (2002) recognises that gendered power relations have implications for men too. She argues that feminist social work should be based upon egalitarian principles and recognise that power dynamics underpin relationships and personal behaviours. However, men, like women, are not a homogenous group; indeed great diversity exists among men. Dominelli identifies the need for a commitment not to impose gender stereotypes on either sex and to *seek solutions that enable women to transcend the limitations imposed by simply being deemed mothers who look after their children, and men as fathers who provide economic support for their offspring* (2002, p97). This involves assisting men to find satisfaction in adopting more nurturing and egalitarian roles. Men need to take responsibility for their behaviour where appropriate and to be - assisted to understand their role in oppressing others, in order that they may challenge it. Dominelli suggests:

> *Working with men requires a reconceptualisation of masculinity in accordance with feminist insights and a holistic approach to men and the relationships in which they engage. Men's emotional needs have to be brought centrally into the equation.*
>
> (p104)

This section has identified ways of intervening with families that are grounded in feminist thinking and which contribute to breaking down oppressive practice. If you are on placement or have been on placement recently, you may wish to attempt the following exercise to further consolidate your thinking.

ACTIVITY **4.9**

> *Thinking about a family you have worked with or are working with, identify ways in which feminist practice can assist you to work in empowering ways with families.*

Being a safe practitioner

At the beginning of this chapter, we drew attention to the fact that all social work students, whether male or female, need to reflect upon their own experiences of family life in order that they can be safe practitioners. The following exercise draws attention to this.

ACTIVITY **4.10**

Jim was a social work student on the BA Social Work course. He had been attracted to a career in social work because his own experiences of family life had not been easy. His father had been violent to his mother for a long as he could remember; he drank heavily and Jim could remember countless nights where he had returned home and started to push his mum around. Jim's father had always belittled him and made him feel useless; he was regularly hit as a child and Jim lived in constant fear of him. When Jim was 14, he discovered that his sister had been sexually abused by their father over a number of years. Social Services were called in by the school and Jim's father was eventually sent to prison, where he committed suicide some months after being sentenced. From an early age, Jim had pledged to himself and his family that he would work to help others who had similar experiences to those of his family.

In the second year of his course, Jim was allocated a placement in a family support team. He was assigned the case of Mr and Mrs Baker, with the remit of working with them to see what services could be provided to assist the Bakers in caring for their 12-year-old son who had learning disabilities, and their six-year-old daughter who had begun bed-wetting and also to show some aggressive behaviour recently.

Mr Baker was a large, outgoing man, with tattoos, who used to be a biker, and Mrs Baker was a quietly-spoken woman. Over time, Jim began to see qualities in Mr Baker that concerned him. He didn't feel comfortable with the man and tried to visit in the afternoon when Mr Baker was at work. He began to feel concerned that the six-year-old daughter's behaviour might have arisen because she was being sexually abused by her father.

What are the potential issues of concern in this case study?

Hopefully you will have recognised the potential danger of social workers being unable to separate out their own experiences of family life from those of their service users. In this case, Jim is in real danger of projecting issues from his own childhood onto the service users with whom he is working. In this case, there is a real concern about whether the worker can remain objective. The reverse scenario could apply: sometimes workers who have experienced abuse in their own childhoods find abuse too painful to see, or deal with. Either way, there is a real risk of professional danger. Beckett (2003) suggests that social workers are honest and think hard about the kinds of parental behaviour they find most unforgiveable and that which they find easier to understand. Equipped with this understanding they are more able to approach their practice in a way that is professional, objective and safe.

C H A P T E R   S U M M A R Y

Early in this chapter, we acknowledged that social work can be both a help and a hindrance to families. This can depend upon a whole range of factors, not least whether intervention has been requested or imposed, upon the nature of the intervention, the dynamics between the family and the worker, the contexts that surround intervention and the process by which it is carried out. The complexities that underpin social work intervention in families are never-ending. A sociological perspective, however, can assist social workers to understand the diversity of family life in the UK, and the differential pressures that impose themselves upon families.

FURTHER READING

For an accessible introduction to feminist theories, see **Abbott, P, Wallace, C and Tyler, M** (2005) *Introduction to sociology: Feminist perspectives*. Abingdon: Routledge.

Jowitt, M and O'Loughlin, S (2005) *Social work with children and families*. Exeter: Learning Matters, provides an overview of the principal elements of social work with children and families.

For a consideration of changing family formations and the position of lone parents, see **Rowlingson, K and McKay, S** (2002) *Lone parent families and gender, class and state.* Harlow: Prentice Hall.

Chapter 5
Community

Introduction

Both the Subject Benchmark Statements for Social Work and the National Occupational Standards liberally utilise the notion of 'community'. The Benchmark Statements highlight the need for students to understand *the relevance of sociological perspectives to understanding societal and structural influences on human behaviour at individual, group and community levels* (Quality Assurance Agency for Higher Education, 2000). Meanwhile, the National Occupational Standards emphasise the need for social workers to be able to comprehend the risks that different communities face, as well as their specific needs (Topss, 2002). However, neither the Benchmark Statements nor the National Occupational Standards explain precisely what they mean by 'community' or 'communities'. Their apparent reluctance to do so is, to a certain extent, understandable, because as we will show, within the political and academic sphere there is no agreed definition of 'community'. Like many of the sociological concepts examined in this book, the term 'community' is contested and open to a variety of different meanings. Indeed, Bell and Newby identified 98 different definitions for the term (cited in Popple, 1995, p2).

Certainly, the word 'community' has been used in many different ways by sociologists and politicians of competing political orientations, each of which have sought to appropriate it to justify different policies and practices. Marjorie Mayo (1994, p48) concludes that the word is *notorious for its shiftiness*, arguing that there is a case to answer whether sociologists should continue to use it at all. For others, though, it is precisely the 'shiftiness' of the concept – its ambiguity and its multiplicity of meanings – that provides the main rationale for its continuing importance to us as sociologists. As Anthony Giddens (1994) argues, *On each side of the political spectrum today we see a fear of social disintegration and a call for the revival of community* (p124). Just what is it, then, that makes the concept equally popular among academics and politicians who, ideologically, have very little in common?

ACTIVITY 5.1

Get together in a group to try and identify as many different usages of the word 'community' as you can. See if you can beat Bell and Newby's total of 98 different definitions. Here are some examples to set you on your way:

- *community care;*
- *community policing;*
- *community play area;*
- *cyber community.*

Types of community

While conducting the above task, you may have thought about placing the different types of community you identified into broader categories. Below, we outline the three most common kinds of community referred to in academic literature – aesthetic communities, communities of interest and 'traditional' geographical communities. Once you have read these sections, you may want to return to this task and categorise your list of communities.

Aesthetic communities

Most of you will probably have never come across the term 'aesthetic communities' before, but according to some sociologists, such as Zygmunt Bauman (2001), they have become a key feature of modern life. Normally, when we imagine a community, we envisage a neighbourhood, a geographical area or physical space. We also tend to think of communities as permanent, long-standing entities that are steeped in stability and tradition. However, aesthetic communities are different. They are, as their title suggests, 'aesthetic': related to taste, fashion, 'the immediate' and the 'here and now'. According to Bauman, they are often built around superficial areas of identity or interest. Hence, aesthetic communities might emerge around particular fads, fashions, soap operas, television shows, movies, pop groups and celebrities within the entertainment, or sports industries. We will refer to these as 'idol-centred' aesthetic communities. Alternatively, aesthetic communities can, Bauman argues, sometimes develop in response to one-off true, or supposed panic-arousing events or issues. We will refer to these as 'spontaneous' aesthetic communities.

Idol-centred aesthetic communities

As already intimated, idol-centred aesthetic communities are often built around the 'cult of celebrity'. In the UK, for example, all the UK's popular soap operas have their own online 'communities' or forums. In these 'community forums' fictional soap opera characters become almost 'real', to the extent that their dramatised lives and the storylines they help create become the subject of heated debate and discussion. There is also an online 'Big Brother Community', where tens of thousands of participants discuss in intimate detail the daily happenings on the popular Channel 4 reality television show. Another example is the online football club message boards. These tend to be populated by regular contributors who begin by discussing their football teams, but then frequently diverge and come to know each other very well, albeit in cyberspace. While these kinds of communities may lack a physical entity or visibility, in some ways, like 'traditional' communities, they do provide their participants with a sense of belonging. Indeed, they have emerged, some argue, partly in response to the decline in traditional community ties and bonds. People need to feel a sense of belonging, and in increasingly individualised, consumer-orientated societies, aesthetic communities, to a certain degree, perform that function. Following the private and professional lives of actors and other celebrities has today, Bauman argues, become much more than idle curiosity. Indeed, for many it has become a way of life – or a 'surrogate' community. These 'idol-centred' aesthetic communities offer their participants more than entertainment *per se* and their subjects become role models, or people to relate to and empathise with. Their private lives are dissected in the full glare of the media spotlight. Their abusive childhoods, their failed relationships, their alcoholism, their substance misuse and other problems are exposed to an avid audience. By becoming engrossed in the storylines, dramas and real lives of their 'idols', those who participate in aesthetic communities are reassured that their own loneliness and their own problems are not unique. In this way, *The idols accomplish a small miracle: they make the inconceivable happen; they conjure up the experience of community without real community, the joy of comfort without being bound* (Bauman, 2001, p69).

Spontaneous aesthetic communities

As their title suggests, 'spontaneous' aesthetic communities arise in response to one-off, often temporary events that arouse concern. For instance, residents in a particular area may come together to campaign for the provision of better leisure facilities for children. Other spontaneous campaigns may emerge in opposition to local authority proposals for a particular area. For instance, the resettlement of asylum seekers to a residential area may lead people in a particular locality to develop a campaign, or 'community' of opposition. Similar protests have occurred over fears about homeless people, mental health service users or paedophiles being resident in particular areas. Although different in some respects to idol-centred aesthetic communities, these kinds of aesthetic communities share certain common characteristics with them – they are temporary, the 'community bonds' are often one-off and short-lived, and little is expected in the way of long-term commitments or ethical responsibilities: *Whatever their focal point, the common nature of aesthetic communities is the superficial and perfunctory, as well as the transient nature of the bonds emerging between the participants* (Bauman, 2001, p71).

ACTIVITY 5.2

- *Do you agree with Bauman's point that 'aesthetic communities' are an increasing feature of contemporary life?*

- *In the discussion above we have referred to two kinds of 'aesthetic communities'. Try to identify as many examples of aesthetic communities as you can, placing them in one of the two categories outlined above.*

- *Do the aesthetic communities you have identified perform any positive welfare functions?*

- *Can you think of any negative aspects that may be associated with aesthetic communities?*

In terms of the advantages of aesthetic communities, they can certainly provide those engaged in them with an 'emotional premium', a sense of belonging and worth. This may especially be the case with idol-centred communities. As social workers, we can see how they may provide isolated, emotionally vulnerable people with a link to the outside world, allowing them to communicate with others about issues they feel they can relate to, and have in common. In addition, they require little in the way of personal commitment on the part of participants. Indeed, by their very nature, people are free to drop in and out of them as they please. In this sense, the fact that the bonds created by aesthetic communities are short-lived can be seen as a good thing. Campaigns initiated by spontaneous aesthetic communities can also have a positive impact, sometimes leading to the provision of community services that would otherwise be lacking. They can also serve an educational function, providing community activists with the confidence and skills that may lead them to engaging in more substantive community work.

However, aesthetic communities, and in particular the campaigns that can stem from spontaneous aesthetic communities, are not without their shortcomings. Indeed, they can cause particular problems for social workers. Ill-informed spontaneous protests against homeless people, people with substance-misuse problems, asylum seekers and suspected paedophiles can, for instance, make it very difficult for those charged with providing services to these groups to perform their roles effectively.

ACTIVITY 5.3

By way of illustration, it might be worth briefly mentioning a campaign that developed in Preston, in opposition to the use of the city's leisure facilities by people living in one of its homeless shelters. Out of a desire to promote healthy living and to better integrate homeless people into the community, the management of the shelter had paid for supervised visits for its residents to one of the city's leisure centres. An article in the local newspaper, which was headlined Blast For Homeless Gym Deal, articulated the concerns of a residents' group opposed to the initiative:

> Parents have complained that people from a Preston homeless shelter are using facilities at one of the city's most popular leisure centres. Some city residents say they do not want to share facilities ... with people from the city's ... homeless shelter ... A father-of-two, who did not wish to be named, said: 'I have been in the shelter and I have seen alcoholics, drug users and people with serious problems and it worries me that my children could be sharing facilities with these kind of people.' A woman from Ribbleton said she had seen members of the homeless community using the climbing wall in the centre as part of a recent charity fund-raiser. She said: 'That is fine, when there is someone there with them, but you cannot have someone there all the time. I would be really uncomfortable using the facilities knowing certain people could be about.'

As is often the case with such spontaneous protests, the comments lacked any understanding of, or sympathy for the difficulties faced by the service user group in question, or any appreciation of the impact their protest may have had on the self-esteem and confidence of those affected by it. As the manager of the leisure centre explained, the reality was that their fears were entirely unwarranted: I am surprised people are targeting the homeless because we have not had a single problem with any of them, they are a brilliant bunch (Lancashire Evening Post, 4 May 2007). Sociologically this is interesting, as it provides an example of how an already excluded group of people can be further marginalised by the included majority.

Task: In this task we want you to split into three groups. The purpose of the task is to assist you to work on your skills developing and summarising an argument and then presenting it clearly.

The first group will represent the homeless shelter and will articulate the case for allowing its residents to use the leisure facilities. The second group will put forward the case for the local residents opposed to the proposal. The third group will represent the management of the leisure facilities, who will obviously be concerned about its 'reputation' and the views of local residents.

An additional problem with spontaneous aesthetic communities is that they have in the past turned into little more than lawless witch hunts. For instance, impulsive protests against suspected paedophiles have, in some cases, targeted perfectly innocent people, including in one case a paediatrician, due to confusion about the distinction between 'paedophile' and 'paediatrician'. Some also argue that they have also made it very difficult to monitor the whereabouts of known paedophiles, thus exacerbating rather than mitigating the threat they pose.

More generally, aesthetic communities – whether idol-centred or spontaneous – are more about personal fulfilment and 'personal belonging' than they are the achievement of community goals in a wider sense. While this is not necessarily a bad thing, it can arguably serve to impede the inculcation of the sort of values that are needed to facilitate the development of a community spirit based upon long-term commitments and recognition of genuine, shared obligations and duties and norms. It is this latter form of community that we are told by commentators and politicians is becoming increasingly less common and in need of strengthening and support. Moreover, it is towards the strengthening of this latter form of community that community development and community social work have been mostly directed in recent years.

Communities of interest

Communities of interest are said to be comprised of people who share common characteristics, interests or identities. According to Delaney (2003), *In this view of community, people from diverse backgrounds can come together in communal activism united by a bond of common commitment and the solidarity that results* (p122). Communities of interest are more permanent than aesthetic communities, often entail a good degree of personal commitment and are frequently based around substantive and progressive goals. Unlike aesthetic communities, therefore, the focus here is not on personal fulfilment, but on the achievement of wider social transformation, such as gender equality, or the removal of prejudice or discriminatory, disabling barriers. Thus, such communities may be based on gender, ethnic grouping, disability, sexuality, occupation, or indeed any other substantive area of common interest. As we discussed in Chapter 1, it is commonly thought that the last few decades have seen a proliferation of such communities. We have, according to Fiona Williams (1992), seen *the fragmentation of traditional class politics and the emergence of a politics of identity based on, for example, ethnicity, gender and/or sexuality* (p205) and disability. People, she argues, have lost faith with traditional 'class-based' politics and now when they want to initiate change they do so through these 'classless' communities of interest, which they see as better able to represent their diverse needs and particular concerns.

ACTIVITY 5.4

Spend some time researching the growth of the mental health service user movement. You might wish to look at various sources to assist you, for example the Community Care journal and books such as Beyond the water tower, *written by the Sainsbury Centre for Mental Health in 2005.*

ACTIVITY 5.4 *continued*

- *Think about when the mental health service user movement began and why.*
- *What are the issues and challenges facing it?*
- *What are its achievements?*
- *You might also want to consider the mental health user movement's response to the Government's recent controversial Mental Health Bills.*
- *To what extent is the mental health service user movement a community of interest?*

Most would welcome the gains made by 'communities of interest' in terms of the development of civil rights and anti-discriminatory legislation. The achievements of the feminist, anti-racist, mental health and disability rights movements, to name but four, have been hugely significant, not least in the sphere of social work theory and practice. Postmodernist sociology is particularly welcoming of the work performed by communities of interest. As we discussed in Chapter 1, it sees the emergence of new social movements as being linked to the failure of traditional politics and universal welfare provision to meet the needs of particular groups. While we would caution against an uncritical celebration of the rise of a 'politics of identity', there can be little doubt that communities of identity have increased in number, and their influence in terms of policy and practice is significant.

'Traditional' geographical communities

Sometimes also referred to as 'communities of place' or 'spatial communities', with geographical communities the principal defining characteristic is the geographical locality. While in recent years, the term 'community' has been used to denote very large spatial areas (such as the European Community, or even the 'global community'), when we think of community in a geographical sense, typically we envisage a relatively small territorial area or locality – a 'neighbourhood', consisting of an electoral ward perhaps, or an estate or a village. Those living within the 'community' obviously share geographical space, but, crucially, they are also often said to share a sense of belonging, identity and loyalty to their particular areas. Close geographical proximity and years of shared experience are frequently seen to have inculcated certain common values and norms. There is, therefore, a sense of permanence, of shared responsibility and duty, and mutual support. In this sense, they are different from aesthetic communities discussed above and correspond more closely to what most people think of when they hear the term 'community'. Moreover, it is these geographical communities that have provided the focus for much community development policy and practice, and it is towards an analysis of this type of community that the rest of this chapter is devoted.

There is a long history within community studies of examining small, geographical communities, much of which has sought to explore the role that close networks, ties and feelings of reciprocity have played in facilitating the development of common bonds, cohesion and stability. One of the most influential of these is *Family and kinship in east London*, written by Michael Young and Peter Willmott (1962). In this classic mid-1950s study, Young and Willmott documented the extended kinship net-works and close neighbourly ties among the working-class community in London's Bethnal Green. Their investigations revealed how a complex web of reciprocal family and neighbourhood ties provided the basis for the development of community cohe-sion and solidarity. The key to this community spirit, they argued, was residential stability and geographical proximity of kin, which facilitated the development of mutual aid strategies. They feared that post-war slum clearance and housing reloca-tion policies were in danger of destroying this residential stability, and in doing so shattering the community bonds that been built up through decades of shared experi-ence and mutual support.

Young and Willmott's work is the most influential of a long line of community studies that have used geographical localities as the central focus of analysis. While the focus of these studies has been on particular geographical areas, the main intention of researchers, as with Young and Willmott, has been to examine the webs of relation-ship, trust and familiarity that are thought to be mainstay of 'community life'. Such studies, and the policy recommendations that stem from them, have been influenced by a number of key assumptions:

- Firstly, it is assumed that close-knit, cohesive communities, with a common set of bonds and values, were commonplace in the past, and, moreover, that they continue to exist today in well-functioning neighbourhoods. 'Community', in this sense, is seen as good, desirable thing and something to be celebrated and encouraged.

- Secondly, it is felt that the loyalty, shared values and feelings of reciprocity that have traditionally bound communities together has, in many areas, somehow degenerated or been lost, and that this is the principal cause of the economic and social ills facing particular areas. There is, to cite Taylor (2003, p17), a *community deficit*. Communities are *deficient in some way, whether in skills, in networks, in moral cohesion, or in responsibility*.

- Thirdly, it is assumed that it is possible to create conditions that are conducive to the restoration of community, and, importantly, that this reinstatement of community values is the solution to the problems that certain areas face.

- Finally, it is assumed that it is possible to strengthen, or create, mechanisms which will enable those within the particular locality to themselves rebuild the ties that have been lost.

A paradise lost?

Many of these assumptions have faced criticism for offering an overly simplified, 'romanticised' view of community life in both the past and the present. However, there can be little doubt that they are largely shared by the general public and policy-makers alike. For example, most people today would probably agree with the claim that community life, once the bedrock of cohesion and stability, is in decline. In one recent survey, nine out of ten Britons said that they felt that community life was breaking down (cited in O'Grady, 2007). The question of whether there is any less community spirit in Britain is now rarely asked – the focus instead is on why there is less, and the notion that community is in decline is invariably taken as given. If we ourselves cannot recall more civilised, interdependent and mutually supportive communities, there are countless others – newspaper editors, politicians, bishops, or even our own older relatives – who are more than happy to recount to us their recollections of a 'lost', cherished community, where law-abiding people were more prepared to come together to care and help each other. All the evidence, we are told, seems to point to a lost 'golden age' of community that today, for some reason, is far less commonplace than it was in the past.

At the same time, as our third assumption above indicates, many, not least leading politicians, seem to believe that it is possible to re-create or recover the community spirit and way of life that has been lost. As Bauman (2001, p3) argues, in mainstream political debates, community is held out as the kind of societal organisation which is not, regrettably, available to us at present, *but which we should dearly wish to inhabit and which we hope to repossess*. The term 'community', then, is invariably utilised by politicians to denote much more than just a geographical space; it is used to describe a time, a place or a state of being that is 'safe', that offers a haven to the dangers, trials and tribulations of what is seen an increasingly insecure, hostile and threatening world.

The politics of community

There does indeed seem to be a political consensus that the trials and tribulations of modern life have led to a breakdown in community. According to David Cameron (2006), the Conservative leader, *we are experiencing a crisis of community. Social networks are shrinking. Neighbourhoods are suffering ... Too many of us are strangers in our own streets. People don't feel at home in their own communities – they don't feel that the public space is their space*. The current Labour government is also concerned about community, so much so that it has created a Department for Communities and Local Government. The Department's aim is to *create strong, cohesive communities in which people feel comfortable and proud to live, with a vibrant civic culture and strong local economy* (Ruth Kelly, cited in Communities and Local Government, 2006). As well as agreeing that community is 'in trouble', politicians also agree that it can be 'retrieved' or 'recovered'. The following quote, taken from the report published by the Labour government's Commission on Integration and Cohesion (2007), sets out a future vision of community life in Britain:

> *Imagine the open communities of 2020 ... thriving and prosperous places where people from all different backgrounds are equal, and where everyone matters – whether old or young, settled or new, Black or White. There are local places where all groups feel that they are treated fairly, and that they have a responsibility to others that transcends the differences between them. Places where people are not fearful of meeting their neighbours, and where they don't see individual differences as a barrier to the success of the whole community.*

> (p2)

Sociologically, this kind of interpretation of the concept of community is often traced back to the German sociologist Ferdinand Tonnies' seminal work, Community and society, *where he distinguished between the terms* Gemeinschaft *('community') and* Gesellschaft *('society'). Writing in 1887, Tonnies bemoaned the breakdown of kinship, order, communal ties and shared interests, which he referred to as* Gemeinschaft, *associated with the onset and progression of industrial capitalism. The family ties and small-scale, personal kinship bonds that had hitherto characterised social relationships, were, he feared, gradually being replaced by the development of a more complex, fragmented, atomistic* Gesellschaft, *where individuals pursued their own isolated self-interests. In short, as far back as 1887, Tonnies was concerned about the decline in community, its impact on wider society, and he yearned for a return to a more convivial, harmonious and better world which had been shattered by industrialisation and modern life. As the following extract shows, his work does have a contemporary resonance, for his comparisons between a harmonious, convivial past and a fractious divided present continue to find expression in social and political debates today:*

> *In the Middle Ages there was unity, now there is atomization: then the hierarchy of authority was solicitous paternalism, now it's compulsory exploitation; then there was relative peace, now wars are wholesale slaughter; then there were sympathetic relationships among kinsfolk and old acquaintances, now there are strangers and aliens everywhere; then society was made up of home- and land-loving peasant, now the attitude of the businessman prevails; then man's simple needs were met by home production, now we have world trade and capitalistic production; then there was permanency of abode, now great mobility; then there were folk arts, music and handicrafts, now there is science.*
>
> (Tonnies, 1957, p3)

But what, exactly, do politicians today mean when they call for a restoration of 'community values'? This is an important question, because some sociologists have questioned whether the harmonious, idyllic, trouble-free 'community' that politicians and commentators often hark back to has ever really existed. They argue that notions of neighbourliness and security frequently associated with community can sometimes serve to mask the segregation, division and exclusion that are characteristic features of many localities in modern 'developed' societies. Hence, 'community' can, to cite Taylor (2003), *become a spray-on solution to cover the faultlines of economic decline and social fragmentation* (p2).

Theories of community and community breakdown

We now move on to look at different interpretations of community, and the main explanations that have been advanced for its alleged demise. In doing so, we want to make use of two theoretical approaches outlined earlier in our chapter on social exclusion – moral underclass discourse and redistributive discourse. We will add to this a third approach, which we refer to as the 'middle way' discourse. Advocates of the middle way seek to position themselves in between what they see as the two 'extremes' of right (moral underclass discourse) and left (redistributive discourse).

Moral underclass discourse and community breakdown

Those of you who have already read Chapter 2 will be unsurprised to discover that the moral underclass discourse locates the causes of community breakdown with the morally corrupting nature of state welfare and what are perceived to be other well-meaning, but morally degenerative government interventions. These, it is argued, have created dependent, feckless 'welfare communities', and in doing so destroyed the family bonds, mutual support, self-help and voluntarism that was the mainstay and lifeblood of community life in the past. Whereas once people looked to their family, friends, neighbours and other informal community support networks for assistance, now there is an expectation that the state will unconditionally provide for any unmet needs. In this sense, the 'cushion' of the welfare state *has diminished opportunities for people to be of service to each other, impairing the quality of life and encouraging us to look outwards to the 'authorities' instead of inwards to our own strengths and skills, for solutions to shared problems* (Green, 1996, pix).

This approach, therefore, sees the solution to the disintegration of community as lying not with what it sees as 'top down' state-sponsored initiatives (which are thought to be the cause of the problem), but with reduced levels of welfare provision, the restoration of civic and community values, and the encouragement of initiatives designed to stimulate mutual support, voluntarism and community self-help. In its more orthodox manifestations, moral underclass discourse simply calls for the withdrawal of state welfare, convinced that previously recalcitrant, 'dysfunctional' people will be forced to become self-reliant, active and responsible members of their community. If such individuals were forced to bear moral and financial responsibility for their actions (for example, their idleness and promiscuity) they would, it is argued, soon conform to community norms and values. Moreover, in the absence of statutory assistance and welfare, voluntary and charitable community services, which are more attuned to the causes of community breakdown and the diverse needs of the locality, will inevitably emerge to deal with any problems that do emerge. In this sense, the restoration of community will entail a return to a pre-welfare state era, which is said to have been characterised by altruism, mutual support and voluntarism (Green, 1996).

Moral underclass discourse and community policy

For a glimpse of the policy-making impact of this kind of analysis of community, we need look no further than some of the wider social policy initiatives introduced by Conservative governments in the 1980s and the 1990s. These were designed with a view to reducing the state's responsibility for welfare, and encouraging private, or voluntary community provision. Of course, informal mechanisms of support have always been significant providers of welfare, but the ideologies of self-help and 'community care' were thereafter pursued with the utmost of political vigour.

Community care

In the 1980s successive Conservative administrations introduced a number of initiatives designed to promote 'community care'. The rhetoric that underpinned these policies implied that a desire to improve the lives of service users was at the heart of the shift. The initiatives were, it was argued, motivated by a desire to close impersonal and oppressive state institutions and to deliver more humane, personalised, tailored packages of care in community settings. More services, it was assumed, would be provided by the voluntary and private sectors and the family (crucially, with appropriate support), and this would lead to improvements in the standard of care and increased choice and control for service users and their relatives.

ACTIVITY *5.5*

In small groups, share your perceptions and experiences of community care. These might come from:

- *personal experiences of having a family member who is cared for in the community;*
- *placement experience of providing services;*
- *working as a carer for an agency;*
- *living close to a community-based project – for example, supported housing;*
- *media reporting on community care.*

What are the issues, advantages and challenges around this policy? Try to think of these from the perspective of service users; carers; family members; professionals; and members of the public.

Discussion

Few would disagree with the principle that in many instances it is better to provide support for people in community settings. However, when community care policies were rolled out in the 1980s and 1990s, social workers, welfare professionals and academics questioned the Conservative government's motives and expressed concern (and have continued to express concern) at the direction of community care policy. Indeed, it quickly became apparent that the government's community care strategy was driven more by concerns about costs than it was standards of care. To a government that was ideologically committed to rolling back the state and cutting public expenditure, the rhetoric of community care proved useful in its justification of the closure of large, expensive psychiatric hospitals, and its attempts to limit spending on nursing care. The introduction of a more mixed economy of care meant that a great deal of direct care provision was provided by private-sector agencies, which raised real issues pertaining to the quality of care when profit is the key underpinning factor. The possibility that communities may have been ill equipped to cope with the often complex needs of service users was also rarely acknowledged, and *community care became synonymous with 'care at home' and in practice relied on informal care from families [predominantly women] to look after those in need* (Pierson, 2002, p138). We have not got the space to engage in a detailed analysis of the gendered nature of community care here, but we would agree with Pierson's (2002) suggestion that much needs to be clarified before embracing the concept. As he points out, *If it is little more than an another ideological device to extract unpaid, low-prestige labour out of women then it an oppressive concept in its own right* (p139).

There is little doubt that properly funded, well co-ordinated, service user-led care in the community can contribute to improvements in the lives of many people. However, where care is poorly resourced, badly co-ordinated and service-led, the consequences can be disastrous. In such circumstances, some service users have fallen through the professional net and have come to be a serious risk to themselves and others. Some service users daily receive shoddy services with very poor standards of care which gives no consideration to their basic human right to dignity and respect. In addition to this, very many carers feel unsupported and unable to cope. This is not to draw attention away from very many positive outcomes of community care; however, where it is poorly funded, inadequately supported and motivated by the pursuit of profit, service users' experiences of community care can be sadly lacking.

Moral underclass discourse, social work and community

As intimated above, moral underclass discourse sees the social work profession, as it is currently organised, as part of the problem. It too readily assumes that 'the poor' in deprived communities are victims of circumstance. Social workers assume naïvely that the problems facing certain communities are due to external forces beyond their control, and that residents are justly entitled to support and compensation for their 'plight'. The ethos underpinning the social work profession was, it is argued, not always organised in such a manner. In its earlier incarnations social work was very different, less 'indiscriminate' in its propensity to deliver welfare, and more concerned about questions of character and culpability. In advocating a model for the future, therefore, those such as Green (1996) and Whelan (2001) look backwards, to the late nineteenth and early twentieth century work of the Charity Organisation Society (COS).

The foundation of the COS in the nineteenth century is often seen as heralding the beginning of social work in Britain. Initially organised and run on a voluntary basis, it adopted a personal casework approach, seeking to determine not just levels of need, but also levels of moral culpability. Assistance was conditional and those who were deemed undeserving of support, or 'not likely to benefit' from support (a euphemism for 'undeserving'), were simply turned down, and forced to rely upon their own devices. Advocates of moral underclass discourse defend the apparent harshness of this approach:

> *This was not due to hard-heartedness, as critics maintained, but to the conviction that not everybody asking for assistance was in a position to benefit from it, and that to give relief heedlessly was to make a bad situation worse ... So, for example, a man who is poor because he is addicted to drugs or alcohol will not benefit from cash handouts, as he is extremely likely to spend the funds on his addiction. (This point might seem too obvious to need making, were it not for the fact that the state welfare system today ignores it.)*

> (Whelan, 2001, p22)

For proponents of the moral underclass debate, social work can potentially have a role in helping us recover community life, but it will entail a very different kind of practice to that taught in universities today, which, according to Whelan (2001, p96), renders social workers *unfit to operate in the real world. Structural issues surrounding race, gender and other politically correct causes*, he argues, have *assumed supreme importance, whilst the idea that social workers should help their clients to modify their habits and develop the skills necessary to participate in mainstream society seemed to have evaporated entirely*. From this perspective, then, welfare, and more specifically social work, should once again be devolved to a community level, organised primarily by the voluntary or charitable sectors, and geared towards modifying behaviour and ensuring that all are encouraged to respect community values and norms.

Redistributionist discourse and community breakdown

As outlined in Chapter 3, redistributionist discourse adopts a structural approach when explaining social problems. Not surprisingly, therefore, instead of focusing on individual culpability, redistributionist discourse draws attention to the forces that impinge on communities, which serve to undermine the development of cohesion and shared values. Hence, community breakdown is linked to factors such as economic decline, the restructuring of the labour market, the residualisation of state welfare, and changes at an ideological level. Regarding the economy and labour market, the decline of traditional manufacturing industries, such as textiles, mining and steel, has, it is argued, torn the heart out of many communities, wiping out millions of jobs, and destroying the aspirations and dreams of younger generations. Industries that once provided employment for whole neighbourhoods or communities have disappeared, leaving in their wake exclusion, hopelessness and division. Hence, the camaraderie and feelings of reciprocity that evolved from shared workplaces and social experiences have been shattered not by moral breakdown, but by social and economic dislocation. These trends have adversely affected economic activity and social interaction at a community level, and small-scale enterprises – local butchers, newsagents, social clubs, pubs and grocers shops – have closed, unable to cope with decline in demand for their goods and services (this process has, of course, been exacerbated by the proliferation of large, multinational supermarket chains). These local shops and leisure facilities previously provided geographical spaces where people within communities were brought together, facilitating the development of community ties and shared interests and values.

At the same time, the welfare support mechanisms which would previously have helped communities cope with such changes – for instance, welfare benefits, advisory and support services – have been withdrawn or cut, exacerbating the difficulties communities face. Meanwhile, at an ideological level, decades of neo-liberal dominance have served to foster and sustain a culture of selfishness, greed and other traits that make the development of shared community values difficult. Certainly, the ethic of competition, reward and 'just deserts' has gathered pace in the past couple of decades, and advocates of redistributionist discourse argue that this has impacted negatively upon community cohesion and support for the kind of collective action that is necessary to create a community ethic.

For supporters of redistributionist discourse, any solution to community decline must begin by tackling the chronic unemployment, poverty and hopelessness that are seen to have contributed to a dislocation of community. Redistributionist discourse would not deny the importance of moral underclass discourse's emphasis on community self-help, but it draws attention to two main factors that currently militate against solutions which focus primarily upon community activism.

Firstly, there is a much wider recognition of the wider social, economic and ideological environments within which communities (and community activists) must operate. Thus, the notion that communities can themselves solve the fundamental structural problems that lie at their neighbourhoods is, they argue, naïve. These problems – for instance, educational inequality, chronic unemployment, underemployment, low incomes, inadequate welfare benefits and the emergence of a individualist consumer culture – are national in nature, and while communities and community activists can mitigate their symptoms, they are powerless to deal with their origins. As Mayo (1994, p11) argues, *Neither voluntary effort in general, nor community-based self-help in particular, can be expected to fill the widening gap between social needs and public provision.* Governments, therefore, need to begin by acknowledging their responsibility for ensuring that all communities benefit from, for instance, decent educational and employment opportunities and adequate incomes.

Secondly, and on a more practical level, poverty, unemployment, and the daily struggle to make ends meet means that many people are simply unable to participate in activities designed to promote 'community cohesion'. Referring to Maslow's hierarchy of needs, Taylor (2003) argues that *There are many in marginalised communities whose main preoccupation is physical survival, so self actualisation is a long way up the hierarchy of needs* (p78). From this perspective, people can only develop the kinds of solidarity recommended by policy-makers if they have the time and resources to do so, a luxury currently lacking in many communities across Britain. Mayo (1994) agrees:

> If communities are realistically to play an enhanced role in a restructured welfare state they will have to be provided with public resources to make that option viable.
>
> (p11)

Redistributionist discourse, social work and community

While redistributionist discourse places much greater emphasis upon wider structural factors, as hinted at above, it does also believe that social workers can play a significant role in mitigating community decline and fostering community action at a local level. Indeed, countless textbooks have been written detailing the virtues of community work and outlining the ways in which practitioners, such as social workers, can utilise their skills to help initiate progressive change in deprived communities. Twelvetrees (2001) argues that community workers on deprived housing estates can help people form and organise their own autonomous representative organisations, such as tenants' associations, youth groups, play groups, senior citizens' associations and food co-operatives. While moral underclass discourse might interpret such work as 'professional busy-bodying' and representative of a 'nanny state', redistributionist discourse would emphasise its importance in empowering members of the community and encouraging them to become directly involved in improving the fabric of their own localities. This kind of work, which Twelvetrees (2001) refers to as the *community development approach*, is seen as being valuable for two reasons. Firstly, and most obviously, it helps initiate material improvements which all members the community stand to benefit from. Secondly, and just as importantly, bringing members of the community together and encouraging them to work collectively to solve some of the problems they face, helps facilitate the development of the sort of values, networks and feelings of reciprocity upon which healthy communities depend. By working together, people come to realise there really is something such as society and that they, and the communities within which they reside, stand to benefit from collectivist as opposed to selfish, individualist action.

There is, however, another important way in which redistributionist discourse feels that practitioners can facilitate the development of healthy, vibrant communities; that is, by engaging in what Twelvetrees (2001) refers to as *social planning*. By this, he means working directly with policy-makers – locally, regionally, nationally and even internationally – with a view to sensitising them about the needs of particular communities, and harnessing opportunities and resources that can be used to promote community development. Supporters of redistributive discourse see this aspect of community work as crucial. Practitioners can, and, it is argued, should, use their advocacy, organisational and networking skills to influence policy debates and promote a wider awareness of the structural problems that deprived communities face. They can do this in a 'consensual' way by, for instance lobbying policy-makers and applying for grants on the community's behalf, but where necessary they should not rule out helping to organise direct political action campaigns and even protests based upon civil disobedience. That said, redistributionist discourse approaches to community tend to stop short of engaging in a wider critique of capitalism itself. It is assumed that the basic foundation of society is sound and that causes of community dislocation can be solved through gradual social reform.

The 'middle way' and community breakdown

Those adhering to what we have referred to as the 'middle way' (others sometimes refer to it as the Third Way) seek to chart what is claimed to be a non-ideological route between what are perceived to be the 'extremes' of both right and left, or to use our typology between moral underclass discourse and redistributionist discourse. Influenced by the work of sociologists such as Anthony Giddens (1998), and associated in the UK with post-1997 Labour governments, middle-way interpretations of community breakdown tend to combine structural and behavioural elements. Rhetorically, each is often given relatively equal prominence, but as we will see, the relative influence of structural versus behavioural explanations in shaping Labour's community development strategy (which, as intimated, has been justified by middle-way discourse) is a matter of much debate.

The influence of redistributionist discourse on the middle way can be found in its acknowledgment of the government's responsibility to provide the environment and opportunities for communities to develop and thrive. On the other hand, moral under-class discourse can be detected in the strong emphasis the middle way places on the role that communities themselves, the private sector, and 'third sector' organisations, such as voluntary associations and charities, can play in reinvigorating community life. Moral underclass overtones can also be found in the focus the middle way places on the need for community members to fulfil responsibilities, duties and to behave appropriately.

These days, advocates of 'middle way' solutions to the problems of community break-down appear to include the leaderships of both the Conservative and Labour Parties. As we have seen, Conservatives have traditionally tended to embrace moral underclass discourse and Labour politicians redistributionist discourse. However, now both have sought to distance themselves from what they see as the 'extremities' of their parties' former positions. David Cameron, for example, has criticised the 'Old Right' who believed that the only way of restoring 'community' was by cutting the supply of state services:

> *The fact is, we cannot arbitrarily withdraw welfare benefits for the most needy of our fellow citizens. Yes, if we did that, no doubt in 20 years' time people would have become more self-reliant – but think of the misery of those 20 years. Some people will always need help and support – and we should not imagine that government simply withdrawing from the social field will automatically and instantly cause new, independent bodies to spring up in their place.*
>
> (Cameron, 2006)

Likewise, the former Labour Prime Minister, Tony Blair, has bemoaned the 'top down' state interventionist solutions to community regeneration, which had traditionally been favoured by the 'Old Left', and under his leadership Labour shifted towards a 'middle ground', accepting the validity of behavioural interpretations of community decline and the need for voluntary and private sector initiatives.

The New Deal for Communities

One of the Labour government's flagship policies for strengthening communities, the New Deal for Communities (NDC), is a good example of a policy initiative driven by middle-way discourse. Introduced in 1998, the NDC set aside £2 billion for investment over a period of ten years in some of the country's most deprived communities. In all, 39 of what were described as some of poorest communities were to be given resources to help them tackle five key themes: poor job prospects, educational underachievement, high crime levels, poor health and poor housing and urban environments. There can be little doubt that the communities chosen were in need of investment. On average in these communities only 42 per cent of over 16s were in full-time work (18 per cent lower than the national average). Overall unemployment in 2001–04 stood at 8 per cent, three times the national average, and average weekly income was only £241, almost half the national average (Office of the Deputy Prime Minister, 2005, p121). The government, though, was keen to emphasise that this

The New Deal for Communities — *continued*

would not simply be a 'top down', redistributive initiative of the kind previously associated with 'Old' Labour. Too much, Tony Blair argued, has been imposed from above, when experience shows that success depends on communities themselves having the power and taking the responsibility to make things better (Social Exclusion Unit, 1998a, pi). The Prime Minister's comments here hint at the NDC's middle-way influences, with his emphasis on the need for communities themselves (and not just government) to take responsibility for improving their neighbourhoods. Indeed, at times the government has given as much prominence to the importance of community self-help as it has to the need for wider structural improvements, such as additional resources and greater opportunity. This does seem to mark a significant break with 'Old' Labour's redistributionist strategies:

> *Without effective self-help, it is unlikely that any other measures of community regeneration, however well-resourced, will provide long-term solutions to long-term problems ... To put the matter another way: the regeneration of poor neighbourhoods will take more than physical rebuilding; more than the improvement of local services; more even than economic opportunity*
>
> (Home Office, 1999, p1)

While some of the NDC initiatives have a redistributive element at their core, much of the funding has been devoted to 'supply side' measures, designed to stimulate and incentivise communities and community members to solve their own problems. Hence, many of the worklessness schemes funded by the NDC have focused less on actual job creation and more on motivating and encouraging people to take up opportunities that are deemed to be readily available. Likewise, in education, NDC funding has been used to offer inducements for pupils to work harder, by providing financial rewards to those who pass a certain number of GCSEs, rather than to tackle the structural causes of educational disadvantage.

Many have welcomed the government's acknowledgement of the failure of previous community regeneration schemes, as well as its embrace of the principle that community members themselves should be at the heart of any development strategy. However, much of this is not new, and some argue that the experiences of middle-way initiatives such as the NDC to date suggest that they may be in danger of repeating the same mistakes of earlier regeneration initiatives, such as Community Development Programmes in the 1960s and 1970s. Space prevents us from engaging here in a detailed critical evaluation of the NDC, but a general concern shared by many is the lack of resources that have been devoted to tackling the structural causes of community decline. For example, the £2 billion allotted to the NDCs sounds like a great deal of money, but when placed, for instance, in the context of the problems these 39 communities face (and the £800 million spent on the Millennium Dome during the same period) its significance becomes clearer. Others have criticised the ends to which resources have been put. One concern is that the focus has been on 'supply-side' measures which are designed to stimulate and motivate community members to solve their own difficulties, rather than deal with the intractable structural problems their communities face. We touched on this point earlier, when discussing redistributionist discourse views on the potential of community self help to deliver progressive change, and we will return to a more specific critique of the current vogue for self-help strategies in our Marxist section below.

Middle-way discourse, social work and community

Some of the funding provided by 'middle-way' initiatives, such as the NDCs, has been devoted towards addressing some of the structural causes of community breakdown, by directly creating employment for, for example, classroom assistants, nursery nurses and construction workers employed on environmental work. In many cases, practitioners have played a crucial part in helping to organise and arrange funding for these, and in this sense, there is still a role in middle-way initiatives for what Twelvetrees calls the social planning approach to community work. However, given the emphasis it places upon self-help and encouraging voluntarism and activism, middle-way discourse places primacy upon the community development approach. Practitioners must, to quote one influential government report, provide *support in a way which fosters independence rather than dependence* (Home Office, 1999, p17):

> *It will sometimes seem easier to an outside agency, whether local authority, police service or voluntary organisation, to analyse a situation, identify 'the problem' and then solve it. But the chances are that it won't stay solved. It is more likely that a long and slow process of helping the community identify the issues and deal with them will yield greater long-term benefits.*

In summary, therefore, middle-way discourse does see an important role for community social workers, but that role remains firmly rooted in the community development tradition. Practitioners are to be enablers rather than providers and all efforts should be aimed towards stimulating community-led initiatives. Table 5.1 on page 124, summarises the approaches to community breakdown.

Traditional sociological theories of community breakdown

The functions of community

As we saw in Chapter 1, functionalist sociology often reverts to a biological analogy when explaining how society works. Society, like the human body, is said to have certain functional prerequisites – or basic needs – which must be met if it is to work effectively. Whereas the heart, the brain, the lungs, the kidneys and so on work together to keep the body functioning healthily, institutions such as the family, education, religion and the community, do the same for society. The point is, if one of these constituent parts – for example, community – malfunctions, then the health of the whole of society is seen to be threatened and remedial, 'curative' action is necessary to prevent the spread of the 'disease'.

So, what are the functions of community? Firstly, communities provide the 'stage' upon which shared norms and values are played out. As we saw in Chapter 1,

Table 5.1 summarises the approach to community breakdown.

	Causes of community breakdown	Solutions to community breakdown	Practice implications
Moral underclass discourse	• Well meaning, but morally degenerative government interventions, which reward and encourage dependency and 'deviancy', and destroy self-help and voluntarism. • Low levels of motivation and aspiration at a community level.	• Reductions in levels of welfare support, aimed at reducing dependency and forcing communities to take responsibility for their own lives and situations. • Promotion of individualism. • Encouragement of initiatives designed to stimulate mutual support, voluntarism and community self help.	• Emphasis placed on the virtues of private, voluntary and charitable provision and practice. • Rejection of structural analysis and a focus on modifying welfare-induced dysfunctional behavioural patterns. • Practice should be geared towards inculcating appropriate norms and values, and stimulating self-help, hard work and thrift.
Redistributionist discourse	• Economic decline and unemployment. • Welfare cuts. • Poverty and inequality. • Dominance of individualistic, neo-liberal ideology.	• Substantially improved work opportunities. • Moderate levels of income redistribution. • Improved welfare benefits. • Repudiation of individualist, neo-liberal ideology. • Encourage the development of a community spirit/ethic.	• Practice underpinned by an understanding of wider structural causes of community decline. • Encouragement of community action, but with an awareness of the limitations of self-help strategies. • Promotion of strategies designed to arrest inequalities in economic and social resources.
Middle-way discourse	• Economic decline and unemployment. • Low levels of motivation and aspiration to engage in self-help.	• Provide the environment and opportunities for communities to develop and thrive. • Emphasis is placed on the duty and the responsibility of community members to avail themselves of opportunities that are available. • Tackle the 'culture of aspiration' that is said to contribute to the failure of communities to engage in self help. • Encourage the development of a community spirit/ethic.	• Some role for social planning work, but a rejection of old style, 'top down' redistributive initiatives. • Celebration of voluntarism and self-help, with only a tacit acknowledgment of its limitations. • Promotion of strategies that encourage community members to solve their own problems.

Durkheim used the term *collective conscience* to refer to the totality of beliefs and sentiments, which exists to shape the behaviour of individuals such that they fit into society as a whole. The community can act as the platform for the manifestation of the collective conscience, by perpetuating systems of mutual obligation and co-operation. If in Britain today, powerful sentiments exist around courtesy and respect, for example, this can be demonstrated very clearly in communities – examples might include pervasive but largely unspoken norms which discourage playing loud music late at night; promote being respectful of speed limits; and not swearing in public or spitting on the pavement. Although of course there are implications here for individuals, it is the *patterns of relationships* and supporting norms that functionalists regard as being key; these are self-perpetuating and reinforcing as the expectations that underpin behaviour in communities create accepted behaviours, which in turn reinforce the expectations that exist, and so on.

Secondly and very much linked to this, communities can perform a useful and powerful social control function when individuals fall short of shared norms and values. For instance, in an area where unacceptable behaviour occurs, such as playing loud music late at night, neighbours may get together to ring the police or go round together to try to address this issue. In this case, the individuals involved are overtly influencing the offending neighbour by making it clear that the behaviour is not acceptable. However, for functionalists, communities may also play a more covert and silent, but very significant role in enforcing norms; for example, when members of a community take pride in their homes, gardens and communal spaces, this contributes in an unspoken way to the shared 'emotional' ownership of an area. Similarly, neighbours who automatically keep an eye on their neighbours' property or make it known that they are watching if vandals are hanging around can contribute to implementing social control.

Thirdly, a functionalist perspective on community would point to how communities contribute a powerful component to our social identities, which in turn assists members of society to feel that they belong to something greater than themselves. As we saw at the beginning of this chapter, belonging to a community varies considerably; for some this entails a tangible experience demonstrated by attending a community centre, participating in a local concern, chatting with others in the 'local', or popping in to neighbours' for a coffee. For others, our social identity may be more shaped by being part of a less tangible entity, such as an online community, or by being part of a particular interest-based community.

Fourthly, communities can offer individuals support, either through organisations and agencies, or through neighbours and more localised informal support networks. An example of this can be seen more and more on our TV screens following the tragic death of a child – the local community rallies round to give support, for example by laying flowers, writing messages of support, and showing solidarity with the child's family.

We can see then how for functionalism the community fulfils various roles for the well-being and cohesiveness of mainstream society. Importantly, functionalists are not so much interested in individuals here, but the way that 'community' can contribute to the smooth running of the system. Of course, functionalists are well aware of the potential dysfunctional aspects of certain communities – for example, high rates of crime, riots and gang violence – but they perceive these as warning signs of societal malfunctioning, which, with appropriate interventions, are solvable. In this sense, we can see how each of the three discourses on community that we outlined earlier – moral underclass, redistributonist and the middle way – could be said to share a common functionalist heritage. All three, to varying degrees, view community break-down as a 'disease' or 'malfunction', which, whilst temporarily disturbing to the equilibrium of society, is capable of 'cure'. Of course, the solutions offered by each do differ, but there is a general agreement that it is possible to 'smooth over the cracks' and assist communities to function well again.

A Marxist approach to community and community breakdown

In previous chapters we have seen how Marxists reject functionalist claims that capitalist societies are, on the whole, essentially well-functioning totalities, subject to only sporadic, relatively small-scale, 'curable' problems. In fact, the problems associated with community breakdown, such as poverty, unemployment, social division, crime and poor housing are, Marxists argue, an inevitable and intractable feature of a system based upon competition, exploitation and injustice. Moreover, these problems are far more common and endemic than any of the above approaches is prepared to acknowledge. Even redistributionist discourse, the most radical of the three approaches outlined above, seems to accept that targeted interventions, aimed at a relatively small number of communities, can help overcome social dislocation and create a more harmonious and just capitalism. In this sense, Marxists argue that the rhetoric surrounding community regeneration policy, even in its more progressive redistributionist form, can serve an ideological function, diverting our gaze from the bigger picture of social division and exclusion. It persuades us that only a small number of communities are 'malfunctioning', and that their 'sickness' is a result of abnormal, pathological and parochial factors which are capable of cure. The reality, for Marxists, is that these social and economic problems are symptomatic of a much wider malaise that lies at the heart of capitalist societies, which will only be overcome with the abolition of capitalism and the creation of a socialist society.

Marxism, social work and community

What role, then, do Marxists see for community practitioners? Firstly, there needs to be a recognition that practice itself cannot change society or solve the multiple problems and difficulties communities face. Although practitioners can have as their aim the creation of a more fair, just society, they cannot themselves achieve the large-scale changes that are needed to affect fundamental improvements. That is not, though, to suggest they cannot perform a positive role by engaging in radical, transformatory practice. One of the problems with much community development work, Marxists argue, is that while it has made the lives of many people somewhat easier, less intolerable and unpleasant, it has not been truly transformative (Ledwith, 2005). So although it has helped alleviate some of the symptoms of the injustices that characterise capitalist societies, it has failed to draw attention to, address or challenge their root cause – the system itself. Marxists therefore claim that practitioners engaged in community development work often perform a contradictory function. On the one hand, they help to mitigate the worst effects of capitalism – by affecting moderate improvements in the material circumstances of sections of the poor – yet on the other hand, they help 'prop' the system up by diffusing potential discontent, and perpetuating the myth that capitalist societies are, on the whole, characterised by solidarity, cohesion and integration. Marxists therefore insist that the work of community practitioners in capitalist societies must be shaped by an acknowledgement of wider economic and social inequality, and be driven by a desire to initiate fundamental social and economic change.

In practical terms, then, practitioners may wish to engage in propaganda and political education work, designed to stimulate a community-level awareness of the wider structures that contribute to the problems they face. Practitioners can also play a crucial organising role, assisting communities to challenge oppressive structures, through campaigns, demonstrations and sit-ins. In addition, they can help community organisations to develop links with other radical community associations and movements, with a view to increasing their collective strength. In relation to the current emphasis placed on self-help, Marxists insist that practitioners must have an awareness of the limitations of such an approach. As Ledwith (2005), a prominent advocate of transformative practice, argues:

> If we are uncritical in our practice, we may find ourselves naively supporting policies that emphasise participation as a further erosion of rights in favour of responsibilities, rather than a process leading to social justice and equality. The end result of this would be a continued transfer of resources away from the most vulnerable communities, with an increased emphasis on local self-help as an inadequate response to the structural forces of discrimination.
> (pp19–20)

Of course, Marxists would never dismiss the potential of community empowerment *per se*, and they accept that community self-help and organisation must be part of a strategy for empowerment, harnessing the collective strength of the poor. However, they argue that the current vogue for community self-help constitutes little more than a *masking defence against calls for redistribution* and represents a *neo-liberal wolf dressed up as a populist sheep*:

> Self-sufficiency, the idea that 'left to their own devices' (and their current resources) poor communities would lift themselves out from poverty just fine, makes for an attractive myth but a regressive policy.
> (Berner and Phillips, 2005, pp20 and 24)

The concern here, to cite Ledwith (2005), is that while the rhetoric of self-help has an undeniable appeal, it *places the responsibility for tackling poverty onto the very groups who are most targeted by oppressive forces, denying the reality of structural power that permeates communities and perpetuates poverty* (p24). Hence, the idea that poor communities can 'develop themselves', which finds expression in much community development policy and rhetoric, is seen by Marxists as being fundamentally and dangerously flawed. It assumes, incorrectly, that communities do not need to benefit from a fundamental redistribution of resources and that the current structure of wealth and power distribution can be ignored. It also harms demands for realistic levels of funding for tackling the problems that many communities face, and, overall, reinforces the view that the poor are poor because they have failed to help themselves (Berner and Phillips, 2005).

CHAPTER SUMMARY

The sociology of community seems to be less fashionable than in previous years. If we cast our minds back to when we were A Level sociology students, the topic did seem to feature in most introductory sociology textbooks. Now, however, 'community' seems to have been inauspiciously removed as a substantive subject in most texts, partly, no doubt, due to what we described earlier as the perceived 'shiftiness' of the concept – its ambiguity and its multiplicity of meanings. However, as you have hopefully witnessed while reading the chapter, the concept of community lies at the heart of debates about the future of social welfare and social work policy and practice, and it is crucial that those of you who will be responsible for implementing future policy have a firm understanding of the different conceptualisations of the term. We hope that this chapter has stimulated your interest in and understanding of the topic and, at the same time, gone some way towards making a case for the rehabilitation of the sociology of community. Hopefully, those of you who do go on to engage in community work are now in a position to give some consideration to the ideological origins of different policy initiatives, as well as their limitations.

FURTHER READING

Those of you interested in radical, transformatory community work will find Margaret Ledwith's book a useful text: **Ledwith, M** (2005) *Community development: A critical approach*. Bristol: Policy Press.

For a moral underclass discourse perspective on community work see: **Green, DG** (1996) *Community without politics: A market approach to welfare reform*. London: CIVITAS.

In the following influential text, Alan Twelvetrees discusses different approaches, but the book focuses mainly on the skills needed by community workers: **Twelvetrees, AC** (2001) *Community work*. Basingstoke: Palgrave.

For a more theoretical and critical text, see: **Popple, K** (2005) *Analysing community work: Its theory and practice*. Maidenhead: Open University Press/McGraw-Hill.

Chapter 6
Moral panics

This chapter will help you begin to meet the following National Occupational Standards and General Social Care Council's Codes of Practice.

Key Role 2: Plan, carry out, review and evaluate social work practice, with individuals, families, carers, groups, communities and other professionals

- Apply and justify social work methods and models used to achieve change and development, and improve life opportunities.
- Work with groups to promote individual growth, development and independence.

Key Role 3: Support individuals to represent their needs, views and circumstances

- Advocate with, and on behalf of, individuals, families, carers, groups and communities.

Key Role 5: Manage and be accountable, with supervision and support, for your own social work practice within your organisation

- Provide evidence for judgements and decisions.

Key Role 6: Demonstrate professional competence in social work practice

- Implement knowledge based social work models and methods to develop and improve your own practice.
- Manage complex ethical issues, dilemmas and conflicts.
- Identify and assess issues, dilemmas and conflicts that might affect your practice.

General Social Care Council Code of Practice

Code 1.1: Treating each person as an individual.

Code 1.4: Respecting and maintaining the dignity and privacy of service users.

Code 1.5: Promoting equal opportunities for service users and carers.

Code 1.6: Respecting diversity and different cultures and values.

It will also introduce you to the following academic standards as set out in the social work subject benchmark statements.

3.1.1 Social work services and service users

- The social processes (associated with, for example, poverty, unemployment, poor health, disablement, lack of education and other sources of disadvantage) that lead to marginalisation, isolation and exclusion and their impact on the demand for social work services.
- Explanations of the links between definitional processes contributing to social differences (for example, social class, gender and ethnic differences) to the problems of inequality and differential need faced by service users.
- The nature and validity of different definitions of, and explanations for, the characteristics and circumstances of service users and the services required by them.

3.1.3 Values and ethics

- The moral concepts of rights, responsibility, freedom, authority and power inherent in the practice of social workers as moral and statutory agents.
- The complex relationships between justice, care and control in social welfare and the practical and ethical implications of these, including roles as statutory agents and in upholding the law in respect of discrimination.

3.1.4 Social work theory

- The relevance of sociological perspectives to understanding societal and structural influences on human behaviour at individual, group and community levels.

Introduction

Some of you may already be familiar with the term 'moral panic', as it is now commonly used to describe what are perceived to be exaggerated societal responses to particular issues or problems. In sociological and social work literature we find frequent reference to moral panics. Moral panics are said to have occurred over issues such as youth crime, asylum, satanic child abuse and paedophilia. As we will show, the basic premise is that the threat said to be posed by a particular issue or social group is out of all proportion to the danger actually posed. Society, it is argued, is frequently 'whipped up' into a frenzy of concern over particular issues, and this leads to inappropriately harsh policy responses. As social workers, we will quite often be working with individuals and groups who are said to be the subjects of moral panics and hence it is important for us to understand the concept's origins and meaning. This chapter will consider how the term 'moral panic' emerged and developed, and will discuss different relevant sociological perspectives. You will be encouraged to make sense of the ways in which individuals and groups can become labelled by the media, politicians, welfare professionals and institutions and assess how social work can, on the one hand, help generate and foster moral panics, and on the other hand, empower service users to move beyond labelling.

What is a 'moral panic'?

Societies appear to be subject, every now and then, to periods of moral panic. A condition, episode, person or group of persons emerges to become defined as a threat to social values and interests; its nature is presented in a stylised and stereotypical fashion by the mass media; the moral barricades are manned by editors, bishops, politicians and other right-thinking people.

(Cohen, 2006, p1)

The term 'moral panic' was coined by Stan Cohen to explain what he felt was the exaggerated level of media, societal and political concern generated by disturbances between 'Mods' and 'Rockers' in British seaside resorts in 1964. The catalyst was a sporadic outbreak of violence in Clacton on a wet, cold and miserable Easter Sunday in 1964. A few groups of young people with little else to do began scuffling with each other, throwing stones and engaging in other minor misdemeanours. A few windows were broken and some beach huts were vandalised. The young people began to break off into two separate groups, 'Rockers' and 'Mods'. The total estimated cost of the damage was no more than £500, yet the day after, the incidents were portrayed in most national newspapers in wildly inflated terms. The emotive language used such as 'riot', 'orgy of destruction' and 'siege' conveyed images of a besieged town being laid to waste by a rampant, lawless mob.

As a young sociologist, Cohen was fascinated by the reactions to the events as they unfolded. He identified the creation of 'folk devils', or newly created deviant groups. In this instance, these were Mods and Rockers, two groups of young people differentiated by their distinctive style of dress and musical tastes. Prior to the trouble on Easter Sunday, the differences between the two groups were not fully established, but they were later reinforced partly as a consequence of the overstated emphasis placed by the media on their distinctiveness. Cohen described how the media exaggerated, simplified and distorted the events, amplifying levels of concern to such a degree that the occurrences in Clacton assumed a national significance out of all proportion to the danger they posed. Doom-laden predictions were made about the 'threat' posed to societal norms and values by the gangs of so-called 'mindless hoodlums'. The media's sensationalist portrayal of similar events in other seaside towns in 1964 served to reinforce the perception of the mods and rockers phenomenon as a widespread evil menace that needed to be tackled. Few assumed the events were a 'transient' phenomenon, and they were presented as being representative of a general breakdown in moral values, law and order and societal well-being. As Cohen (2006) noted:

> it was clear throughout that it was not only property that was being threatened, but 'all the conventions and values of life'. As the Birmingham Post (19 May 1964) put it, drawing on Churchill's 'we will fight them on the beaches' speech: the external enemies of 1940 had been replaced on our own shores in 1964 by internal enemies who 'bring about disintegration of a nation's character'.
>
> (p38)

Cohen drew attention to the emotive labelling that was used to describe and demonise the participants as 'hooligans', 'thugs' and 'wild ones'. These terms became part of the prevailing mythology and were attributable to all young people wearing certain clothes and belonging to specific social groups. Cohen (2006) quoted the prosecutor at the first trial in Clacton after the events who listed the following traits of the offending youth: *no views at all on any serious subject; an inflated idea of their own importance in society; immature; irresponsible; arrogant; lacking in any regard for the law, for the officers of the law, for the comfort and safety of other persons and for the property of others* (p40). These themes were picked up by the press, who incorporated them into their headlines, which described those participating in the disturbances as *ill conditioned, odious louts, retarded, vain, young, hotblooded paycocks, and grubby hordes of louts and sluts*. This had the effect of further reinforcing the negative images associated with the labels, touching a chord with the general public and moral crusaders who became drawn into the newly created moral panic and demanded swift measures to be implemented to counteract the 'threat'. Cohen went on to describe how politicians harnessed the moral panic around mods and rockers to justify the introduction of coercive criminal justice policies.

Since the publication of Cohen's seminal work on moral panics, sociologists have subsequently utilised the concept to describe what they see as the exaggerated levels of concern that surround certain social groups and problems. Importantly, as we will show, the subject matter of moral panics is often linked to the areas of life that social workers intervene in.

In summary then, a moral panic can be defined as a socially constructed process that occurs when there is a reaction to a social event, which produces a heightened sense of awareness and concern in society. As we have seen above, the moral panic begins with a problem being identified; its causes are then simplified and key participants stigmatised. The media then pick up on the issue and campaign for 'something to be done'. The authorities respond, often harshly, but in many cases the media's appetite for the more lurid and inaccurate aspects of the debate remains as insatiable as ever, and its continued stereotypical reporting of the issue leads to calls for still more stringent action to be implemented.

ACTIVITY 6.1

You may wish to do this exercise in a small group.

With reference to the above definition of a moral panic, scan the newspapers over the duration of a two-week period and try to identify any current moral panics.

- *What are the key features of these?*
- *Who are the 'folk devils'?*
- *Which groups or interests are 'manning the moral barricades'?*
- *How are the folk devils seen to challenge the moral fabric of society?*
- *What responses have there been and by whom?*
- *What solutions have been proposed to deal with the folk devils identified in your moral panic?*
- *Are there any practice implications for social workers stemming from the responses and solutions?*

You may wish to use online newspaper databases for this exercise or simply purchase a selection of different newspapers. It might be useful to collect quotations from different newspapers to compare the ways in which the issue is being presented.

In the above exercise, you were probably able to identify a range of current issues that have appeared in the media that are currently generating a great deal of concern. Many of the issues you identified may have had important implications for social work intervention. However, moral panics are not helpful for social workers, who have an obligation to adopt a measured and non judgemental approach when working with certain popularly stigmatised groups of service users.

Moral panics frequently seem to assume a relentless momentum, so why are moral panics so persuasive? We have developed the following model for understanding moral panics which may help you to address this question.

The power of the media
The mass media in Britain are considered by many sociologists to be a very powerful means by which reality is constructed. In terms of moral panics, the media are able to advance the momentum of moral panics by reporting aspects of social issues in simplistic, sensational and often inaccurate ways.

The presentation of the issue is often accompanied by powerful images and emotive language

The media are able to show visual images of issues in such a way that the audience not only hears or reads about the issue, but sees a range of persuasive and sometimes disturbing visual images. In the current world of instantly available news in a variety of mediums, the public can have access to news 24 hours a day if they wish.

Moral panics are often backed by politicians who seem plausible

It is not uncommon for politicians to feed moral panics by making statements at particularly pertinent times to reinforce and heighten levels of concern. Indeed, as we will see later Marxists argue that politicians often seek to initiate moral panics over particular issues in order to divert attention away from the real structural causes of social problems.

Moral panics often feed into long-established, pre-existing fears and prejudice

The success of moral panics is often linked to the fact that their subject matter frequently taps into pre-existing public fears, striking a chord with their audience. This means that the public are often familiar with and sympathetic to the narrative as presented by the media, politicians and moral entrepreneurs. This has the effect of reinforcing existing anxieties and fears

Moral panics are often characterised by circular, self-supporting arguments

Quite often the momentum assumed by a moral panic is strengthened by the perpetuation of arguments and responses which are mutually reinforcing. This can derive from the impact of the initial response to the issue, which is often out of all proportion to the threat posed. Indeed, in many cases, the reaction apportions an unwarranted prominence to the 'problem group', which in turn exacerbates the perceived level of anxiety.

Moral panics are often based on a compelling mixture of myth, fact and lies such that it is often difficult to separate the three

The subject matter of moral panics is regularly reported and debated in such a way that it is difficult to separate out fact from fiction. Sections of the media in Britain are well known for their overdramatised and sensationalist reporting of certain issues and this often results in a heady combination of truth and lies. Similarly, it has been argued that politicians often distort and simplify issues seeking to make political capital out of moral panics. The impact of this, along with all the other factors identified above, results, some suggest, in persuasive and relentless moral panics.

Asylum and moral panics

In the introduction to the third edition of *Folk devils and moral panics*, Stanley Cohen (2006) identifies current debates about asylum seekers in the UK as providing a particularly good example of the kind of hysteria that can be generated by a moral panic. According to Cohen, when discussing this issue, the media, politicians and moral crusaders invariably propagate inaccuracies and simplistic stereotypical myths, focusing on the 'pull' factors which are said to entice people to Britain, rather than 'push' factors that may lead them to flee their countries of origin. Hence key influences on asylum trends such as war, conflict or persecution are disguised or dismissed and the overwhelming imagery associated with asylum seekers tends to be negative. Asylum seekers are portrayed as economic migrants or benefit tourists rather than human beings and genuine refugees. This view has contributed to policy developments which have been geared towards reducing, and in many cases removing entirely, the welfare entitlements of asylum seekers. These policies have had direct practice implications for social workers, who in many cases have been left to deal with the consequences of the state-enforced destitution of asylum seekers. We will now consider how the model we outlined can help us to understand the creation of a sustained and persuasive moral panic around asylum.

Power of the media

A large proportion of the British population have probably never knowingly seen an asylum seeker, yet opinion polls tell us that they are widely perceived to be an unambiguously unfavourable group. Indeed, in a 2005 MORI poll, the British public said that they were more concerned about asylum seekers than they were about terrorism and defence, crime, education, the National Health Service, drug use, the environment, the economy, taxation, unemployment, poverty, and a host of other issues besides. In this respect, debates over asylum serve to highlight the sheer 'opinion-forming' power the media possess. Asylum seekers are widely seen, to use Stanley Cohen's (2006) words, as the *visual symbols of society's ills*. There can be little doubt that the media have helped to construct this negative perception of asylum seekers. In the absence of any direct contact with asylum seekers or refugees, it is the sole reference point for most people's information – it is *the* opinion former.

The presentation of the issue is often accompanied by powerful images and emotive language

In the case of the asylum debate, the repeated publication and broadcasting of images of unkempt, dishevelled asylum seekers clambering over border fences, or desperately trying to cling on to trains bound for Britain, reinforce the notion that Britain is about to be 'flooded' with a 'deluge' of 'asylum cheats'. Likewise, inaccurate media generalisations about the 'generous' levels of support provided to asylum seekers help generate and perpetuate the popularly held misconception that the assistance given to asylum seekers is 'lavish', acting as a magnet, encouraging 'bogus' asylum claims. Thus, according to dominant conceptions of the asylum debate, it is the irresistible lure of the 'honey pot' of welfare that drives asylum applications, rather than the incidence of war and political persecution. As one fairly representative headline in the *Sun* put it, *We resent the scroungers, the beggars and crooks who are prepared to cross every country in Europe to reach our generous benefit system* (cited in Cohen, 2006, pxx). With moral panics, the language used to frame debates is also important. As well as being overwhelmingly negative towards the 'folk devil' in question, like the above quote from the *Sun*, it often seeks to invoke a sense of impending doom, or disaster. In the specific case of the asylum debate, terms like 'flooded', 'deluge' and 'wave', all of which are widely used by the media and politicians to describe the 'influx' of asylum seekers, convey the image of crisis and an impending natural disaster, which must be thwarted at all costs.

RESEARCH SUMMARY

Insight or incite? The media's coverage of the asylum debate

In 2003, Article 19, an international human rights organisation dedicated to promoting freedom of expression and freedom of information all over the world, published What's the story?, *an exploration into the ways asylum seekers and refugees are represented in the media. The research, based upon content analysis of the media and interviews with asylum seekers and refugees themselves, sought to assess the impact media coverage had on the everyday lives of asylum seekers.*

Findings

- *Media reporting of the asylum debate is characterised* by the inaccurate and provocative use of language *and* meaningless and derogatory terms.

- *Little or no attention is devoted to analysing the 'push' factors that force individuals and families to flee from their homelands and seek refuge in other countries.*

- *Media discussions of the issue focus overwhelmingly on 'numbers', but the statistics cited are frequently unsourced, exaggerated or inadequately explained.*

- *Images used tend to concentrate on the stereotype of the* threatening young male, *with women and children rarely seen. Refugee women, in particular, expressed frustration at the media's lack of interest in issues that affected them.*

- *Reports rely almost exclusively on official figures, politicians and the police as sources of information. The voices of refugees and asylum seekers themselves are only very rarely represented.*

- *Asylum seekers and refugees* feel alienated, ashamed and sometimes threatened as a result of the overwhelmingly negative media coverage. *Many interviewees felt that this contributed to the prejudice, abuse or aggression they experienced from neighbours, and, importantly for us, service providers.*

(Article 19, 2003, p10)

The researchers concluded that the media have a crucial role to play in informing public policy debate about asylum seekers and refugees, and that they must ensure that reporting of the issue does not prejudice the rights and welfare of vulnerable individuals. It called for an end to the use of meaningless, derogatory language, and the introduction of press guidelines prohibiting the use of threatening and pejorative labels. More generally, the authors demanded a more balanced approach. A far greater level of consideration should be given to illuminating the human rights situations in countries from which asylum seekers arrive, and a greater acknowledgement of the problems they face in terms of accessing services and resources should be made (Article 19, 2003).

Moral panics are often backed by politicians who are plausible

Critics argue that moral panics over asylum and immigration, which reinforce the portrayal of the vast majority of asylum seekers as 'bogus', serve a number of 'functions' for politicians in developed countries. Firstly, they disguise Western governments' culpability in contributing to, or failing to alleviate, the 'push factors' (global poverty, famine, war, persecution and conflict) that drive asylum seekers to make the difficult decision to leave their homes and seek refuge. There is, in fact, remarkably little evidence to suggest that the 'lure' of welfare is a significant influence in driving asylum claims, while there is a direct correlation between asylum claims and persecution, war and conflict. Secondly, the portrayal of asylum seekers as 'welfare tourists', 'economic migrants' or as an 'economic burden' means that the blame for unemployment, housing shortages and stretched health and education services in deprived areas is skilfully placed on the shoulders of asylum seekers rather than politicians themselves. In this way, the failure of politicians to reverse decades of economic decline is obscured, and economic and social ills are mistakenly (but, for politicians, usefully) seen to be the result the relatively recent arrival of what in some cases is a couple of dozen asylum seekers. Finally, the overwhelmingly negative representation of asylum seekers provides justification for politicians to circumvent their legal obligation to provide support to people seeking refuge from persecution, and to restrict asylum seekers' eligibility for welfare assistance. In fact, there can be little doubt that politicians in Britain – both Conservative and Labour – have drawn on negative, stereotypical images of asylum seekers to justify cutting their benefits and to deflect attention from other political issues.

Moral panics often feed into long-established, pre-existing fears and prejudice

Here in the UK, we like to think of ourselves as a tolerant society, with a long and just record of providing refuge to genuine victims of political persecution and human rights abuses. The recent 'backlash' against asylum seekers in media commentary and political debates is often seen as a recent and justifiable reaction to an 'abuse' of our hospitality. In fact, refugees, even those fleeing Nazi Germany in the 1930s, have always been treated with suspicion, fear and hostility, being portrayed as either economic migrants or an 'alien threat' to national security (Winder, 2004). More recently, since the London bombings of 7 July 2004, asylum seekers have become linked with fears about terrorism nationally and internationally, which acts as further justification for tighter controls and vilification by certain sections of the media.

However, moral panics about asylum seekers have also tapped into a long-established fear of migrants, the origins of which can be traced back to notions of genetic, moral and intellectual superiority which have their roots in Britain's imperial history. Hence, Commonwealth migrants who came to Britain in the post-war years were greeted with hostility and abuse, and the blame for society's economic and social ills – such as poor housing and unemployment – was placed firmly on their shoulders. Fear of 'the other' therefore, is a pervading theme in British history and permeates moral panics which are linked to immigration and asylum.

Moral panics are often characterised by circular, self supporting arguments

Hysteria about asylum seekers has developed a momentum that has in many respects become self-perpetuating. Asylum seekers are often portrayed by the media as being scroungers who come to Britain to take advantage of welfare benefits, with little acknowledgement of the fact that they are legally unable to work and are therefore required to claim benefits to survive. Similarly, the policy of dispersing asylum seekers to deprived inner-city districts, where health, education and housing resources are already stretched, serves to support the notion that asylum seekers are a burdensome drain on limited resources. In many areas this has led to an increased incidence of racist attacks and abuse, and a reinforcement of the perception that asylum seekers are the cause of community ills, shifting attention away from the underpinning structural causes of social problems.

Moral panics are often based on a compelling mixture of myth, fact and lies

If media and political commentaries are to be believed, the UK is the preferred destination of choice for 'bogus' asylum seekers. It is, we are told, easier to claim asylum in this country than any other European country, and this, together with the 'lavish' welfare support offered to asylum seekers, has contributed to a scenario whereby 'we' (far more so than any other European country) are 'inundated' with false asylum applications. The UK has, according to this interpretation of the asylum debate, become a haven for (at best) foreign scroungers, or (at worst) foreign criminals and terrorists. Is this an accurate depiction of the asylum issue or, as organisations such as the Refugee Council have argued, is it based on a confusing, yet compelling, mixture of half-truths, myths and lies?

Firstly, Home Office statistics belie claims that we are 'inundated' with unprecedented numbers of asylum seekers, showing that asylum applications to the UK are lower than they were in 1995. Indeed, contrary to popular belief, UK asylum applications have seen a dramatic fall in recent years, by 31 per cent in 2004 and 25 per cent in 2005 (Home Office, 2006), a far higher reduction than any other European country. Moreover, when measured in terms of applications per 1000 inhabitants, statistics show that the UK receives far fewer asylum claims than most other European countries, contradicting claims that 'we' are the preferred destination of choice for asylum applications.

Secondly, as we have shown, asylum seekers are invariably portrayed as bogus 'welfare tourists', with little or no credence given to the possibility that they may be genuine victims of war, torture or persecution. In fact, research shows that asylum seekers coming to the UK are from nations that are characterised by some of the most horrific conflicts and human rights abuses. Indeed, as intimated above, all the evidence shows that asylum trends are correlated to the incidence of war, conflict and human rights abuses, and not the generosity of welfare payments. This leads us to our third point, regarding welfare. While it is true that asylum seekers are often dependent on state support, this not because they do not want to work. On the contrary, it is because UK law prohibits them from working while their claims are considered. Nor do asylum seekers get large handouts from the state. Indeed many are made destitute as punishment for not fulfilling complex, strict eligibility criteria, and those who do receive assistance are only entitled to an amount that is lower than the normal level granted to UK citizens. Contrary to popular belief, therefore, asylum seekers do not jump the queue for housing, do not get routinely housed in the Ritz Hotel in London and do not receive special perks such as mobile phones, colour televisions or cars. Research suggests that the majority of asylum seekers are living on the margins of society, in dire poverty, often in housing that is unfit for human habitation.

Finally, despite fears perpetuated by some sections of the media that asylum seekers are in fact hardened criminals or even terrorists in disguise, the Home Office itself has stated that there is no evidence that asylum seekers are any more likely to commit crimes than anyone else. Indeed, asylum seekers are more likely to be the victims of crime, particularly race-related crimes, a reflection, no doubt, of the suspicion and hostility generated by moral panics surrounding the asylum debate (Refugee Council, 2006).

The above model for understanding the development of moral panics will hopefully have demonstrated to you why levels of concern around asylum seekers have been so relentless. As Cohen (2006) argues, *the overall narrative is a single, virtually uninterrupted message of hostility and rejection Moreover, successive British governments have not only led and legitimated public hostility, but spoken with a voice indistinguishable from the tabloid press* (pxix). You may wish to track the progress of this issue by keeping a watchful eye on newspaper reporting in the future.

The problem of youth

Asylum is just one of many topics we could have considered in some detail to illustrate Cohen's ideas. In this section, we want you to apply some of the theories and concepts we have outlined above to another issue that is increasingly dominating the media and political debates – the behaviour and conduct of working-class youth.

Young people are regularly identified by sociologists as being the subjects of moral panics. Certainly, 'youth' and youth cultures are generally constructed in terms of the problems they cause for others, and in recent years, there has been a fairly persistent concern around youth crime and in particular about threats to society posed by a so-called 'new generation' of anti-social, disaffected young people. Very real fears exist about the apparent growing criminality of British young people, but some argue that these anxieties are overstated, and that reporting of the issue has taken on a momentum and energy of its own (Muncie, 1999). In this sense, 'hoodies' and 'chavs' have become latter-day folk devils, in the same way as Mods and Rockers did in the 1960s.

ACTIVITY 6.2

Earlier, we identified a number of key factors that contribute to the creation and momentum of moral panics. In this exercise, we want you to revisit the model we introduced earlier and consider the extent to which these factors may have contributed to the development and reinforcement of moral panics about young people's behaviour. Here we list again the core components of our model for you to discuss and develop in relation to youth crime. You may wish to do this exercise in a small group, perhaps drawing from newspaper articles to assist you.

The power of the media
How influential have the media been in shaping views around youth crime or about youth in general?

The presentation of the issue is often accompanied by powerful images and emotive language
How do the emotive images and language used in the media serve to shape our opinions about young people and their behaviour?

Moral panics are often backed by politicians who are plausible
What have politicians had to say about the issue and why?

Moral panics often feed into long-established, pre-existing fears and prejudice
Here, you might want to consider the claim that there is a long tradition of fear and hostility towards the behaviour of young people. You may wish to ask friends and family about their views on 'youth'.

Moral panics are often characterised by circular, self-supporting arguments
To what extent has the reaction to sections of 'youth' and their behaviour served to apportion an unwarranted prominence to the 'problem group', exacerbating the perceived level of anxiety?

Moral panics are often based on a compelling mixture of myth, fact and lies such that it is often difficult to separate the three
Can you find any examples of ways in which the behaviour of young people has been distorted by the media?

It is important to recognise that while some young people are guilty of engaging in damaging, disruptive behaviour, the key point is that this is a small minority. Yet, according to those such as Muncie (1999), it is the 'anti-social', delinquent behaviour of the small minority that finds greatest exposure in media headlines. By contrast, the silent law-abiding, unremarkable majority rarely receive a mention. Why? According to Cohen (2006, pviii), young working-class males constitute, for newspaper editors, *one of the most enduring of suitable enemies* and hence regularly find themselves the subjects of moral panics. Thus, over the past half-century, Teddy Boys, Mods and Rockers, football hooligans, punks, muggers, joyriders, chavs and hoodies have all been portrayed as dangerous and menacing folk devils. In response, governments, wanting to be seen to be responding firmly to the threat posed by youth, have sought to introduce coercive methods of control, sometimes feeding and reinforcing moral panics. Muncie (1999) argues that the state response to the 'problem of youth' has consistently been greater surveillance, coercion and law-and-order initiatives with a strong social control agenda. This can clearly be seen in relation to anti-social beha- viour, which, in recent years, has resulted in early intervention programmes, which may lead to issues in relation to labelling (see below), and the use of ASBOs. Ironically, the often impossible conditions imposed by ASBOs are regularly breached by young peo- ple, which criminalises them over and above the original impact of their offence. This is an example of the circular, self-perpetuating nature of moral panics we talked about earlier. A young person may be given an ASBO for a relatively minor misdemeanour, may then inadvertently end up breaking a condition, and thereby find themselves in court potentially facing a more serious sentence which in some cases may be custodial.

We saw earlier how moral panics over asylum seekers could be said to serve a political 'function'. The same, it has been argued, is true over moral panics over working-class youths. Marxist sociologists, for instance, argue that by focusing attention on indivi- dual bad behaviour and pathologising groups of young people, the structural causes of the extreme social exclusion many of them experience is effectively sidelined. Thus, not only are young people conveniently blamed for broader structural ills (thus absol- ving politicians of blame), societal attention is diverted away from real difficulties, such as homelessness and unemployment, that impinge on the lives of tens of thou- sands of young people.

Sociological considerations of 'moral panic'

As in previous chapters, we now wish to interrogate the concept of moral panic from different theoretical standpoints. Perhaps the most pertinent position to begin with is labelling theory, which is central in terms of understanding the processes by which moral panics come to exist.

Labelling theory

Labelling theory remains as pertinent to social work today as it was when it was first developed. Rooted in symbolic interactionism, the concept was introduced in 1938 by Tannenbaum, but it is frequently associated with the work of Howard Becker in the 1960s. To develop the concept, Becker (1963) used the example of a brawl involving young people. In a low-income area of town if a fight breaks out between gangs of young people, neighbours might be alarmed, the police might be called and arrests might be made (or in the present day, an ASBO might be slapped upon the offending youths) and they might find themselves in court facing a charge of breach of the peace. Becker's argument is that a brawl that breaks out between middle-class youths in a more affluent area of town is likely to have a very different outcome. Neighbours might come out of their houses and diffuse the situation or break up the fight, assuming the acts to be 'youthful high spirits'. The police may not be called at all, but if they were called, Becker suggests that they would be more likely to have a polite but firm word and move things on. No sign of an ASBO here! Importantly, Becker's point is that although the acts may be the same, the interpretation of them and the context in which they occur are not.

He uses the term 'labelling' to make the point that *Deviant behaviour is behaviour that people so label*; in other words, there is no such thing as a deviant act *per se*, it is only when it becomes interpreted and labelled as such that it takes on the properties of being deviant.

Labelling then, refers to a process whereby sometimes evocative labels are applied to individuals, often by powerful agents of social control such as the police, the legal system, medical professions or social workers. The labels applied often evoke powerful imagery or stereotypes, so for example, the labels 'asylum seeker', 'mentally ill' or 'yob' may evoke a range of different images and assumptions. In relation to moral panics, the concept of labelling is important, as the 'actors' in the moral panic are usually given a range of powerful labels. For example, asylum seekers are frequently labelled as being 'scroungers', 'criminals', 'bogus', 'irresponsible' by the media and politicians. People with mental health problems are often labelled in sections of the media as being 'dangerous', 'violent' or 'evil'. It is labels such as these that can feed into media and political hysteria concerning a particular group.

It is vitally important of course, that such damaging, dehumanising and discriminatory labels do not impinge upon social work practice. Social workers are bound by moral and ethical codes of practice to protect vulnerable service users and to ensure the integrity of the profession. However, social work does not take place in a vacuum and social workers as human beings will be bombarded with the same images from the media as anyone else. It is therefore essential that social workers learn about and understand the ways in which labelling can impact upon practice. Furthermore, social workers as potentially powerful agents of the state also play a part in assigning labels to individuals with whom they work.

ACTIVITY 6.3

Jason is a 12-year-old boy who has come to the attention of the local Youth Intervention Project (YIP). As a student social worker on placement with YIP you have been given Jason to work with in a preventative way. On your first visit to Jason, he is sitting hunched up wearing a dark hoodie, with the hood over his head. You find engaging in conversation with him difficult. He seems unresponsive, preoccupied and uninterested in taking up any of the opportunities you suggest. You return to the office after half an hour feeling that you have been unable to effectively engage with Jason, and when discussing him with your supervisor, you describe him as sullen, uncommunicative and unco-operative.

Your supervisor failed to challenge you and you continued to work with Jason based on your first assessment of him. Let us assume that Jason has recently committed a minor act of vandalism in the grounds of the local park one night. He has been referred to the multi-agency panel which considers low-level offending. You attend the panel and share your views on Jason as being difficult, unwilling to engage and possibly a high risk to the community in terms of future offending.

However, it may be that if you had approached Jason differently at the very beginning (or indeed, if your supervisor had challenged some of your early perceptions), you

ACTIVITY *6.3* *continued*

would have discovered that Jason's reaction to you was based upon a fear of authority and a general state of withdrawal linked to being bullied by some older pupils at school. However, as a student social worker, your opinion of Jason might be assimilated by the other professionals around the table who might unquestioningly take on board your views.

In this instance, Jason has been assigned a label which may well stick with him for a long time. There is always a danger that professionals, who undoubtedly possess a great deal of power, can create a 'dominant view' of a particular service user, such that all future behaviour by the service user is interpreted in this light, seeking to confirm the original judgement about that person. In such instances, the service user may be powerless to challenge this view. The worst-case scenario here would arise if Jason internalised the views of the professionals around him and came to see himself as delinquent or deviant in some way, and began to act accordingly. This would be an example of a self-fulfilling prophecy.

The concept of the self-fulfilling prophecy is central to labelling theory and is used to describe the process whereby individuals who are labelled *internalise* the characteristics of the label assigned to them and start acting according to its defining features. In other words, they begin to see themselves in the light of the label applied. Lemert (1972) refers to this as a symbolic reorganisation of the self. It can therefore be understood how powerful agents of social control, including social workers, who are fundamentally involved in the assigning of labels, can actually be seen to contribute to criminal or deviant behaviour.

Becker (1963) notes that once an individual has been successfully labelled in a particular way, this can often become their *master status*, which comes to define them, over and above all other statuses. So, once a person has been labelled a 'criminal' for example, this then becomes the dominant means by which others see them, as opposed to other labels the person might have as well, such as son, father, artist, student and so on. The master status becomes in effect the *defining status*, and brings with it a range of other images and characteristics often associated with the label.

ACTIVITY *6.4*

Labelling

To some extent, we are all labelled at various times throughout our lives. Working with someone you trust, take some time out to think about labels you may have been given throughout your life. Some examples might include 'disabled'; lone parent; unemployed; victim of domestic violence; offender; alcoholic; drug user.

How did the labels come to be assigned to you? What was the impact of these? What assumptions were assigned to the label?

If you are on or have been on a placement in your social work degree, think about the ways in which service users you have worked with have been labelled and the potential impact of these labels. How can social workers challenge these labels and work in a more empowering way?

Labelling theory is useful in the study of moral panics as it enables us to think about the processes by which moral panics might be constructed. It is also helpful for social workers who need to understand the ways in which individuals come to be assigned identities which can ultimately shape their lives.

Labelling theory has, however, been criticised for being deterministic, in that it assumes that a person who has been labelled has no ability to reject that label, and has no option other than to commit further acts of deviancy. In this sense, the labelling process can be cited as an 'excuse' for future deviancy. Who is to say, for example, that it is the label of 'deviant' that has encouraged a young person to engage in further criminal acts? It may be that they would have chosen to engage in that behaviour anyway. Furthermore, it may be that the initial labelling may have had a positive effect, reducing rather than amplifying deviance. From a different perspective, Marxists have also criticised labelling theory, arguing that while it recognises class differences in the ways in which labels are assigned, it stops short of a more sustained, structural analysis. It fails to acknowledge, for instance, the unequal distribution of power in society, or the fact that the solution to the problems identified by labelling theorists involves a far greater level of structural reform than they are prepared to contemplate. In response to this criticism, symbolic interactionists defend the validity of micro-level analysis which is concerned with small-scale interactions and the processes by which meanings are applied.

Functionalist perspective

As we discovered in Chapter 1, the concept of value consensus is central to functionalism. As moral panics are usually based on issues that potentially disrupt value consensus or seek to threaten the *status quo*, functionalists are likely to take the view that ultimately, a moral panic has the effect of separating out 'folk devils' from the rest of society, uniting the majority of society in order to clarify shared norms and values in the face of the threat. In effect, the storm caused in the wake of the moral panic will ultimately result in a celebration of the 'majority view', reaffirming and re-establishing the moral equilibrium. Although Durkheim did not specifically use the term moral panic, his writings on crime enable us to develop a Durkheimian perspective on 'moral panics'. Durkheim's view was that crime was both inevitable and functional; it was functional because it enabled society to change and develop, and because importantly it provided the means by which shared norms and values could be clarified. In drawing attention to rules that have been broken, a line is drawn between 'normal' and the 'deviant' members of society, ensuring punishment or vilification of the latter and providing clarification for the former regarding what is and what is not acceptable conduct. Applied to moral panics then, this Durkheimian interpretation could be extended to argue that moral panics provide a vehicle by which the folk devils or outsiders, such as young criminals or asylum seekers, are highlighted because of the threat they pose to shared norms and values. The reaction to the threat is the stigmatisation of the offending individuals and society stamping down hard through legislation and policy to ensure that the moral consensus remains intact.

Functionalist theories of the media are concerned with ways in which the media contributes to the well-being and maintenance of society. The media serves different functions to this end; in particular, it transmits social norms and values, and performs a key role in terms of socialisation, ensuring that children and adults alike are shaped in terms of society's values, norms and cultural fabric. In relation to moral panics then, the media can draw attention very powerfully to folk devils at times of anxiety, to ensure that moral boundaries are drawn around deviant norms or behaviours. The overall effect is that although a warning siren may be sounded regarding the specific aspect of dysfunction, importantly the overall consensus is preserved. This can be seen clearly in relation to moral panics around aspects of youth culture. In the 1970s, a new subculture began to emerge in the form of punk rock, when mostly working-class young people began to hang around in groups wearing bondage trousers, ripped clothes, safety pins and, bin-liners and having brightly coloured, often spiky, unconventional hair. The overwhelming message from the punk movement was discordant and anti-establishment, with a groundswell of anger against the monarchy, the political establishment and the police. This, some have suggested, was related to the significant unemployment of the time and the ensuing economic disadvantage and social alienation felt by many young people. However, despite protracted media hype concerning the anarchistic drive of punk rock, eventually the movement found itself at least partly incorporated by the establishment, as 'designer' punk clothes were advertised on the pages of *Vogue* magazine and commercial enterprises sought to institutionalise the movement by mass reproduction of certain aspects of it. In effect, by popularising punk, or as Dick Hebdidge (1979) suggests by *incorporation*, the punk movement became safe, and ceased to be a threat to shared norms and values. Nevertheless, a warning siren had been sounded that all was not well, giving those in power the opportunity to respond. Thus it can be seen that the media here along with other aspects of society, collectively overcame the threat to collective values. The panic generated by the punk movement was effectively 'managed' and attention shifted away from the underpinning issues which had perhaps led to the emergence of the movement that was so opposed to conventional norms.

Functionalists then, see a positive role for moral panics, as the means by which attention is drawn to any threat to the value consensus and the means by which shared social norms are reaffirmed and celebrated.

Functionalist perspectives on moral panics can be criticised. Firstly, we can question whether moral panics, in reality, serve to act as 'warning sirens' for society. While our example of the punk movement seems to provide evidence to support this notion, there are numerous instances where the warning sirens have simply been ignored. Moreover, they have heralded the beginning of a process whereby 'folk devils' are stigmatised and pathologised, arguably for reasons other than the reinforcement of 'shared norms and values'. As we show below, for Marxists the vilification of 'hoodies', asylum seekers and the like is motivated less by a desire to reinforce a 'shared value consensus', and more by a wish to promote ruling-class culture, values and ideals. Indeed, for Marxists, the very notion that there exists a 'shared value consensus' is contentious and open to debate.

A Marxist perspective

As we have seen above, functionalists argue that there are positive benefits to moral panics occurring in society. Marxists also suggest that moral panics serve a purpose; however, their interpretation differs in one important respect. Rather than suggesting that moral panics are useful to the whole of society, Marxists believe that they serve positive functions for the powerful ruling classes. As suggested above, moral panics serve to shift attention away from underlying structural causes of society's socio-economic problems, laying the blame instead on visible, scapegoated 'deviant' individuals or groups. This has the effect of individualising the causes of socio-economic ills, which leads to solutions based upon modifying 'deviant' behaviour, rather than addressing deep-seated structural inequalities. In the example of asylum that we used at the beginning of this chapter, a Marxist perspective would focus upon ways in which asylum seekers are blamed, for example, for housing inadequacies, unemployment and racial tensions. Solutions, therefore, are directed at deterring and stigmatising asylum seekers rather than addressing the chronic underfunding of public services and mitigating the inequalities that are a feature of capitalist societies. Similarly, 'hoodies' or other young people are pathologised and blamed for urban decline and the breakdown of law and order, with little attention given to the chronic poverty and economic decline which shapes the lives of those living in deprived communities. Solutions, therefore, tend to focus upon tighter control and surveillance of the lives of young people, rather than upon more fundamental issues, such as lack of educational opportunity, meaningful employment policies and affordable housing.

In explaining the emergence and reinforcement of moral panics, Marxists, like functionalists, are particularly interested in the role played by the mass media. However, whereas for functionalists the media acts as a positive 'moral guardian' of societal values, for Marxists it is a conservative guardian of ruling-class interests. Marxists regard the media as an important component of the superstructure, which, as shown in Chapter 1, is seen to promote and transmit ruling-class culture, values and ideals in an uncritical way to the masses. There is no single authoritative Marxist interpretation of the mass media in capitalist societies, but one influential explanation has emerged, based on Antonio Gramsci's concept of 'hegemony'. Basically, according to Gramsci the ruling classes in any society cannot rule for any period of time simply through coercion alone, and a subtler means of gaining the the consent of the masses is required. Hegemony, therefore, refers to means by which the ruling class obtain the consent of subordinate groups to their own domination, by imposing an appealing world view, or 'common sense'. 'Hegemonic status' is achieved when the ruling class have successfully managed to represent its own values and ideals as those of society as a whole, and created a terrain favourable to resolving economic and social problems in a way that is conducive to its interests. The media is, for Marxists, one of the crucial mechanisms by which this process is accomplished. It uncritically transmits messages that serve to uphold prevailing ruling-class ideologies, thus ensuring that the consent of the masses for their own domination is manufactured and maintained. To a certain extent, this process may be 'unconscious' – the ruling class may not directly control the media, but the pervasive, all-encompassing nature of ruling-class values means that events and issues are unconsciously and instinctively reported in a way that reproduces and reinforces the ideals of dominant groups. In this sense, the importance of the media lies not just in its transmission of moral panics, but also in its reproduction and sustenance of dominant values. In some other respects, though, the media's bias is more deliberate. For example, key sections of the media are often owned by powerful individuals or corporations who themselves have a strong desire to preserve the *status quo*. Hence, national newspaper proprietors and commercial broadcasters, most of whom are likely to be averse to paying 'punitive' rates of taxation to fund decent public services, are more than happy to promote cheaper, 'individualised', 'behavioural' solutions to social problems.

Irrespective of the causes of the media's 'bias', in relation to moral panics, Marxists suggest that media representations of certain events do undoubtedly distort and simplify, providing inaccurate, yet persuasive interpretations of issues that detract attention away fundamental problems inherent in capitalist societies. In this way, the structural causes of unemployment, poverty, urban decay, crime and a host of other social problems are 'individualised'. 'Folk devils' are identified, stigmatised and blamed for situations which in reality are the result of more deep-rooted social problems. For Marxists then, the extent of the media's opinion-forming potential should not be underestimated. As we intimated in our asylum example, for many people it is their only 'portal' through which to view certain issues. It can provide an immensely powerful means of shaping the belief systems of its audience such that the messages inherent within particular moral panics become engrained in the consciousness of the nation. In this way, claims such as 'all asylum seekers are bogus', or 'the care of mentally ill people in the community poses a "grave threat" to society', or 'the welfare system is "rife" with abuse', or 'youths who wear hooded tops are hooligans', all become established, unquestioned facts, rather than debateable assertions.

Like the other theoretical approaches outlined above, Marxist analyses of moral panics have also faced criticisms. Firstly, Marxist explanations, though powerful, are, some argue, just that – explanations. The logic of Marxism, its detractors argue, seems to suggest that as long as capitalism exists and the ruling classes continue to profit from the obscuration and division generated by moral panics, then groups will continue to be labelled, stigmatised and subjected to punitive forms of control. The 'solution', then, for Marxists, lies in the abolition of capitalism and the creation of a more fair society, based upon the principles of equality and egalitarianism. However, while it is fine for Marxist academics to theorise about the need for, and the prospects of, a radical transformation from capitalism to socialism, what happens in the meantime? Do stigmatised asylum seekers, mental health service users, marginalised young people and other subjects of moral panics have to await the 'triumph of the proletariat' before their plight is addressed? This is an interesting critique, but as we saw in Chapter 1, the claim that Marxism fails to offer any readily accessible or deliverable solutions for 'the here and now' is one that Marxists strenuously refute. In their defence, Marxists argue that such claims are based on a simplistic and dogmatic interpretation of Marxist thought. Certainly, few Marxists today would dismiss the need to engage in immediate political action to mitigate inequalities within capitalist societies. Indeed, many of those involved in the radical social work movement, or its more recent manifestation the Social Work Manifesto Group are Marxists, and they campaign vigorously for an immediate end to the stigmatisation and oppression of vulnerable groups.

Marxist approaches have also been targeted by those generally critical of the overall concept of moral panics. For some, such as Norman Dennis and George Erdos (2005), the 'moral panic' concept is itself a 'social construction', 'invented' by biased, left-wing academics who use it, wrongly, to deny the culpability of the certain 'deviant' groups for moral and social breakdown, and to inappropriately apportion blame for social problems on the shoulders of political and economic elites. We examine this critique in further detail below. In its total dismissal of the moral panic concept it does, to a certain extent, represent a criticism of all the theoretical approaches we have examined, but the sort of critique adopted by Dennis and Erdos is most often directed at 'left-wing' academics and politicians.

ACTIVITY **6.5**

Returning to the moral panic you selected in Activity 6.1, apply firstly a functionalist and then a Marxist perspective to it, to develop two contrasting arguments. When concentrating on the functionalist perspective, you might wish to think about which aspects of value consensus are under threat by the moral panic and what responses there were. When looking at Marxism, you may want to consider what functions the moral panic serves for the ruling class.

How do your two analyses differ?

Moral panics or genuine fears?

Having provided you with a detailed and perhaps persuasive overview of the moral panics, we will now end by looking at an alternative approach to the concept advanced by Dennis and Erdos (2005). These authors argue that the concept is fundamentally flawed. A key feature of moral panic arguments, they insist, is the notion that it is the politically powerful, or the ruling class, who are said to exaggerate concerns about particular issues, in an attempt to 'scapegoat' certain groups, and divert attention away from their own culpability in creating or failing to alleviate social problems. Using data from various surveys on crime and anti-social behaviour, Dennis and Erdos argue that it is, in fact, those living in poor, deprived areas that report the highest levels of anxiety about crime, disorderly behaviour and moral breakdown. On crime specifically, they argue that data *shows that if or to the extent that the fear of crime is exaggerated, it is the poor who do the exaggerating, not the rich*. This, they insist, contradicts one of the main arguments in theories based on the moral panic concept.

However, their more fundamental point is that this fear of crime and other social problems among the poor is not based upon media-induced 'naïvety' or 'irrationality'. On the contrary, worry about social problems in these areas is associated with the actual incidence of social problems. Dennis and Erdos castigate those such as Cohen for, in effect, accusing decent, honest working people in deprived communities of 'conjuring up', or 'imagining' the high levels of crime and the lack of respect for common values that they are forced to endure on a daily basis. If only the 'liberal intelligentsia' (that is, left-wing academics, media commentators and politicians) lived in the residential areas affected by these genuine social ills, they might be forced to reappraise their own 'fantastical' denials of growing levels of moral breakdown. From this perspective, therefore, the 'moral panic' concept, which as we have seen purports to expose common myths and misconceptions, is itself rejected as a delusion. In its representation of genuine fears about endemic social problems *as a defect of the aged, the timid and the ill informed*, it is guilty of incorrectly dismissing people's very real anxieties about their security, their homes and their livelihoods (Dennis and Erdos, 2005, p57).

> *The error and folly have not lain, therefore, with a benighted public that has succumbed to unrealistic fears of crime, or has been stampeded into a moral panic by a sensationalist gutter press. The error and folly has lain with ideologically driven academics, and the broadsheet, radio and television journalists who depend on their 'findings'.*
>
> (Dennis and Erdos, 2005, p67)

Moreover, and paradoxically, Dennis and Erdos argue that the moral panic concept can serve a political function, in that it allows politicians to claim that popular anxieties about crime, immigration, drug use, and a whole range of other social ills, are 'disproportionate'. In this respect, the left-wing liberal intelligentsia may have scored an 'own goal'. In their haste to 'bash' the politically powerful, they have inadvertently provided ruling elites with a 'get-out' concept, which allows them to dismiss people's concerns as unwarranted, and claim a higher degree of success for their policies on, for instance, 'law and order', 'community cohesion' and 'asylum' than is actually the case.

The arguments presented by Dennis and Erdos certainly provide an interesting alternative to the ideas presented above. However, it is worth noting a few points of caution. Firstly, as the authors themselves acknowledge, much of the statistical evidence for their arguments is based on surveys examining people's perceptions of moral breakdown, vulnerability and crime, rather than their actual incidence. The problem here, as most sociologists would acknowledge, is that perceptions about the threat posed by groups such as 'hoodies', 'muggers' or, to cite another of our earlier examples, asylum seekers, are often exaggerated or inflated, partly as a result of inaccurate, sensationalist media and political commentaries. Dennis and Erdos would no doubt dismiss such suggestions as 'misguided paternalism', but as our asylum example showed, the media's influence in shaping our perception of certain problems and groups, and inflating the prominence of particular issues, cannot be denied. Secondly, while Dennis and Erdos accuse advocates of moral panics of constituting a left-wing intelligentsia, they say little about their own ideological dispositions. In fact, both authors have written extensively for CIVITAS, a right-wing think-tank, and both have long bemoaned the impact of what they see as deteriorating moral values, 'liberal' criminal justice policies, and 'corrupting state welfare' on levels of permissiveness, responsibility and lawlessness. In short, Dennis and Erdos are not without their own 'ideological baggage'.

Relevance of the moral panic concept for social work

Social work does not take place in a vacuum; rather, social workers are functioning members of society who both absorb aspects of popular culture and contribute to it. As we saw in Chapter 1, it is simply not possible for social workers to enter their professional practice uninfluenced by societal misconceptions and prejudices. Just like other members of society, social workers will of course read newspapers, watch the news, discuss issues with their families, friends and colleagues, and both consciously and unconsciously absorb vast amounts of information about social life. So, a fundamental consideration is, to what extent do the moral panics impact upon judgements made, and the ways in which social workers intervene with people?

Critical practice

Payne, Adams and Dominelli's (2002) concept of critical practice can be helpful here. Critical practice requires that social workers continually question their 'knowledge' and taken-for-granted assumptions about life. Similar to the idea of social workers developing a sociological imagination that we talked about in Chapter 1, critical practice makes structural connections and locates service users within wider contexts. So, in relation to service users who are seeking asylum in this country, the social worker who is implementing critical practice will move beyond the stereotypical and face-value messages that he or she is bombarded with daily in the media, and will contextualise their work with the service user within an understanding of the bigger picture of that person's life. By locating the service user, the social worker will hopefully be able to develop an understanding of the way in which structural factors have impacted upon the individual's functioning. Or, to think about this in terms of the model we developed in Chapter 1, the social worker will be able to use their sociological imagination and perceive the service user's 'private troubles' as 'public issues'.

Critical practice then, considers the context of the scenarios in which social workers intervene and examines the situation from different perspectives. Payne *et al.* (2002) quite rightly note the interface between our personal and professional lives and they make the point that in order to implement critical practice in social work, we need as individuals to continually challenge our thoughts, our emotions and our actions. Where our beliefs and values are concerned, it is not possible to separate out the personal from the professional, therefore as workers, it is imperative that we are continually reflecting and challenging our taken-for-granted assumptions that form part of our conscious and, importantly, our subconscious. You will remember that earlier in this chapter we talked about the power of the media, and how media images and language can both shape and constrain our intellects. It is vital therefore that in relation to the subject matter of moral panics, social workers engage in critical practice to ensure that they are able to step back from media reports, for example, to develop a more grounded approach to the issue. This involves consideration of the issue from different perspectives and being able to understand the bigger picture, the context in which action unfolds. As Fook (1999) suggests, we must continually engage with contexts in order to deconstruct and critically reconstruct the social world as it is presented to us. This involves challenging our assumptions that develop from the messages that shape our consciousness.

C H A P T E R   S U M M A R Y

This chapter has examined different theoretical debates relevant to moral panics and assessed the importance of the concept to you as students of social work. The exercises we included to support the analysis should have helped you appreciate the importance of being aware of the origins of some of your own views and prejudices. As we have stressed, much of what we know and think about certain issues and social groups stems not from direct experience, but from powerful images presented in the media and by politicians, many of which are inaccurate and based on popular stereotypes and myths. We hope that reading this chapter will encourage you to think critically about the negative way certain groups are presented and the need for you as practitioners to challenge your own value base.

FURTHER READING

Pearson, G (1983) *Hooligan: A history of respectable fears.* Basingstoke: Macmillan. This classic book argues that moral panics are not a new phenomenon, by examining historical societal reactions to 'hooliganism'.

Goode, E and Ben-Yehuda, N (1994) *Moral panics: The social construction of deviance.* Oxford: Blackwell. This text will provide you with an excellent introduction to the concept.

Finally, we would recommend you read Cohen's original text. It provides a fascinating clearly written, accessible insight into the evolution of his ideas: **Cohen, S** (2006) *Folk devils and moral panics.* 3rd edition. Abingdon: Routledge.

Chapter 7
Education

A C H I E V I N G   A   S O C I A L   W O R K   D E G R E E

This chapter will help you begin to meet the following National Occupational Standards and General Social Care Council's Code of Practice.

Key Role 2: Plan, carry out, review and evaluate social work practice, with individuals, families, carers, groups, communities and other professionals
- Interact with individuals, families, carers, groups and communities to achieve change and development and to improve life opportunities.

General Social Care Council Code of Practice

Code 1.1: Treating each person as an individual.

Code 1.5: Promoting equal opportunities for service users and carers.

Code 1.6: Respecting diversity and different cultures and values.

It will also introduce you to the following academic standards as set out in the social work subject benchmark statements.

3.1.1 Social work services and service users
- The social processes (associated with, for example, poverty, unemployment, poor health, disablement, lack of education and other sources of disadvantage) that lead to marginalisation, isolation and exclusion and their impact on the demand for social work services.
- Explanations of the links between definitional processes contributing to social differences (for example, social class, gender and ethnic differences) to the problems of inequality and differential need faced by service users.

3.1.4 Social work theory
- The relevance of sociological perspectives to understanding societal and structural influences on human behaviour at individual, group and community levels.

Introduction

Education holds particular relevance for social workers working within children and families settings and within the education welfare sector. It is a core area of socio-logical debate, and is a topic which holds resonance for students who have themselves experienced the nuances of the education system. As you progress through this chapter, we would like you to reflect upon your own experiences in the education system and consider how factors such as the messages you received from teachers or from home, shaped your experience.

The functionalist theory of education

In common with the approach outlined in previous chapters, functionalists are inter-ested in the role that the education system plays and the crucial functions it performs for the benefit of society. Firstly, Durkheim (1972) identified the function of socialisa-tion. The social learning that takes place in schools supplements that which occurs within families (primary socialisation). Socialisation is the mechanism used to instil what are seen to be appropriate societal norms and values in children's minds. Schools do this in a range of different ways: overtly through the curriculum, or more subtly via what has been referred to as a 'hidden curriculum'. By the latter we mean the other, less obvious ways that schools seek to inculcate the values, skills and modes of behaviour which are deemed important and necessary for society. For example, some schools use a points system to reward appropriate behaviour and to punish that which is deemed to fall outside acceptable bounds. For Durkheim (1972) the social training of the young was necessary to ensure conformity and the acceptance of dominant values so that children learn to fit into mainstream society:

Society can survive only if there exists among its members a sufficient degree of homogeneity; education perpetuates and reinforces this homogeneity.

(p203)

More generally, the culture and discipline of the school environment teach children the importance of norms such as good manners, timekeeping, a positive attitude and respect for authority. In this way, education also performs a social control function. It is in schools that children learn about deference to authority and obedience, which ultimately prepares them for their future lives in the workforce.

A further important function of the education system concerns the fit between the education system and the economy. For society to operate smoothly and efficiently, it is necessary to have appropriately skilled workers to fulfil the requirements of the economy. The education system ensures that appropriate training is given to society's future workers, so that all constituent parts function effectively. As children get older, they are encouraged to think about their future careers and embark upon educational training to this end. This function can be most sharply understood when there is a shortage of a certain type of worker, needed to keep both society and the economy ticking over – indeed, a good example of precisely this can be found with the social work profession in recent years. Over the past decade or so, the government identified a chronic shortage of appropriately skilled social workers and so the response was the introduction of the new social work degree crafted alongside a huge recruitment campaign which sought to increase the numbers of trained social workers. In order to achieve this aim, the government reduced the minimum age for qualifying social workers to allow and facilitate school leavers at 18 to begin to train (the argument was that preventing 18-years-olds from training meant that they tended to embark on alternative careers and were then 'lost' to the profession). Additionally, universities were encouraged to raise their numbers for social work training courses significantly. In this way you can see the fit between the education system and society, and how each part functions to support the overall functioning of the whole.

Linked to the above, Davis and Moore (1945) identify a further function of education – that of role allocation. This is the argument that for society to function efficiently, it must ensure that all roles needed to keep the economy ticking over are filled. It would obviously not be good for society if all pupils trained to be social workers! Similarly, if insufficient pupils wanted to be doctors or footballers or bus drivers, then of course society would have significant unmet need. Clearly, the extent to which children 'choose' to be what they ultimately end up becoming is a matter of great debate and as we hinted in Chapter 1, for very many members of society, their choices are constrained choices. However, for functionalists such as Durkheim, and Davis and Moore, the education system performs a significant task in allocating roles to individuals by sorting pupils according to talent and ability. In 'Some principles of stratification', Davis and Moore argue that stratification (or the hierarchical division of society into layers) is necessary for societies who must place and motivate individuals in the social structure. They note that some positions are: *inherently more agreeable than others ... some require special talents or training and some are functionally more important than others (p24).* This latter point is interesting, as it raises questions about which jobs are more 'functionally important'.

ACTIVITY 7.1

In small groups, look at the list of jobs below and try to rank them according to which are most functionally important. Another way of doing this exercise is to hold a 'balloon debate'. If you choose to complete the exercise this way, you will each need to take one of the roles outlined below and mount a convincing argument as to why your role should stay in a sinking balloon. The idea is that the group needs to decide the order each role should be thrown out of the balloon in order to save the other individuals.

Town planner
Public toilet cleaner
Social worker
Sewerage worker
Premiership footballer
Estate agent
Nurse
Doctor
Refuge disposal worker
Waiter
Care worker
Lawyer
Brain surgeon
IT expert
Plumber
Car assembly line worker
Postman
University lecturer

How did you come to your decisions?
Was there any disagreement among you?

The chances are that you had some difficulty deciding upon the relative extent to which roles were functionally important (or not). Furthermore, the way that society rewards different roles does not necessarily give an indication of functional importance. We only have to compare the wages of a premiership footballer with those of a refuge disposal worker to sharply consider this argument. As football fans ourselves, we are not suggesting that footballers are not important (clearly our Saturday afternoons would never be the same without football!); however, what we are saying is that if we consider which role is more important for the smooth running and maintenance of society, clearly the refuge disposal worker is more critical than the footballer, even though the wages of the former are in no way comparable to those of the latter. Notwithstanding these criticisms, Davis and Moore were clear in their argument that society needed to attach different rewards to different positions and that the existence of differential rewards would ensure that the most talented individuals in society would be motivated to train to fulfil the most important positions. They pointed to the sacrifice that individuals who remain in education are required to make in order to allow them to fulfil their dreams. Unlike their peers who can begin earning much sooner, those staying on must defer their rewards until such time they have finished their training.

According to functionalists, the education system is the institution in which individuals compete to find their natural place in society. By the formal system of examinations, and to an extent via more informal systems that we talked about earlier, individuals are sifted and sorted so that they find their 'natural' place within a stratified society. The most talented and skilled individuals are motivated by the rewards attached, to train for longer and harder to fulfil the most functionally important roles. The reverse argument then, must also be true for functionalists – the least skilled and talented individuals who do not do so well within the education system will find their way into less well-paid roles. Functionalists argue that this system is inherently fair because all individuals have the same opportunities to do well. Their belief is that the education system is a 'meritocracy' or a system which allows pupils to achieve success proportionate to their talents and abilities, as opposed to one in which social class or wealth is the controlling factor.

Davis and Moore's ideas have been criticised by sociologists who identify a range of shortcomings with their argument. In particular, Melvin M Tumin (1953) questioned the very notion of 'functional importance' by suggesting that for any social system to survive, all social roles are equally important to maintain the *status quo*. Furthermore, he questioned Davis and Moore's assertion that only a limited number of individuals in society have the talents that can be trained into skills. Tumin argues that there may well be very many individuals who have talents, but various obstacles exist which prevent the conversion of talent to qualifications. Obstacles might include access to education, subtle processes within the education system that motivate some but dissuade others and the ability of some professions to restrict access. We will consider some of the barriers within the education system later on in this chapter, but for now it suffices to identify factors such as negative labelling of some pupils based on class, race or gender and the power of teachers to potentially shape a pupil's educational career by the messages they give and the influence they can yield.

Moreover, Tumin is very critical of the idea that those who stay in the education system are undergoing some kind of sacrifice. He notes that the cost of training is usually borne by parents who themselves have had privileged positions; and that any loss of earnings in the early years is more than made up within the first ten years when trained professionals finally enter the labour market in significantly higher-paid roles than their contemporaries who left school earlier. Tumin further identifies the 'psychic and spiritual rewards' and the opportunities for self-development that those who go on to University enjoy: *There is ... access to leisure and freedom of a kind not likely to be experienced by the persons already at work (p390).*

Marxists such as Bowles and Gintis are also critical of Davis and Moore's ideas, arguing that education merely perpetuates existing inequalities. These ideas will be considered later on in this chapter.

A level playing field?

In this section, we examine further the functionalist claim that education acts as a meritocracy. Certainly, at first glance the evidence may seem to support functionalist assumptions. For example, in the UK, formal secondary education is available to all children and young people, irrespective of their social class background. It is free, compulsory and relatively well resourced, and in state-funded schools (the vast majority of all schools), it is delivered through a national curriculum. This, theoretically, ensures that all children receive the same standard and level of education. It is therefore perhaps reasonable to assume that the UK's education system mitigates the impact of different family backgrounds and social class on educational experience and attainment. In short, common sense would suggest that a free, standardised education, delivered through a national curriculum to all, should provide children from disadvantaged backgrounds with a route out of poverty and social exclusion. After all, if all children have the same levels of opportunity, then surely the quality of their educational experiences, and their qualifications at the end of their school careers, will have been determined by the amount of effort they have put in to their schooling?

In this meritocratic interpretation of education, academic outcomes are seen to mirror intelligence plus 'merit' or effort, reflecting the work and commitment pupils are prepared to put into their schooling. Pupils start their school careers, it is assumed, with a 'level playing field' and if they are prepared to work hard, they will succeed academically. Conversely, if they fail to apply themselves, or choose not to attend school or to misbehave, then at best, they will fail academically, and at worst, they may be excluded from school. From this perspective then, all children start with the same chances and they get out of education what they put in. If we accept this interpretation of education as valid, we can perhaps see how education has the potential to 'flatten out' class differences and equalise educational opportunities and ultimately life chances. It can perform an intrinsically progressive function, providing disadvantaged children with the same opportunities to succeed academically as more advantaged children. As the famous US educational philosopher, John Dewey wrote, *It is the office of the school environment to see to it that each individual gets an opportunity to escape from the limitations of the social group in which he was born, and come into contact with a broader environment* (cited in Bowles and Gintis, 1976, p21). Tony Blair, the UK's former prime minister, saw the role of education in precisely these terms. Education, he argued, had the potential to create a 'true meritocracy', and his aim was to provide a system that enabled *the full potential of every individual to be liberated* (cited in Webster, 2001).

As well as guaranteeing 'just deserts', an education system based upon meritocratic principles also ensures that intelligence, aptitude and effort are rewarded, and that those who 'succeed' in education, and subsequently in their professional lives, are the most talented.

However, the notion that the education system acts as a meritocracy has generated much criticism. In the following exercise we would like you to use your analytical skills and draw up a critique of the concept.

ACTIVITY 7.2

Thinking carefully about the education system, in what ways can you criticise the principle that it is truly meritocratic?

You will hopefully have identified the fact that not all children begin school at the same, equal, starting line, and therefore it is unlikely that education can ever truly provide an equal platform for children to enter the 'race' on an equal footing. Some children clearly have considerably more privileged home lives that positively impact upon their school experiences. Conversely, some children have difficult experiences at home that can negatively impact upon them in school. Other 'home-related' factors can include the physical environment, such as the space a child has or does not have to study. Some children, for example will have their own room, with a desk, a computer, internet access, very many books, and other 'mod cons' which make the home environment conducive to studying. Conversely, other children may share a room with several others, they may live in a chaotic, noisy environment, will not have a computer or internet access (which is immediately disadvantaging as much homework is increasingly based around this resource) and may not have the material benefits that their peers have. Children from disadvantaged backgrounds may not have had the experiences that children from privileged backgrounds will take for granted.

Other factors within school can mean that some children are held back while others are pushed forwards; children may be labelled in particular ways by teachers which can result in self-fulfilling prophecies, an issue we will consider later in this chapter. The micro culture within schools tends to be very middle class, and this can sometimes be alien to working-class children. This manifests in terms of the language codes used by teachers (see for example the ground-breaking work done by Basil Bernstein in 1971 around elaborated and restricted codes); the value systems of teachers; and the cultural gulf between the home lives of some children and the expectations within schools. Furthermore, there may be factors linked to the school itself – some schools have been identified as 'failing schools' while others excel at targets and are awarded specialist status. It is possible that where schools are publicly labelled as 'failing', the children will to an extent internalise this deep in their subconscious and understandably see themselves as failing too. We will return to many of these factors later on in this chapter in more detail, but it is pertinent to note that any concept of the education system truly being a meritocracy or a level playing field where children who work hard and achieve their potential will be rewarded is significantly flawed. The data we present in the next section serves to illustrate the extent to which this is the case. As we will see, if the aim of education is to flatten out social class differences then it has been proven to be a spectacular failure.

Educational achievement and disadvantage

All the available research shows us that children from disadvantaged backgrounds tend to perform less well at school, and gain fewer qualifications than those from more advantaged backgrounds. As Raffo *et al.* (2007) argue:

> Put simply, the poorer a child's family is, the less well they are likely to do in the education system ... Far from offering a route out of poverty, education simply seems to confirm existing social hierarchies.

(p1)

Moreover, social class differences in attainment rates seem to hold true throughout an individual's educational career. Let us begin with the secondary school. The receipt of free school meals is often seen as an indicator of disadvantage, since eligibility is based upon parents' entitlement to means-tested income support. How, then, do the educational attainment rates of children receiving free school meals compare with those who do not? In the UK, the data consistently show that children who receive free school meals are far less likely to achieve five A*–C grade GCSEs than those who do not receive free school meals. In 2005/06, only 32.6 per cent of children in receipt of free school meals did so, whereas the equivalent figure for non-free school meal children was 60.7 per cent (Office for National Statistics, 2007).

As Table 7.1 illustrates, data contrasting the educational performance of children from different socio-economic groups seem to confirm the links between low income and educational underachievement. Nearly eight out of every ten children from higher professional families achieve five or more A*–C grade GCSEs, compared with only just over three out of every ten from unskilled manual families.

Table 7.1 Attainment of five or more A–C GCSEs by social class of parents (2002)*

Social class background of children	Per cent obtaining five or more A*–Cs
Higher professional	77
Lower professional	64
Intermediate, skilled manual	52
Lower supervisory, semi-skilled manual	35
Routine, unskilled manual	32
Other	32

Source: Haezewindt, 2004, p12

Social class differences in educational attainment continue into further and higher education. In 2002, 87 per cent of young people whose parents were working in higher professional occupations continued with full-time education at 16, compared with only 60 per cent of those whose parents were in manual occupations (Haezewindt, 2004, p16). With regards to higher education, less than 20 per cent of young people from skilled manual, partly-skilled and unskilled backgrounds participate in higher education, compared with 50 per cent from the higher social class groups (professional, intermediate and skilled non-manual) (Haezewindt, 2004; see also Connor et al., 2001).

Social class is not the only variable that seems to influence educational attainment, and children from certain minority ethnic group backgrounds also fair less well than their white equivalents. As Table 7.2 illustrates, black African, black Caribbean, Bangladeshi and Pakistani pupils performed consistently below the national average at GCSE level.

Table 7.2. Attainment of five or more A*–C GCSEs by ethnic group, 2005

Ethnicity	Per cent obtaining five or more A*–Cs
All pupils	55
White	55
Bangladeshi	53
Pakistani	48
Black African	48
Black Caribbean	42
Gypsy/Roma	15

Source: DfES, 2006b

Alarmingly, children in care are among the worst performing of all children in the UK, with only 12 per cent of them achieving 5 or more A*–C grades at GCSE level. The DfES has referred to this as *shocking for twenty-first century Britain* (DfES, 2007, p65). These low levels of education at secondary school have a knock-on effect in terms of progression. Thus, whereas 38 per cent of all 19-year-olds are at either college or university, only 19 per cent of 19-year-old care leavers are in college and only 6 per cent in university (DfES, 2006a, p68).

ACTIVITY 7.3

In this task we want you to consider the sort of factors which may have contributed to the low levels of educational attainment among looked-after children. In doing so, we want you to critically engage with the functionalist claim that all children start their schooling with a 'level playing field', and that educational success is simply a reflection of merit and effort alone. What variables, for example, may detrimentally affect the educational potential of looked-after children? When considering this question, you may want to consult the following recent DfES Green and White Papers, both of which draw attention to the forces that impinge on looked after-children's educational opportunities:

- *DfES (2006a)* Care matters: transforming the lives of children and young people in care. *Green Paper.*

- *DfES (2007)* Care matters: time for change. *White Paper.*

While undertaking this task you may have identified a number of factors that impact detrimentally on the educational opportunities available to looked-after children. Research, for example, has shown that looked-after children are far less likely than their peers to go to higher-performing schools, so geographical residence may be a factor. The disruption caused to looked-after children's education by multiple placements is also significant. For instance, one in ten children leaving care in the year ending March 2006 had been subjected to nine or more placements while in care. At the same time, only 65 per cent of children who had been in care for over two and a half years had been in the same placement for two years or more. We must put this in the context of research findings which suggest that on average pupils who move schools during Key Stage 4 attain 75 points lower at GCSE – equivalent to between one and two grades in every subject (DfES, 2007, p69). Furthermore, children who are in care are likely to be experiencing varying amounts of emotional distress associated with the very reasons why they are being looked after in the public care system. For children who are separated from their birth families, coping with psychological anguish, and dealing with a range of personal and social problems, there is little wonder that they fall short of average educational achievement.

Not only are poorer children, looked-after children and children from minority ethnic groups less likely to achieve better qualifications, they are also more likely to be excluded from school, and to be diagnosed as having special educational needs. The school exclusion rate among looked-after children is very high – around ten times higher than the average (DfES, 2007, p14). Clearly being excluded from school compounds existing disadvantage. The White Paper *Care matters* recognises this and makes a strong case for ensuring that children in care are only excluded as a last resort, and this should only be done following discussions with the local authority regarding provision for the child. Various measures to address the concerns relating to looked-after children who are excluded have been introduced, including the commission of a review by Ofsted to look at schools' practice in relation to the exclusion of children in care in 2009.

School exclusions and ethnicity

Here we will concentrate briefly on the issue of school exclusions and the experiences of minority ethnic group children, an issue that has rightly generated a good deal of controversy in recent years. The controversy stems from statistics which show us that black pupils are three times more likely to be excluded from school than their white counterparts. The Social Exclusion Unit's (1998b) Report, *Truancy and school exclusion*, pointed out that 16 per cent of excluded children are from minority ethnic group backgrounds, a much higher percentage than would be expected statistically. More recent statistics suggest that there has been little change. In England in 2003/04 the permanent exclusion rates of Traveller of Irish Heritage and Gypsy/Roma pupils were over four times that of the average for all pupils, while permanent exclusion rates for black Caribbean pupils and other black pupils were almost three times higher than those for white pupils (DfES, 2006b, p87). All these ratios had increased since 2002/03.

In this exercise we would like you to consider some of the factors that might account for the different ethnic rates of school exclusion outlined above.

Some of your explanations may have focused on cultural factors. For example, it has been suggested that Black Caribbean pupils may experience considerable levels of peer pressure to adopt the norms associated with urban street culture. This culture, it is argued, places a primacy on unruly behaviour and non-compliance with authority, including school authorities. From this perspective, higher levels of school exclusions among Black Caribbean pupils are a reflection of their rejection of mainstream school values, and their attempts to look 'cool' in front of their peers. Needless to say, there are problems with this kind of interpretation. For example, research shows that working-class white pupils who conform to the discipline and goals of the school are just as likely to be taunted for being 'nerds' and 'geeks' as their black Caribbean counterparts (Strand, 2007). More importantly, though, such explanations fail to acknowledge potential structural determinants of school exclusion, in particular racism.

An alternative explanation then is that pupils from black and minority ethnic group backgrounds are treated differently from their white peers by teachers and the school authorities. Certainly, this is the perception of black pupils who have themselves been excluded from school. As Ofsted suggests:

> *many Black pupils who find themselves subject to disciplinary procedures perceive themselves to have been unfairly treated ... Black pupils were more likely to be excluded for what was defined by schools as 'challenging behaviour'. The length of fixed-term exclusions varied considerably in the same school between Black and white pupils for what are described as the same or similar incidents.*

(cited in Wright et al., 2005, p3)

Wright *et al*. (2005) interviewed a number of black excluded pupils, and they found that nearly half of those excluded believed that racism or racial stereotyping had played a part in their exclusion from school. Is there any justification for such claims?

Some research has drawn attention to the fact that in schools where exclusions are most commonly occurring, the teaching staff tended not to be representative of the ethnicity of the pupil population. While this may not necessarily be a problem, studies suggest that in some instances this 'imbalance' is accompanied by the existence of inaccurate, stereotypical and indeed racist assumptions about the behaviour of children from different ethnic backgrounds. For example, in a DfES-funded study on school exclusions, the head teacher in one such large comprehensive school, with 75 per cent of pupils from minority ethnic backgrounds, complained about the challenge he and his staff faced from *West Indian boys [who] tend to be loud and aggressive* (Parsons et al., 2004, p66).

In fact, research suggests that pupils from minority ethnic group backgrounds who are excluded are less likely than white excluded children to have had prior behavioural problems, attendance issues, or be classified as having special needs difficulties. In addition, they are less likely to be classed as having low educational attainment and are far less likely to be excluded for reasons of ongoing, persistent misconduct (Parsons et al., 2004). Statistics suggest that black and mixed-heritage pupils are far more likely than other groups to be excluded for one-off violent offences (41 per cent of all those excluded compared with 29 per cent of excluded white pupils). The reasons for this are not clear, but one suggestion is that teachers and the school authorities, influenced by stereotypical views on the 'aggressiveness' of black youth (such as those held by the head teacher mentioned above), are less tolerant of relatively isolated bouts of bad behaviour when committed by black children. Inaccurate assumptions about the educational potential and behaviour of black pupils have been well documented within the sociology of education, and there is plenty of evidence to suggest that black children are sometimes inappropriately labelled as challenging, aggressive and as troublemakers, and that their behaviour is interpreted in the light of the label (Wright et al., 2005). This was the conclusion of a recent study sponsored by the Department for Children, Schools and Families into the educational experiences of pupils from minority ethnic group backgrounds (Strand, 2007, p99). It is also endorsed the interpretation favoured by a secret high-level official report into differential ethnic rates of school exclusions, which was leaked to *The Independent* in December 2006. The author of the report, Peter Wanless, Director of School Performance and Reform at the DfES, argued that the exclusions gap was *caused by largely unwitting, but systematic, racial discrimination in the application of disciplinary and exclusions policies*. Black pupils, he argued, were disproportionately denied mainstream education and the life chances that go with it.

> *It is argued that unintentional racism stems from long-standing social conditioning involving negative images of black people, particularly black men, which stereotype them as threatening. Such conditioning is reinforced by the media portrayal of black 'street culture'. It encourages school staff to expect black pupils to be worse behaved and to perceive a greater level of threat.*

> (cited in Griggs, 2006, p8)

Wanless also rejected 'cultural' explanations for different rates of exclusion, stating that there was a *comparatively weak basis for arguing that street culture has a more persuasive influence on black young people than it has on other young people* (p8).

Sociological explanations for educational inequality

The evidence we have presented so far leads us to question the notion that true equality of educational opportunity exists in the UK. As we have seen, educational experiences and outcomes vary between social classes and ethnic groups. In the following section, we look at sociological explanations which purport to account for these unequal outcomes. We begin with the symbolic interactionist perspective, because it follows on from the preceding discussion on labelling and school exclusion.

The role of the school: symbolic interactionist perspective

Symbolic interactionists are interested in the micro processes of communication within schools that can contribute to the relative success or failure of individual pupils. Drawing upon Howard Becker's work on labelling, it is possible to see how teachers can potentially assign labels to pupils in their class, which has a powerful impact upon them and can lead to their education and subsequent career being shaped in particular ways. One of the earliest experiments was carried out in 1968 by Rosenthal and Jacobsen. They conducted IQ tests on school children at the beginning of the school year before the teachers had had an opportunity to form an opinion about their pupils. Without looking at the actual results, the researchers grouped children into so-called ability groups, telling teachers that a certain number of pupils had above-average ability and could be expected to 'spurt'. They then returned to the school some months later and retested the pupils. They compared both sets of test results and to their astonishment found that the pupils who had randomly been selected to be in the 'above average', 'spurters' group had improved their actual IQ scores significantly. Rosenthal and Jacobsen concluded that there must have been something in the way that the teachers interacted with the so-called 'star' pupils that contributed to their success. Although this study can be criticised on many fronts, not least because of the ethical issues around carrying out such a study, it does give us an indication of how potentially powerful teachers can be in shaping the attitudes and abilities of pupils, possibly by giving them additional attention, responding more positively to them, or pushing them to a higher level. Conversely, other pupils may be labelled as failures, be provided with less encouragement and be more likely to be perceived and treated as troublemakers. The expectations that teachers have of pupils can influence the pupils, who may internalise the expectations and act accordingly. This is called a self-fulfilling prophecy.

More recently, useful research carried out by Stephen Waterhouse (2004) found that teachers construct conceptions of pupils' identities over time, as they form impressions of them. This involves categorising or labelling children in relation to the social boundaries of the school and largely involves categories of 'normal' and 'deviant' pupils. Waterhouse found that 'deviant' pupils were of great concern to teachers and occupied a significant amount of time; by contrast, the 'normal' pupils were to some extent invisible in comparison. Furthermore, he found that once children were categorised as 'deviant' or 'normal' there was a tendency to interpret other behaviours in light of the master label assigned:

> Once the dominant category of 'normal' or 'deviant' was adopted by the teacher, it then became the pivotal identity for interpreting other [behaviours] – even in those episodes of classroom life in which the child was apparently not demonstrating behaviour typical of the dominant 'deviant' or 'normal' type .

(p74)

Waterhouse cites one of the teachers in the study predicting future behaviour: *Today he's been good. But I think this afternoon he'll probably be naughty because he has to stay in because the dinner ladies can't control him* (p75). It is clear from this research that teachers are involved in categorising and labelling pupils as part of their core business of assessment and relating to their pupils. Although Waterhouse's research did not set out to measure the impact of labelling on specific pupils, he does identify the positive outcomes associated in two schools that had adopted new initiatives with the aim of reducing pupil exclusions. By adopting a range of measures based upon an emphasis on inclusion, both schools significantly reduced the numbers of school exclusions. Measures included an incorporative ethos and a culture in which the pupils were seen as being entitled to be there and entitled to support; positive interactions with the pupils by teachers and the senior management; and high-profile 'crowd control' whereby a visible presence signalled *strong behavioural expectations, and at the same time creating spontaneous opportunities for informal, supportive and generally positive interactions with pupils* (p80). If such measures are regarded as constituting a form of institutional labelling of pupils, by consciously reconstructing the pupils as being positive members of the school community, it is possible to see how self-fulfilling prophecies were occurring here both for the pupils and the staff. Indeed, the number of pupils to be excluded in both schools decreased significantly.

If we accept as a general point that it is likely that teachers label and categorise pupils according to their educational ability and their social attributes, this could potentially have a significant impact upon large numbers of children. Of course, for some pupils the impact will be positive, but for others it will be negative and may contribute to poor outcomes for some children. The labelling of children linked to their social class background, their gender, race or other factors (such as their status as a looked-after child, for example) can significantly impact upon their educational experiences and outcomes. Indeed, our own students are usually very aware of the subtle but powerful labelling that they themselves have experienced and the impact it has had upon them.

However, in addition to the largely unconscious labelling that may be done by individual teachers, children are also labelled more formally by being streamed into ability groups. However subtly or otherwise this process is carried out, children are usually aware that they are in the 'top group for maths' or the 'bottom group for English' and such *institutionalised labelling* may also play a part in how children perceive their own ability. In some areas of the UK, there are systems of selective education where children can enter an 11+ examination which they need to 'pass' in order to go to a selective grammar school. The impact of such a system can be far reaching for some pupils, who can perceive themselves as 'failures' if they do not pass the test. Such institutionalised labelling can have a significant social impact upon geographical areas, where there is a two-tiered system perceived to be in operation, with great stigma or pride attached to which school a child attends. However, there are a range of difficulties associated with the IQ test that is the highly sought-after passport to grammar school; rather than genuinely testing intelligence, the 11+ may actually test the ability of the child to do the test. It is argued that middle-class pupils are at an advantage here as their parents are more likely to be able to pay for a private tutor to assist their child and/or purchase (expensive) test papers to practise with. There are other criticisms of the 11+ system, not least the immense stress that it can put children (and their parents) under. Furthermore, the two-tier system can simultaneously disadvantage some children while advantaging others.

Genetically determined intelligence?

A radically different explanation for unequal educational outcomes shifts the focus away from schools and teachers and onto what are perceived to be pupils' innate abilities or inabilities. According to this interpretation, children from disadvantaged backgrounds, or from different ethnic groups, are simply genetically less intelligent than their better-off, or white counterparts. Hence, intelligence is seen as an inherited trait, determined by genetic rather than cultural, structural and environmental factors. In 1969, the American educational psychologist Arthur Jensen (1969) published a deeply controversial paper which implied that racial differences in educational attainment had a genetic origin. In this paper, which was based on IQ data, he argued that compensatory educational initiatives which were aimed at raising the relatively low levels of educational attainment among black children in the US were effectively a waste of time and resources. Their educational underachievement, he argued, had little to do with environmental influences, such as labelling, poverty and poor educational opportunities, and more to do with their genetically inherited low levels of cognitive ability. Jensen explained social class differences in education in much the same way, and, more recently has hinted at genetic explanations for a range of social ills, and not just educational failure. *Many social behaviour problems*, he states, *including dropping out of school, chronic welfare status, illegitimacy, child neglect, poverty, accident proneness, delinquency, and crime, are negatively correlated with ... IQ independently of social class of origin* (Jensen, 1999).

Jensen's ideas provided the basis for Charles Murray and Richard J Herrnstein's 1994 controversial book, *The bell curve*, which sought to re-emphasise the links between genetics and intelligence. These are the main points made in the book.

- Intelligence is significantly (between 40 and 80 per cent) genetically determined and can be measured objectively through the use of IQ data.

- Social class differences in educational attainment and 'success' are largely genetically determined. Those who rise to the top of American society are there because they happen to be the most intelligent, and not through patronage or privilege. Likewise, those at the bottom are so placed because of their lack of intelligence, and not the absence of sufficient opportunities to succeed.

- Social problems such as illegitimacy, crime and unemployment are linked to genetically determined differences in intelligence.

- Social policies designed to improve educational attainment among children of the lower classes, such as the Head Start initiative in the United States, are doomed to failure.

- Racial differences in intelligence and educational attainment are largely inherited. (This was probably the most controversial of Murray and Herrnstein's findings.)

Not surprisingly, many criticisms have been made of *The bell curve*. For example, studies which show social class and ethnic differences in educational attainment to be due to cultural factors, environmental effects, biases built into the tests themselves, or a combination of all of these, are either side-stepped by the authors, completely ignored or inappropriately dismissed. In addition, evidence highlighting the positive effects of compensatory forms of schooling, which are designed to mitigate the educationally detrimental impact of poverty and disadvantage, are also cast aside. There is, in fact, a good deal of evidence to indicate that targeted interventions, aimed at stimulating the intelligence of children from deprived backgrounds, and providing them with packages of educational support, can have huge impact in terms of improving educational performance. Why then do Murray and Herrnstein persist in pushing the case for genetic interpretations of intelligence? According to Alexander Alland (2004), they are driven by their own preconceived ideological opposition to state-funded welfare programmes, including public education. As we have seen in other chapters in this book, Murray has always been a vociferous opponent of state welfare for the poor, and if, through the use of dubious genetic arguments, he is able to show it to be ineffective, then his arguments against progressive welfare interventions are given greater credence.

To a certain extent, IQ testing has experienced something of a popular renaissance in the UK. Organisations such as MENSA and TV shows such as the BBC's *Test the Nation* have helped rehabilitate IQ testing, portraying it as a neutral, objective test of intelligence and aptitude. However, even the experiences of these populist attempts to generate interest and support for IQ testing have been mired with controversy. By way of example, the 2002 edition of *Test the Nation* famously labelled Burnley football fans as the least intelligent in the country, an outcome that generated much embarrassment to the club's supporters themselves, and much amusement among their rivals. To this day, Burnley supporters remain convinced that Blackburn Rovers supporters (Burnley's bitter rivals) registered themselves as Burnley fans and deliberately answered all the questions incorrectly! The flaws associated with IQ data are many and varied. The example cited here may appear flippant, but does help us understand why we should not take IQ data as 'given'. IQ tests are notoriously fallible and are certainly not neutral – indeed, it is important to realise that they are socially constructed, and the questions asked can be designed and framed in such a way as to secure any outcome the author desires.

We would, therefore, caution against letting our guard down against the inherently problematic assumptions that stem from explanations of educational underachievement that are based on the ideas of those such as Jensen, Murray and Herrnstein. In our chapter on social exclusion, for example, we hinted at the way IQ data have in the past been used to justify a whole range of deeply problematic theories, which, in their 'milder' forms, have been used to justify racist practices, and in their more extreme forms, have been used to justify the extermination of whole races. It is no coincidence that references to Jensen's and Murray and Herrnstein's work can be found in the publicity literature of various racist and white supremacist organisations, from the British National Party in the UK to the Ku Klux Klan in the US.

Poor upbringings and parental shortfall

Other explanations for the educational 'failure' of working-class and black children focus on what are perceived to be their poor upbringings, and the failure of their parents or carers to support and nurture their talents. These kinds of explanations can be divided into two broad 'camps', according to the degree of sympathy or blame they apportion to the parents and carers.

A 'blaming' approach

A less than sympathetic interpretation of parental failure to fully support children can be found within what we have referred to elsewhere in the book as 'moral underclass discourse' (see Chapters 2 and 3). A view that has traditionally been shared by politicians and academics on the political 'right' is that there exists an underclass of problematic families who are incapable of socialising their children effectively. While advocates of this approach do sometimes point to genetic influences, their main focus is on the immaturity, low intelligence, and dysfunctional behavioural characteristics – for instance, labour market drop-out, promiscuity and crime – of certain parents. Again, while we can sometimes find a hint of genetics in these explanations, on the whole these, and other dysfunctional traits, are said to have been encouraged by well-meaning but harmful welfare interventions, which reinforce rather than modify the 'deviant' behaviour of morally degenerate parents. These parents, it is argued, are simply unable to provide their children with the stable environment, intellectual stimulation and appropriate role models that are necessary to inculcate a desire for learning and educational success. Moreover, their lack of ambition and aspiration is passed on to succeeding generations, and children unconsciously absorb their parents' fatalistic outlooks on life. The Conservative politician and former Education Minister, Keith Joseph, was an early advocate of this theory. A *high and rising proportion of children*, he argued in 1974, are *being born to mothers least fitted to bring children into the world.* Many of the parents, he insisted, were of *low intelligence*, and most of them of *low educational attainment.* They were *unlikely to be able to give children the stable and emotional background* they needed, and if they were allowed to propagate unchecked they would continue to *produce problem children, the future unmarried mothers, delinquents, denizens of our borstals, subnormal educational establishments, prisons, hostels for drifters.* Joseph argued that those calling for more educational resources and preventative work with disadvantaged children were missing the point. The nation's 'stock' was being diluted by high birth rates among poor families and parents of low intelligence, and the solution, he insisted, lay in a massive expansion of birth control amongst the lower classes (Clark, 1974, p1). Not surprisingly, Joseph's comments excited a great deal of controversy at the time, and indeed are said to have dented his political ambitions. However, these ideas remain influential today.

Charles Murray is one of a number of academics on the 'right' to embrace this kind of approach. He too draws attention to increased birth rates among what he sees as certain 'dysfunctional' sections of the poor and he too dismisses the notion that targeting additional educational resources at children of the 'underclass' can significantly improve their education opportunities or life chances:

Experience gives no confidence that social services can counteract the effects of bad family environment. On the contrary, research is filled with studies showing how intractable these environments seem to be. Less charitably, some observers, of whom I am one, think a case can be made that activist social policy exacerbates the problems it seeks to ameliorate.

(Murray, 1998, p43)

The best we can say about this explanation is that the emphasis moves away from genetics towards an approach which acknowledges cultural influences on educational attainment. However, when it comes to providing solutions to educational inequalities, it is almost as pessimistic in outlook as genetic interpretations for educational disadvantage.

A more sympathetic approach to understanding parental 'failure'

Not all explanations for educational inequality which focus on a perceived 'parental deficit' are quite as blaming as the perspective outlined above. A more sympathetic version acknowledges the difficult circumstances that militate against parental involvement in education. It accepts the fact that many parents themselves may lack the educational and cognitive skills needed to shape their children's learning careers and stimulate their interest in education. This approach also appreciates that many low-income parents feel that they are too busy coping with the day-to-day stresses of making ends meet to show any meaningful involvement in their children's education (Cauce et al., 2003). There is also an acknowledgment of the way parents' own negative experiences of education can feed into the dynamics of family life, negatively impacting on their children's chances at school. Based upon their own lack of opportunities and negative experiences, it is hardly surprising that parents themselves see little value in educational attainment, and this too will impact detrimentally on the encouragement and support they give their children. They are also likely to show less interest in the range of educational 'choices' available to their children, and be content to see them attend the local 'sink' school.

There are links here to Oscar Lewis's 'culture of poverty' thesis discussed in Chapter 2, which sees negative traits – fatalism, lack of motivation and inability to defer gratification – being learned by successive generations of working-class children as a response to their position in society. From this perspective, any 'solution' must seek to change the outlooks and perceptions of working-class parents. It must encourage them to show a greater interest in their children's education, to motivate them, and to provide them with the nurturing, encouragement and support needed to guarantee educational success. In short, what we need to do is make working-class parents more like middle-class parents. Sharon Gewirtz (2001) has outlined some of the assumptions upon which this interpretation of educational inequality is based:

- Middle-class parents are far better at assessing and engaging with the range of options available to parents in the educational marketplace. They know more about the pros and cons of different of schools in their areas, and hence are more able to make informed choices about the quality and types of schools that their children attend. They are, therefore, more 'tuned in' to the 'choice agenda' in education and better equipped to discriminate between good and bad schools.

- Middle-class parents are more effective at monitoring what schools provide to their children, and intervening when they feel it necessary to rectify what they see as being problematic. They know what to expect from schools in terms of, for example, volume of homework and feedback on their child's progress, and are more prepared to intervene if they feel something is wrong.

- Middle-class parents possess more 'cultural capital' than their working-class counterparts. This concept was introduced by Pierre Bourdieu in 1973 to refer to the social skills, language skills, interests and attributes that middle-class parents confer upon their children that help them to succeed in the education system. It is argued that such parents show a much greater level of interest in their children's education, encouraging and incentivising them, helping with homework and taking them on educational trips of interest. They are less fatalistic and more likely to instil in their children a desire and love for learning.

There can be little doubt that many of these assumptions underpin much of the current government's thinking around education policy and educational disadvantage. For example, there now exists a plethora of information – either online or in leaflet form – aimed at informing working-class parents of the different 'choices' available to them, encouraging them to engage more effectively in the educational marketplace. The government's website for parents, *ParentsCentre* (www.parentscentre.gov.uk/), provides a good example of the sort of information available. *No doubt one of the most important decisions you will make in your child's education*, it states, *will be choosing a primary or secondary school. Making the right choice for you and your child will involve a lot of research and planning*.

The government is also encouraging working-class parents to take a more active role in monitoring what their children's schools do. The introduction of home/school agreements, which set out what parents can expect from schools, were partly designed to this end. Likewise, great efforts are being made to persuade working-class parents to spend more time helping their children with school work.

Once again, these are traits that home/school agreements are seeking to instil in working-class parents, by stipulating the responsibilities and duties they are expected to perform in return for their child's education, including reading with children and assisting with homework. The government's attempts to encourage lifelong learning, as well as the wider introduction of initiatives designed to promote community involvement in schools, are also influenced by a concern to equip parents with skills needed to help their children. Adult education courses, parents are told, can help them support their children at school as well as improve their job-related skills. Finally, the government is also determined to change what it sees as the negative cultural traits possessed by many working-class families, which mitigate against their children's educational opportunities. As David Blunkett, then Education Minister, stated, the government's education policy aimed to *liberate literally millions of individuals from that agonizing sense of low self-esteem and low confidence that has sapped the energy and damaged the lives of so many people in previous generations* (cited in Gewirtz, 2001, p371).

At first glance, all these initiatives seem eminently reasonable. Surely, all parents should have an understanding of the different choices available in terms of their children's schooling? In addition, all parents should show an interest in their children's schools, be prepared to nurture a desire for learning, and assist their children with homework. However, this strategy does have its critics. In particular, it is accused of ignoring the structural constraints that shape educational opportunity and disadvantage.

Structural explanations for educational inequality

With each of the above two 'parental deficit' interpretations, the focus is, to a lesser or greater degree, on the essentially negative personal and cultural attributes of children and families themselves, which are said to predispose them to problematic behaviour and/or lower levels of educational attainment. Other explanations for educational disadvantage focus on the structure of the education system itself – its hierarchical nature, the quality of schooling in disadvantaged areas, and the failure to address geographical inequalities in the distribution of educational resources.

The current government certainly locates at least part of the blame for educational disadvantage within the education system, and a number of reforms have sought to improve the educational experience of disadvantaged children. We have seen the introduction of its Sure Start initiative, an expansion of nursery education, reductions in class sizes, the introduction of learning mentors in schools, the development of numeracy and literacy strategies, and the introduction of citizenship education. However, some argue that a disproportionate amount of emphasis has been placed upon what we referred to above as the 'parental deficit' and too little on wider structural factors. In short, advocates of structural explanations for educational inequality accuse the government of:

- neglecting the impact poverty, stress and ill health have on parents' ability to devote time to assisting their child's education;

- reinforcing negative imagery of poor working-class families, strengthening the view that educational inequality is the fault of parents rather than a lack of opportunity;

- engaging in an uncritical celebration of the ideologies of 'choice' and 'competition' in education.

The latter criticism relates to the way the government has seemingly uncritically accepted the rhetoric of choice, competition and the market in education. This has led, as we saw above, to the development of initiatives designed to educate working-class parents about the range of choices available to their children. It is assumed that this will help counter the deficit in knowledge that working-class parents face, thus equalising their children's opportunities of enrolling at 'good' schools. However, critics argue that this strategy is misconceived, and indeed misleading. As Whitty (2001) argues, *education reforms couched in the rhetoric of choice, difference and diversity often turn out to be sophisticated ways of reproducing existing hierarchies of class and race* (p289). From this perspective, instead of teaching working-class parents how to identify 'good' and 'bad' schools, ministers should be directing their efforts at ensuring that all schools provide an excellent quality of educational experience. In other words, there should not be a hierarchy of schools to choose from at all – rather, all schools should be equally good. This was the key principle underpinning the drive towards comprehensive education in the 1960s and 1970s, but in recent years it has been undermined by a plethora of initiatives designed to encourage choice, competition, specialisation and a hierarchy of schools. This latter development is not without its critics. As Gewirtz notes, with hierarchies comes competition, and in any competition for educational resources, the odds are severely stacked against working-class families. Firstly, the worst resourced and underperforming schools tend to be located in working-class areas, and unlike middle-class families, working-class families are unable to relocate to better catchment areas. Secondly, it is naïve to assume that the cultural capital possessed by middle-class families, which enables them to engage more effectively in their children's education, can be mimicked overnight. Moreover, even if such a resocialisation strategy could be moderately successful, this, in itself, would not be sufficient. As Gewirtz (2001) points out:

> *... however successful the government is in reconstructing working-class parents in the image of the ideal-typical middle-class parent, not everyone can be 'successful' or achieve 'excellence' because there are only a limited number of schools or jobs that are deemed to be 'excellent'. So long as hierarchies of schools and jobs exist, the middle classes will always find ways of getting the best out of the system, of ensuring that their cultural capital is more valuable than that of any working-class competitors.*

(p10)

From this perspective, the financial and cultural capital available to middle-class families has enabled, and will continue to enable them to 'colonise' sectors of state education that they feel are appropriate and 'safe' for their children.

RESEARCH SUMMARY

Middle-class colonisation of educational opportunity?

Are academics right to suggest that the elite sectors of public education have been colonised by the better-off? Certainly, there are significant social class differences in secondary school enrolment, with working-class children severely underrepresented in the 'best' schools. In 2005, for example, a Sutton Trust Report showed that only 3 per cent of children in what are considered to be the top 200 state schools were in receipt of free school meals, compared with a national secondary school average of 14.3 per cent. The report found that children who attended the highest performing schools were from significantly more affluent backgrounds than the population as a whole, implying that middle-class parents do indeed manage to 'colonise' the better publicly-funded secondary schools:

> *The intake of the top 200 schools is significantly more affluent than both the school population as a whole and the local areas in which they are sited. Or, to look at it*

another way, poorer children are much less likely to benefit from a top quality state education than their better-off peers, even if a leading maintained school is on their doorstep.

(p8)

Why is this the case? As well as more obvious factors, such as the geographical location of the 'best' schools in affluent areas (which is the case), the fact that middle-class parents can in some respects 'pay' for their children's education by being able to afford to buy houses in areas where the 'best' schools are is significant. So too is the point that was made above about middle-class parents being more aware of the 'choices' available to them. In addition, many of these schools subject applicants to entrance tests or examinations, which, as hinted at earlier, disadvantage working-class pupils. For instance, 161 of the top 200 secondary schools are grammar schools, each of which selects their pupils by means of what is known as the 11+ test. As we have already explained, while these tests are described as 'neutral', 'objective' tests of intellect and ability, there is no such thing as a neutral test of intelligence. The history of the sociology of education is rife with research which shows that more affluent middle-class parents are able, with the aid of their cultural and financial capital, to coach their children to pass the 11+. They can, as we previously indicated, also draw on their own cultural capital, they are in a better position to purchase practice papers (which are not cheap), and perhaps most of all, they are able to pay for private tuition for their children.

These inequalities at secondary school level are mirrored in the higher education sector, with working-class children being underrepresented at the top 'traditional' universities. For instance, only 10 per cent of those enrolled at Oxford and Cambridge are from skilled manual, partly-skilled and unskilled backgrounds. The equivalent figure for the other pre-1992 'traditional' universities is only 15–20 per cent. However, 30 per cent of those attending post-1992 universities and higher education colleges are from such backgrounds. As a 2007 Sutton Trust Report shows, there is very little chance that children of working-class parents will attend Oxford or Cambridge.

In the light of the findings highlighted above, it has been argued that any genuine widening of educational opportunity will involve a dismantling of the hierarchies that structure schooling in the UK. One solution that has been suggested is a system of 'fair banding' of pupils. Under this system all pupils in a given area are tested by ability. However, rather than using the data to cream off the most able pupils (as with the grammar system), banding is used to ensure that all schools have a mixed ability range of pupils.

Marxist approaches to education

Marxists seek to place the education system in its wider social context. In their much-cited 1976 book, *Schooling in capitalist America*, Samuel Bowles and Herbert Gintis provided a detailed Marxist critique of education systems in capitalist societies. They began by seeking to demolish the 'meritocratic myth', which implies that education is an 'objective competition' that provides all children with the opportunity to 'make it'. Education in capitalist societies, they argued, was never intended to be, and indeed never had been, a vehicle for creating a more fair, equal, socially just society. This, they insisted, was borne out by data on social mobility, which showed that despite the expansion of educational resources and 'opportunity' in the US, social mobility was just as low as in the past. Meanwhile, income inequality and poverty remained endemic, and indeed had increased rather than decreased. Education, they concluded, could not therefore be seen as an engine of opportunity or social improvement. In short, the likelihood of working-class children improving their economic and social status and avoiding poverty in the future was just as low when they wrote their book as it had ever been.

Social mobility in the UK

Bowles and Gintis' comments on social mobility related mainly to US society in the specific context of the 1970s. It might be worth considering briefly data for the UK today, to assess whether this aspect of their analysis could be said to hold true. Surely levels of social mobility in the UK today are higher than they were in the past?

One effective way of ascertaining the opportunities for social mobility in the UK is to assess where children from the least affluent families end up in terms of their earnings or incomes in adulthood. If large percentages of children born into poverty in the UK manage to 'succeed', then this suggests that opportunities for social mobility – or to put it another way, the chances of 'making it' – are high. In fact, data from a recent Sutton Trust study conducted by Jo Blanden and Paul Gregg (2005) suggest that the UK (along with the United States) has one of the lowest levels of social mobility of all developed nations. Moreover, levels of social mobility seem to be worsening rather than improving, with children born in 1970 having fewer opportunities than those born in 1958. This is despite the fact that the percentage of poorer children staying on at school after 16 has increased during the same time period. How did Blanden and Gregg explain this? They found that reductions in social class inequalities in staying on at school had not been matched by reductions in social class inequalities in higher education participation. The clear conclusion, *they argued,* is the big expansion in university participation has tended to benefit children from affluent families more and thus reinforced immobility across generations *(p14).*

Data on higher education participation certainly lend weight to Blanden and Gregg's conclusions. For despite the fact that more people from manual/unskilled backgrounds are attending university than ever before, the gap in higher education participation rates between those from manual/unskilled backgrounds and those from professional, non-manual backgrounds has actually widened. For example, in 1960, 4 per cent of people from manual backgrounds went to university, compared with 27 per cent of those from non-manual backgrounds, a gap of 23 per cent. In 2001, the equivalent figures were 19 per cent and 50 per cent, an increased gap of 31 per cent (Haezewindt, 2004, p17). Clearly the introduction of tuition fees and the abolition of the maintenance grant for higher education students in 1998 may have contributed to this trend. Research shows that many potential university entrants from working-class backgrounds are deterred from applying to universities due to fears about debt.

Blanden and Gregg are not Marxists, and their recommendations for improving social mobility point to the need for improved educational opportunities, particularly in relation to access to higher education. Bowles and Gintis, however, would describe such a strategy as naïve. Social mobility, they would argue, is not an intended outcome of schooling in capitalist societies, and any adequate explanation for the role of education systems *must begin with the fact that schools produce workers* (p10). Capitalist economies need a relatively well educated, technically efficient workforce, and education systems provide this function – in short, they ensure that employers have a pool of workers with sufficient knowledge to carry out the tasks required of them. However, this is not the only role said to be performed by education. It is seen to fulfil other crucially important 'disciplinary' functions. Hence, Bowles and Gintis argue that one of the key aims of education is to nurture the *attitudes and behaviour consonant with participation in the labour force*. Here, they are referring to the inculcation of discipline, the work ethic and other personality traits conducive to preparing young people psychologically for work. *Schools*, they point out, *foster types of personal development compatible with the relationships of dominance and subordinacy in the economic sphere* (p11). Or, put another way, they teach children (future workers) to be docile, to submit to authority, to accept instructions unquestioningly and to accept their station in life as given. This interpretation sounds very similar to functionalist views of education that we outlined earlier, and in some respects it is. There is, of course, one fundamental difference. Whereas functionalists see the functions of education as being desirable and good for the whole of society, Marxists see in them a more sinister element. Education, they argue, is one of the crucial means by which bourgeois values are transmitted. It promotes 'false consciousness' and serves to perpetuate an inherently unjust system – capitalism.

Of course, Bowles and Gintis do not envisage that educational practitioners, whether teachers or lecturers, are aware of the functions they provide for capitalism. On the contrary, these functions have become 'institutionalised' into their professional training and practice over a period of more than a century, and hence are performed in an almost unconscious, 'natural' way. Teachers, lecturers and other educational practitioners may themselves be unaware of the constraints within which they operate, or the extent to which the curricula they teach and codes of practice they follow have become increasingly uncritical, and narrowly focused on ensuring children and young people conform to the needs of capitalism. In recent years, Marxists have pointed to developments in UK education policy, such as the introduction of the National Curriculum as being symptomatic of attempts to severely circumscribe what is taught in schools. The same, it could be argued, is true of professional social work training, the curriculum for which is increasingly influenced by prescriptive Department of Heath guidelines and national training bodies, all of whom have pushed a skills-led, as opposed to a critically-engaged curriculum (Ferguson et al., 2002, p81). We will consider this argument more in the final chapter of this book. In relation to school curricula, however, it is as interesting to think about what is not taught as what is taught. The absence of sociology in the National Curriculum, for example, means that the majority of children will leave school without the insights that a sociological imagination can give them. And while citizenship has now been added as a compulsory subject at secondary schools, some have argued that this too is motivated more by a desire to control than to promote a critical understanding of the world.

Marxist analyses of education do sound very pessimistic. Marxists do, though, have a vision – an optimistic vision which envisages the creation of an equal, socially-just society, where education is not subordinated to the needs of the economy. It will, however, involve the overthrow of capitalism:

> *[W]e believe that the key to [education] reform is the democratisation of economic relationships: social ownership, democratic and participatory control of the production process by workers, equal sharing of necessary labour by all, and progressive equalisation of incomes and destruction of hierarchial relationships. This is, of course, socialism.*
>
> (Bowles and Gintis, 1976, p14)

Marxism and education: an evaluation?

In a sense, it is difficult to disagree with certain elements of Marxist analyses of education. Indeed, it could perhaps be said that Marxists are at least partly guilty of stating the obvious. For example, if recent speeches by senior UK politicians are anything to go by, the shape of secondary education is clearly linked to the imperatives of the market and the economy. While Tony Blair and his successor, Gordon Brown, may extol the 'meritocratic virtues' of education, neither would deny that the government's education policies are geared towards improving economic growth and the country's ability to compete internationally. Indeed, educational policy documents are full of references to the importance of education to the UK's levels of economic performance. So while Marxists are correct to highlight the intrinsic economic functions that education performs, this is neither a particularly novel insight, nor one which leading politicians would deny.

Marxist comments on the failure of educational policy to deliver a true 'meritocracy' are perhaps more innovative and useful. As we have shown, Bowles and Gintis' comments about the lack of social mobility in the US in the 1970s also seem to hold true for the UK today. This is despite increased educational resources, an extended school-leaving age and the massive expansion of higher education. Regarding the higher education sector, a Marxist analysis might also help us understand relatively recent changes to higher education student funding, particularly the drive to force students to fund their own studies. Marxists are not alone in suggesting that this has been influenced by a desire to 'divert' students away from theoretical, critical subjects (such as sociology), towards more business-orientated disciplines. For example, the introduction of tuition fees and the abolition of the maintenance grant, means that average student debt is now over £12,000. This, of course, must be paid off, and it seems logical that potential undergraduates may now think twice about enrolling on a socially critical course which, while intrinsically rewarding and interesting, may not appear to carry the same vocational weight with employers as a skill-focused, or business-related subject.

Perhaps the most illuminating aspect of the Marxist view of education, however, lies in the recognition that the education system maintains, perpetuates and legitimates inequality. An understanding of this seems important to assist us to achieve more realistic understanding of inequality in our society.

C H A P T E R   S U M M A R Y

This chapter has encouraged you to synthesise your knowledge and experience of the education system with sociological theory and to think about the educational experiences of disadvantaged groups and how these can impact upon the rest of their lives. The chapter has considered how factors within and outside the school can contribute to and in some instances determine children's educational experiences, achievement and life chances, and encouraged you to move beyond pathological explanations that focus solely on parental and individual failure. If as social workers we are aiming to significantly improve the lives of the children we work with, it is fundamental that we move beyond a blaming approach, and acknowledge the wider structural causes of unequal educational experiences and outcomes.

FURTHER READING

If you are interested in learning more about the Marxist interpretation of the education system, you might wish to look at the seminal work, **Bowles, S and Gintis, H** (1976) *Schooling in capitalist America*. Abingdon: Routledge and Kegan Paul.

For recent statistical data on evidence of educational inequality see **Haezewindt, P** (2004) Focus on social inequalities: education, training and skills. In **Babb, P, Martin, J and Haezewindt, P** (2004) *Focus on social inequalities*. London: ONS.

For a useful consideration of a range of issues relating to education and social work, see **Horner, N and Krawczyk, S** (2006) *Social work education in children's services*. Exeter: Learning Matters.

Chapter 8
Looking back, looking forwards: The relevance of sociology for social work

Introduction

Having set the scene for a sociological approach to social work, this final chapter aims to draw together some of the key themes throughout the book. We hope to convince you of the need to locate your practice within an understanding of underpinning structures and to critically examine taken-for-granted assumptions about the world in which both you and your service users live. The historical relevance of sociology for social work will be considered along with an argument for its continued relevance in contemporary society.

The uncomfortable intertwining of sociology and social work

There is a longstanding relationship between sociology and social work. As far back as 1903, Charity Organisation Society (COS) workers and volunteers were encouraged to study sociology by those responsible for creating the newly formed London School of Economics (LSE) (Jones, 1983, cited in Dominelli, 1997). The assumption was that in order for social workers to intervene effectively, they needed to be equipped with relevant sociological knowledge about the nature of society to underpin their practice. The LSE's initial efforts to educate its social work students as to the structural causes of social problems were not greeted with universal enthusiasm. This is perhaps hardly surprising, since the core emphasis of the COS was to reform the character of the poor in order to maintain the cohesiveness and well-being of society. Poverty was largely seen by the COS as a morally culpable condition and its interventions were directed at modifying deviant behaviour (rather than providing welfare), and putting the poor back on the 'straight and narrow'. Hence sociology's focus on the structural causes of social problems did not fit entirely well with the COS's more blaming approach. The COS's vision of social work training was very different from that envisaged by sociologists. For the COS, social work training would provide a conservative function, inoculating volunteers and workers from potential 'contamination' which might result from developing an undue empathy with those with whom they worked. In his informative work on the history of social work education, Chris Jones (1996) notes that concern has always existed about the potential of sociology to taint social workers, and that the potentially contaminating influence of sociology was concerning for some in the early days of the COS:

The concern to prevent social workers from being either radicalised or demoralised by their daily experience of contact and involvement with some of the most deprived and impoverished sections of society was a driving force in the creation and development of formal social work education at the beginning of the twentieth century. This notion that a carefully constructed education programme rather than an apprenticeship training regime was essential if field workers were to cope with the pressures of the job and be immunised from disillusionment or even radical contamination.

(Jones, 1996, pp191–2)

According to Jones, such concerns remained prevalent within mainstream state social work training at least until the mid-1970s. There was fear that an overly sociological perspective would spawn radical social workers who would ultimately be a threat to the establishment, by exposing unequal power relations and empowering service users in ways that could potentially threaten the *status quo*. Social workers, as agents of the state, needed to be 'safe', thus the content of the social work training curriculum at the time, and indeed ever since, has been carefully constructed. At times, notably in the 1950s and 1960s, sociology was virtually absent from the social work curriculum. The domination of a psychological perspective marginalised the discipline of sociology, with an emphasis on the individual and casework; and an underpinning need to endorse the prevailing social order by assisting individuals who had fallen by the wayside to come back into mainstream society. Emphasis was placed on the need to resocialise deviant individuals, rather than bringing about change in the nature of society. As Jones (1996) argues, the inclusion of any sociology in the social work curriculum at that time tended to be predicated upon functionalism and a perceived need to understand dysfunctional families. Critical or conflict perspectives were virtually absent from the curriculum.

In the 1970s however, the emerging radical social work movement found a voice, with a resurgence of sociological insights which sought to explain the role of capitalism and the welfare state, and how these were related to the poverty that characterised many service users' lives. The emergence of the radical social work movement coincided with *the creation of the polytechnics, followed by the growth of state social work ... [with] many of the new social science graduates drawn into and attracted by social work careers* (Jones, 1996, p199). Social work began to be perceived as being a potentially radical activity, as social science graduates entered the profession, taking up positions of community workers, and began to align themselves with service users in the pursuit of social justice. There was a subtle shift in emphasis away from service users being regarded as ill-fitting, poorly socialised, social misfits, to a perspective which began to see society as being in need of radical change. However, according to Jones, the insights gleaned from the social sciences began to be perceived as being dangerous once more by employers and agencies. The Central Council for Education and Training of Social Workers (CCETSW), the body that preceded the General Social Care Council (GSCC), noted at the time that employers were pressing for better practical training and a need for social workers to understand the rules and regulations of the organisations they worked for. In their annual report in 1975, CCETSW noted a concern of employers about their employees, that:

> *the education they receive makes them difficult employees, more concerned*
> *to change the 'system' than to get on with the job.*
>
> (cited in Jones, 1996, p203)

It is interesting to note that these employers clearly did not regard changing the system to be part of the job. This provides food for thought in terms of what the role of social work is, and more specifically, what it is not. Employers were concerned once more that social workers were being radicalised by the social science content that they were being taught in their training, and worse, that they were ill-equipped to undertake the task in hand. This coincided with the well-publicised death of Maria Colwell, the inquiry of which criticised social workers for failing to protect the little girl who should have been under their auspices.

In the 1980s and 1990s, the backlash against social workers being educated in the social sciences continued to gather pace, and the Diploma in Social Work, the social work qualification of the time, contained only social science teaching that was directly relevant to practice (Jones, 1996). Jones identifies what he refers to as the 'employer takeover', which began in the 1970s and continued to gain sway thereafter, pressurising CCETSW to ensure that social work courses were 'fit for purpose', with a clear shift away from producing qualifying workers who *thought*, to workers who *did*. There occurred a movement away from *education*, that interrogates, analyses and inspects, to *training* which *cannot be bothered with these questions of deep structure* (Webb, 1996, p182). The competence-based 'can do' curriculum was born and sociology and critical social policy were sidelined once more. Howe (1996) traces the concomitant shift away from 'depth' in social work, to 'surface'; a preoccupation with service provision and the performance of tasks and a move away from deeper work and attempts to understand the individual and the structure in which they are located. Jones identifies these shifts as a purge of all things intellectual, with an embracing of what he calls 'anti-intellectualism' and hostility to the social sciences:

> *Universities are sneered at as being ivory towers far removed from the*
> *pressures of everyday life; theorisation is deemed as escape, or even a*
> *symptom of a cold and uncaring personality; what is demanded of state*
> *welfare workers is obedience and loyalty, not thought ... Consequently,*
> *subjects which were once in the core of the curriculum have been virtually*
> *stripped out.*
>
> (Jones, 1996, pp205–6)

However, social work academics have consistently resisted the obliteration of sociology and continue to urge a sociological presence on curriculum. Indeed, the benchmarks for social work training that accompanied the development of the new social work degree identified the importance of:

> *Sociological perspectives to understanding societal and structural influences*
> *on human behaviour at individual, group and community levels*
>
> *Social science theories explaining group and organisational behaviour,*
> *adaptation and change.*

Nevertheless, it seems that there is still a latent concern to keep social workers 'safe'. This may sound rather conspiratorial but we ourselves can recall very passionate national debates occurring about the direction of social work training when the new BA (Hons) in Social Work was under development in 2003. The 'steer' from the Department of Health's guidelines was certainly very much away from critical, theoretical 'isms' and 'ologies' towards a curriculum that would be more skills and practice focused. Any theory that was taught must, the minister responsible for overseeing implementation of the new degree argued, be geared to strengthening practice skills:

It is no help to service users and their carers if their social worker understands the theory but does not use that understanding to inform and support their practice. That is why I have made it clear that the training requirements should prepare students for the reality of becoming a social worker and that on qualification a person can apply their skills and knowledge to the intervention and support that vulnerable service users need and deserve.

(Smith, 2002, p5)

On one level, the minister seems to be making a fair point, but you can perhaps see why such comments were interpreted by some as an attempt to introduce a less critical, less social science-based curriculum.

ACTIVITY 8.1

Think about your own experiences as a social work student.

- *Do you think the balance of social work training is correct?*
- *Is there an appropriate balance between what might be referred to sociologically related teaching and practice-focused training?*

Take a look at the Benchmark statements for social work education *and the* Department for Health guidance Requirements for social work training. *The benchmark statements were written principally by academics, whereas the Requirements were Department of Health guidelines. Is there any difference in the weight each affords to the respective importance of social science content and practice training?*

The documents can be found here:

Benchmark Statements: www.qaa.ac.uk/academicinfrastructure/benchmark/honours/socialpolicy.asp
Requirements for Social Work Training: www.dh.gov.uk/prod_consum_dh/groups/dh_digitalassets/@dh/@en/documents/digitalasset/dh_4060262.pdf

---

The GSCC's code of conduct for social workers can arguably also be interpreted as part of a process of de-radicalising the profession, and a watering down of the traditional social work value base. Although the intention of the GSCC code was to identify standards of conduct and practice within which social workers should work, many interpret the code as at least encapsulating the value base of the profession, if not standing alone in its entirety as the new value base. In the next exercise, we would like you to spend some time analysing the GSCC code of conduct and comparing it with the British Association of Social Work's (BASW) code of ethics that was first published in 1975 and updated in 2002.

ACTIVITY 8.2

Have a look at the BASW code of ethics. This can be found online at www.basw.co.uk/Default.aspx?tabid=64

Read through and identify what you believe to be the value statements contained in the document.

When you have done this, revisit your GSCC code of conduct that you will have been given at the outset of your training. This is available at www.gscc.org.uk

What value statements can you find in this document?

How do they compare with those contained in the BASW code?

Although the BASW code of ethics is still very much around today, it is of course the GSCC code of conduct that social workers are required to sign up to, and which comprises the underpinning minimum standards for the registration of social workers. Careful attention to the GSCC code reveals that it is much less robust in emphasising the principles of social justice. Indeed, it could be suggested that this is more a list of skills deemed important for social workers to have, or a list of conduct standards that they should adhere to, rather than a clear value base. Although some of the traditional social work values appear in the GSCC code of conduct (treating people with respect; promoting dignity; respecting confidentiality; promoting independence, etc.) there is undoubtedly much less emphasis on the value of social justice. The closest the GSCC code gets to this is in identifying the need to promote equal opportunities for service users and carers and respecting diversity. Compare this with the much more strongly worded statement in the BASW code of ethics:

> *Social workers have a duty to bring to the attention of those in power and the general public, and where appropriate challenge ways in which the policies or activities of government, organisations or society create or contribute to structural disadvantage hardship and suffering, or militate against their relief.*

(p3)

The BASW code dedicates an entire section to discussing social justice, which according to the code, includes:

- fair and equitable distribution of resources to meet basic human needs;
- fair access to public services and benefits;
- recognition of the rights and duties of individuals, families, groups and communities;
- equal treatment and protection under the law;
- social development and environmental management in the interests of future human welfare;

- and importantly, in the pursuit of social justice: *identifying, seeking to alleviate and advocating strategies for overcoming structural disadvantage* (p3).

With the clear omission from the GSCC code of conduct of any discussion of social justice or structural disadvantage, it does seem that social work in the present day has also fallen prey to influences which seek to de-radicalise the profession. In some senses, this could be construed as removing the 'social' from social work. Many universities up and down the country are at the point of revalidating their social work courses in the near future as they approach the time of a five-year review. Debate has taken place concerning the nature of social work education and training – whether there should be a shift to more specialist training to mirror the changes in practice and the dichotomy of children's and adult services, or whether generic training should continue to be based upon the premise that all social workers should receive education around all service user groups. At the time of writing it seems that the latter model will prevail at least in basic education and training, with the opportunity to specialise post qualifying. This seems to us to be an important decision and the right decision given that service users and the complexity of issues that dominate their lives, rarely fall under one defining category. It seems important that all social workers gain a good education on all issues concerning what Mark Doel (2007) refers to as 'the problems of living'. It will be interesting to see whether the old chestnut of sociological content raises its head or not as the reviews get under way.

Locating your practice

Throughout this book, we have encouraged you to situate or locate your service users within an understanding of the social structures that underpin their experiences, by encouraging you to develop a sociological imagination. The aim of this is to discourage an overly negative and blaming focus upon individuals' problems and to encourage understanding and analysis of the factors beyond the control of individuals that shape and constrain their experiences. So, we have asked you to think about how the structural nature of society can mean that some people's lives are characterised by poverty, disadvantage and oppression. We have asked you to deconstruct some of your taken-for-granted assumptions about your own lives, the lives of your service users and the nature of society at large. We remain passionately convinced of the relevance of sociology for social workers and urge you to keep your sociological imagination alive. Early on in this book, we encouraged you to develop awareness of the endemic poverty that underpins the lives of very many service users and the related consequences of living in poverty for long periods. We have asked you to think about the nature of social exclusion and, related to this, to try to understand the way that moral panics can be engineered by the media and politicians to shift attention away from the structural source of many problems that excluded individuals face. We spent time thinking about families and powerful ideologies that exist, deeply embedded within our culture that provide us with messages about how we should live. We also acknowledged that for very many of our service users, the reality of their family life falls far short of these ideals. We then looked at the nuances of the education system and recognised how factors within and outside the system can contribute to educational 'failure', which can compound existing disadvantage. For service users, these issues are live and real and without a sociological analysis to assist social workers to make sense of the complexity of the challenges they face, social workers can only intervene at best on the 'surface' and are in danger of pathologising service users, further adding to their oppression.

Social workers need to possess skills to assist them to analyse the vast amounts of information they gather about service users, in order to intervene effectively. A sociological perspective will hopefully assist them in this quest. A sociological approach to social work is consistent with the value base of the profession. An awareness of the structural constraints that underpin all our lives can assist social workers to work in ways that are empowering and help social workers to be aware of their own potential power to contribute to the oppression of those we work with. A sociological approach to social work complements anti-oppressive practice and supports and strengthens critical practice, as it sets out the theoretical basis for understanding oppression and disadvantage. A sociological approach sits side by side with critical practice in advocating conscious and collective action to bring about social change. In this book we have introduced you to different sociological approaches, some of which you will accept and others of which you will reject. However, notwithstanding the differences and relative merits of each, we hope that you have been able to analyse the differing approaches to develop a clear idea of what each has to offer. We hope that you will be able to use some of the ideas in this book to help you to make sense of your practice from a sociological point of view, with the aim of intervening in ways that are truly empowering and make a difference to people's lives.

References

Abbott, P, Wallace, C and Tyler, M (2005) *Introduction to sociology: Feminist perspectives.* Abingdon: Routledge.

Adams, R, Dominelli, L and Payne, M (2005) *Social work futures.* Basingstoke: Palgrave.

Alland, A (2004) *Race in mind: race, IQ and other racisms.* Basingstoke: Palgrave Macmillan.

Article 19 (2003) *What's the story? Results from research into media coverage of refugees and asylum seekers in the UK.* London: Article 19. **www.article19.org/pdfs/publications/refugees-what-s-the-story-.pdf**

ATD Fourth World (2006) *Empowering families.* **www.atd-uk.org/ukprogrammes/denise.htm**.

Barlow, A and Duncan, S (2000) New Labour's communitarianism: Supporting families and the 'rationality mistake', part 2. *Journal of social welfare and family law,* 22(2), 129–43.

Barnes, C and Mercer, G (2005) Disability, work and welfare: Challenging the exclusion of disabled people. *Work, Employment and Society,* 19 (3), 527–45.

Barrett, M and McIntosh, M (1982) *The anti-social family.* London: NLB.

Barry, M (1998) Social exclusion and social work: An introduction. In Barry, M and Hallett, C (eds) *Social exclusion and social work.* Dorset: Russell House Publishing.

Bartholomew, J (2006) *The welfare state we're in.* London: Politico Publishing.

Bauman, Z (2001) *Community: Seeking safety in an insecure world.* Cambridge: Polity Press.

BBC (2004) Shocking racism in jobs market. *BBC News Online:* 12 July 2004. **www.news.bbc.co.uk/1/hi/business/3885213.stm**

Becker, H (1963) *Outsiders.* New York: The Free Press.

Becker, S (1997) *Responding to poverty, the politics of cash and care.* Harlow: Longman.

Beckett, C (2003) *Child protection: An introduction.* London: Sage.

Beresford, P, Green, D, Lister, R and Woodward, K (1999) *Poverty first hand: Poor people speak for themselves.* London: CPAG.

Berger, P (1963) *Invitation to sociology.* London: Penguin Books.

Berner, E and Phillips, B (2005) Left to their own devices? Community self-help between alternative development and neo-liberalism. *Community Development Journal,* 40(1) (January 2005), 17–29.

Bernstein, B (1971) *Class codes and control, volume 1: Theoretical studies towards a sociology of language.* Abingdon: Routledge and Kegan Paul.

Blanden, J and Gregg, P (2005) Intergenerational mobility in Europe and North America, London: Sutton Trust.**www.cep.lse.ac.uk/about/news/IntergenerationalMobility.pdf**

Blumer, H (1969) *Symbolic interaction*. New Jersey: Prentice Hall.

Bossley, S (1987) School sociology attacked over 'anti-business bids'. *Guardian*, 13 July 1987.

Bottomore, TB (1963) *Karl Marx – early writings*. London: Watts and Co.

Bourdieu, P (1973) Cultural reproduction and social reproduction. In Brown, R (ed.) *Knowledge, education and cultural change*. London: Tavistock.

Bowles, S and Gintis, H (1976) *Schooling in capitalist America: Educational reform and the contradictions of economic life*. Abingdon: Routledge and Kegan Paul.

British Association of Social Workers (2002) *The code of ethics for social work*. Birmingham: BASW.

Burton, M and Kagan, C (2006) Decoding valuing people. *Disability and Society*, 21(4), 299–313.

Byrne, D (1999) *Social exclusion*. Buckingham: Open University Press.

Callinicos, A (1989) *Against postmodernism: A Marxist critique*. Cambridge: Polity Press.

Cameron, D (2006) Chamberlain lecture on communities. Balsall Heath, Birmingham, 14 July 2006. **www.cforum.org.uk/blog/wp-content/uploads/2006/07/DavidCameronChamberlain lecture.doc**

Campbell, B (1998) Oh yes you do. *Guardian*, 5 November 1998.

Campbell, D and Temko, N (2006) £250,000: the cost of care for every problem family: No 10 backs new 'mentors' scheme to break cycle of dependency and crime. *Observer*, 3 September, p14.

Cauce, A, Stewart, A, Rodriguez, M, Cochrane, B and Ginzler, J (2003) Overcoming the odds? Adolescent development in the context of urban poverty. In Luthar, S (ed.) *Resilience and vulnerability: Adaptation in the context of childhood adversities*. Cambridge: Cambridge University Press.

Child Poverty Action Group (2005) *Poverty, the facts: Summary*. London: CPAG.

Child Poverty Action Group (2006) *Media briefing: The government's child poverty target*, London: CPAG.

Clark, G (1974) Sir Keith Joseph denies bid for Tory leadership as critics amount attack. *Times*, 21 October 1974.

Cohen, S (2006) *Folk devils and moral panics.* 3rd edition. Abingdon: Routledge.

Commission on Integration and Cohesion (2007) Our shared future. **www.integra tion andcohesion.org.uk/upload/assets/www.integrationandcohesion.org.uk/our_shared_- future.pdf**

Communities and Local Government (2006) *About us: Community, opportunity, prosperity.* **www.communities.gov.uk/index.asp?id=1122595**

Comte, A (1974) *The positive philosophy*. New York: AMS Press.

Connor, H, Dewson, S, Tyrers, C, Eccles, J, Regan, J and Aston, J (2001) *Social class and higher education: Issues affecting decisions on participation by lower social class groups*. London: DfEE. **www.dfes.gov.uk/research/data/uploadfiles/RR267.pdf**

Conservative Party's Social Justice Policy Group (2006) *Fractured families*. London: Conservative Party.

Cooley, CH (1902) *Human nature and the social order*. New York: Scribner's.

Daily Express: various dates

Daily Mail: various dates

Daily Star: various dates

Daily Telegraph: various dates

Davies, M (1994) *The essential social worker*. Aldershot: Ashgate.

Davis, K and Moore, WE (1945) Some principles of stratification. *American Sociological Review*, 24, 242–9.

Delaney, G. (2003) *Community*. Abingdon: Routledge.

Denham, A and Garnett, M (2002) From the cycle of enrichment to the cycle of deprivation. *Benefits*, 35(10), 3.

Dennis, N and Erdos, G (2005) *Cultures and crimes: Policing in four nations*. London: CIVITAS.

Department of Social Security (DSS) (1999) *Opportunity for all; tackling poverty and social exclusion*. Cm4445. London: The Stationery Office. Crown copyright.

DfES (2006a) *Care matters: Transforming the lives of children and young people in care*, Cm 6932. London, HMSO. **www.dfes.gov.uk/consultations/downloadable docs/6731-DfES-Care %20Matters.pdf**

DfES (2006b) *Ethnicity and education: The evidence of minority ethnic pupils aged 5–16*. London: DfES. **http:publications.teachernet.gov.uk/eOrderingDownload/DFES-0208-2006.pdf**

DfES (2007) *Care Matters: Time for change*. Cm 7137. London: HMSO. **www.dfes.gov.uk/publications/timeforchange/docs/timeforchange.pdf**

Disability Rights Commission (2005) *Small employers' attitudes to disability: A summary*. **www.drc-gb.org/library/campaigndetails.asp?section=restran&id=722**

Doel, M (2007) *The future's generic*. Standing Conference of Social Work Stakeholders. Birmingham University, November 2007.

Dominelli, L (1997) *Anti-racist social work*. Basingstoke: Macmillan.

Dominelli, L (2002) *Anti-oppressive social work theory and practice*. Basingstoke: Palgrave Macmillan.

Dominelli, L (2004) *Social work, theory and practice for a changing profession*. Cambridge: Polity Press.

DRC (2005) Disability briefing: June 2005. **www.drc-gb.org/uploaded_files/docu ments/ 10_719_Disability%20Briefing%20-%20June%202005%20final.doc.**

Durkheim, E (1972) *Selected writings*. Cambridge: Cambridge University Press.

Engels, F (1968) *The origins of the family, private property and the state*. Moscow: Progress Publishers.

EOC (2006) Facts about women and men in Britain. London, EOC. **www.eoc.org.uk/pdf/facts _about_GB_2006.pdf**

EOC (2007) *Sex and power: Who runs Britain*. London: EOC.**www.eoc.org.uk/pdf/sexand power_GB_2007.pdf**

Featherstone, B (1999) Taking mothering seriously: The implications for child protection. *Child and Family Social Work*, 4, 43–53.

Ferguson, I (2006) Living in a material world: Postmodernism and social policy. In Lavalette, M and Pratt, A (eds) *Social policy, theories, concepts and issues*. London: Sage.

Ferguson, I, Lavalette, M and Mooney, G (2002) *Rethinking welfare: A critical perspective*. London: Sage.

Finn, D (2005) Welfare to work: New Labour's 'employment first' welfare state. *Benefits*, 13(2) (June 2005), 93–97.

Firestone, S (1970) *The dialectic of sex*. London: The Women's Press.

Flaherty, J, Veit Wilson, J and Dornan, P (2004) *Poverty: The facts*. 5th edition. London: CPAG.

Fook, J (1999) Critical reflectivity in education and practice. In Pease, B and Fook, J (eds) *Transforming social work practice: Postmodern critical perspectives*. St Leonards: Allen and Unwin.

Friedan, B (1963) *The feminist mystique*. New York: Dell.

Gans, HJ (1971) The uses of poverty, the poor pay all. *Social Policy*, July/August 1971, 20–24.

General Social Care Council (2002) *Code of practice*. London: GSCC.

Gewirtz, S (2001) Cloning the Blairs: New Labour's programme for the re-socialization of working-class parents. *Journal of Education Policy*, 16(4) (July 1, 2001), 365–78.

Giddens, A (1984) *The constitutional society: Outline of the theory of structuration*. Cambridge: Polity.

Giddens, A (1994) *Beyond left and right: The future of radical politics*. Cambridge: Polity Press.

Giddens, A (1998) *The third way*, Cambridge: Polity Press.

Giddens, A (2006) *Sociology*. 5th edition. Cambridge: Polity Press.

Gillies, V, Ribbens McCarthy, J and Holland, J (2001) *The family lives of young people*. York: JRF.

Gittins, D (1985) *The family in question*. Basingstoke: Macmillan Press.

Goode, E and Ben-Yehuda, N (1994) *Moral panics: The social construction of deviance*. Oxford: Blackwell.

Gordon, D, Levitas, R, Pantazis, C, Patsios, D, Payne, S and Townsend, P (2000) *Poverty and social exclusion in Britain*. York: JRF.

Gramsci, A (1971) *Selections from the prison notebooks*. London: Lawrence and Wishart.

Green, DG (1996) *Community without politics: A market approach to welfare reform*. London: CIVITAS.

Griggs, I (2006) Institutionally racist. *Independent on Sunday*, 10 December 2006.

Haezewindt, P (2004) Focus on social inequalities: Education, training and skills. In Babb, P, Martin, J and Haezewindt, P (2004) *Focus on social inequalities*. 2004 edition. London: ONS. **www.statistics.gov.uk/downloads/theme_compendia/fosi2004/social Inequalities_full.pd**

Hanmer, J and Statham, D (1999) *Women and social work*. 2nd edition. Basingstoke: Palgrave Macmillan.

Haralambos, M, Holborn, M and Heald, R (2004) *Sociology, themes and perspectives.* 6th edition. London: HarperCollins.

Harman, V (2006) Letter to the *Guardian*, 4 May 2006.

Hebdidge, D (1979) *Subculture: The meaning of style*. London: Methuen.

Holman, B (1993) *A new deal for social welfare*. Oxford: Lion Books.

Home Office (1999) *Report of the policy action team on community self-help*. London: Home Office. **www.asylumsupport.info/publications/homeoffice/acu/selfhelp.pdf**

Home Office (2006) *Asylum statistics: United Kingdom*. The Stationery Office, Crown copyright. **www.homeoffice.gov.uk/rds/pdfs06/hosb1406.pdf**

Horner, N and Krawczyk, S (2006) *Social work education in children's services,* Exeter: Learning Matters.

Howe, D (1996) Surface and depth in social work practice. In Parton, N (ed.) *Social work, social theory and social change*. Abingdon: Routledge.

Human fertilisation and Embryology Authority (2007) *Guide for patients*. **www.hfea.gov.uk/en/270.html**

Hutton, J (2006) *Supporting families: The role of welfare*. Speech to the Clapham Park project, 15 December 2006.

Jensen, A (1969) How much can we boost IQ and scholastic achievement? *Harvard Education Review*, 39, 1–123.

Jensen, AR (1999) The G factor: the science of mental ability, *Psycoloquy*, 10(23). Intelligence G Factor. **http://psycprints.ecs.soton.ac.uk/archive/00000658/**

Jones, C (1996) Anti-intellectualism and the peculiarities of British social work education. In Parton, N (ed.) *Social work, social theory and social change*. Abingdon: Routledge.

Jones, C (2001) Voices from the frontline: State social workers and New Labour. *British Journal Social Work*, 31, 547–62.

Jones, C and Novak, T (1999) *Poverty, welfare and the disciplinary state*. Abingdon: Routledge.

Jones, C, Ferguson, I, Lavalette, M and Penketh, L (2004) *Social work and social justice: A manifesto for a new engaged practice.* Liverpool University. **www.liv.ac.uk/sspsw/**

Joseph Rowntree Foundation (1995) *Inquiry into income and wealth: Volumes 1 and 2*. York: Joseph Rowntree Foundation.

Jowitt, M and O'Loughlin, S (2005) *Social work with children and families*. Exeter: Learning Matters.

Kincaid, JC (1973) *Poverty and equality in Britain: A study of social security and taxation*. London: Penguin.

Lancashire Evening Post (2007) Blast for homeless gym, 4 May 2007.

Ledwith, M (2005) *Community development: A critical approach*. Bristol: Policy Press.

Lemert, EM (1972) *Human deviance, social problems, and social control*. 2nd edition. Englewood Cliffs: Prentice-Hall.

Levitas R (2001) Against work: A utopian incursion into social policy. *Critical Social Policy*, 21(4) (1November), 449–65.

Levitas R (2005) *The inclusive society? Social exclusion and new labour*. Basingstoke: Palgrave Macmillan.

Lewis, O (1966) *La vida: A Puerto Rican family in the culture of poverty*. New York: Random House.

Lyotard, JF (1984) *The postmodern condition: A report of knowledge*. Manchester: Manchester University press.

Macionis, J and Plummer, K (1998) *Sociology: A global introduction*. Harlow: Prentice-Hall.

Marsh, P and Doel, M (2005) *The task centred social book.* Abingdon: Routledge.

Marsland, D (1996) *Welfare or welfare state? Contradictions and dilemmas in social policy*. Basingstoke: Macmillan.

Marx, K and Engels, F (1969) *Manifesto of the Communist Party*. Moscow: Progress Publishers.

Mayo, M (1994) *Communities and caring: The mixed economy of welfare*. Basingstoke: Macmillan.

McIntosh, M and Barrett, M (1982) *The antisocial family*. Thetford: Thetford Press.

McLeod, M and Saraga, E (1988) Challenging the orthodoxy: Towards a feminist theory and practice. *Feminist Review*, 28, 16–55.

Mead, GH (1934) *Mind, self and society*. Chicago, IL: University of Chicago Press.

Mills, C Wright (1959) *The sociological imagination*. London: Penguin Books.

Milner, J (1993) A disappearing act: The differing career paths of fathers and mothers in child protection investigations. *Critical Social Policy*, 38, Autumn, 1993.

Milner, J (1996) Men's resistance to social workers. In Fawcett, B, Featherstone, B, Hearn, J and Toft, C (eds) *Violence and gender relations.* London: Sage.

MORI (2005) *Political monitor for Feb 2005*. London: MORI. **www.mori.com/polls/2005/mpm050221.shtml**

Muncie, J (1999) *Youth and crime: A critical introduction*. London: Sage.

Murdock, P (1949) *Social structure.* New York: Macmillan.

Murray, C (1990) *The emerging British underclass.* London: IEA.

Murray, C (1994) *The crisis deepens.* London: IEA.

Murray, C (1998) *Income Inequality and IQ.* Washington, DC: American Enterprise Institute. **www.aei.org/docLib/20040302_book443.pdf**

Murray, C and Herrnstein, RJ (1994) *The bell curve.* London: Scribner.

Novak, T (1997) *Poverty and the underclass.* In Lavalette, M and Pratt, A (eds) *Social policy: a conceptual and theoretical introduction.* London: Sage.

O'Donnell, M (1992) *A new introduction to sociology.* 3rd edition. Cheltenham: Thomas Nelson and sons LTD.

Office for National Statistics (2007) *Ethnicity and identity: Labour market.* **www.statistics. gov. uk/cci/nugget_print.asp?ID=462**

Office for National Statistics (2007) *Social trends 37.* 2007 edition. **www.statistics. gov.uk/ downloads/theme_social/Social_Trends37/ST37_Ch03.pdf**

Office of the Deputy Prime Minister (2005) *New Deal for Communities: An Interim Evaluation.* 121, *www.neighbourhood.gov.uk/displaypagedoc.asp?id=1625*

O' Grady, S (2007) Britain's breakdown in traditional values. *Express,* 16 April 2007.

Parsons, C, Godfrey, R, Annan, G, Cornwall, J, Dussart, M, Hepburn, S, Howlett, K Wennerstrom, V (2004) *Minority ethnic exclusions and the Race Relations (Amendment) Act 2000.* London: HMSO DfES.

Parsons, T (1951) *The social system.* Abingdon: Routledge and Kegan Paul.

Payne, M, Adams, R and Dominelli, L (2002) *Critical practice in social work.* Basingstoke: Palgrave-Macmillan.

Pearson, G (1983) *Hooligan: A history of respectable fears.* Basingstoke: Macmillan.

Pearson, G (2002) Youth crime and moral decline: Permissiveness and tradition. In Muncie, J, **Hughes, G and McLaughlin, E** (eds) *Youth justice critical readings.* London: Sage.

Pierson, J (2002) *Tackling social exclusion.* Abingdon: Routledge.

Popple, K (1995) *Analysing community work: Its theory and practice.* Buckingham: Open University Press.

Prime Minister's Strategy Unit (2005) *Improving the life chances of disabled people.* London: HMSO.

Quality Assurance Agency for Higher Education (2000) *Subject benchmark statements, social policy and administration and social work.* **www.qaa.ac.uk/academicinfrastructure/ bench mark/honours/socialpolicy.asp**

Raffo, C, Dyson, R, Gunter, H, Hall, D, Jones, L and Kalambouka, A (2007) *Education and poverty: A critical review of theory, policy and practice.* York: JRF.

Reder, P, Duncan, S and Gray, M (1993) *Beyond blame: Child abuse tragedies revisited.* Abingdon. Routledge.

Redstockings Manifesto (1969) **http://fsweb.berry.edu/academic/hass/csnider/berry/hum 200/redstockings.htm**

Refugee Council (2006) *Tell it like it is: The truth about asylum.* London: Refugee Council.

Reid, WJ and Shyne, AW (1969) *Brief and extended casework.* New York: Columbia University Press.

Ritzer, G (2000) *Sociological theory,* Singapore: McGraw-Hill.

Rosenthal, R and Jacobson, L (1968) *Pygmalion in the classroom.* New York: Holt, Rinehart & Winston.

Roulstone, A (2000) Disability, dependency and the new deal for disabled people. *Disability and Society*, 15(3) (1 May 1, 427–43.

Rowlingson, K and McKay, S (2002) *Lone parent families and gender, class and state.* Harlow: Prentice Hall.

Sainsbury Centre for Mental Health (2005) *Beyond the water towers.* London: Sainsbury Centre for Mental Health.

Scope (2003) *Ready, willing and disabled.* London: Scope.

Scott, S, O'Connor, T and Futh, A (2006) *What makes parenting programmes work in disadvantaged areas? The PALS trial.* York: JRF.

Scruton, R (1985) Who will cure this social disease? Sociology. *Times*, 8 October 1985.

Smale, G, Tuson, G and Statham, D (2000) *Social work and social problems.* Basingstoke: Palgrave.

Smith, J (2002) Speech by the Minister of State for Health to the Joint Social Work Education Conference, 11 July 2002. **www.swap.ac.uk/docs/gov/minister.rtf**

Social Exclusion Taskforce (2007a) *Context for social exclusion work.* **www.cabinet office. gov.uk/social_exclusion_task_force/context/**

Social Exclusion Taskforce (2007b) Reaching out: Progress on social exclusion, Cabinet Office. **www.cabinetoffice.gov.uk/social_exclusion_task_force/documents/reaching_out/progress _report.pdf**

Social Exclusion Unit (1998a) *Bringing Britain together: A national strategy for neighbourhood renewal.* London: SEU.

Social Exclusion Unit (1998b) *Truancy and school exclusion.* London: HMSO.

Social Exclusion Unit (1999a) *Bridging the gap: New opportunities for 16–18 year olds not in education, employment or training.* London: HMSO.

Social Exclusion Unit (1999b) *Teenage pregnancy.* London: HMSO.

Social Exclusion Unit (2004a) *Breaking the cycle, taking stock of progress.* London: The Stationery Office. Crown copyright.

Social Exclusion Unit (2004b) *Mental health and social exclusion.* London: Social Exclusion Unit.

Strand, S (2007) *Minority ethnic pupils in the longitudinal study of young people in England.* London: HMSO.

Sutton Trust (2005) Rates of eligibility for free school meals at the top state schools. The Sutton Trust. **www.suttontrust.com/reports/RatesOfEligibilityforFreeSchool MealsattheTopState Schools.pdf**

Szasz, T (1972) *The myth of mental illness.* London: Paladin Grafton.

Szasz, T (1973) *The second sin.* New York: Anchor/Doubleday.

Taylor, M (2003) *Public policy in the community.* Basingstoke: Palgrave Macmillan.

Thompson, N and Bates, J (1998) Avoiding dangerous practice. *Care: The Journal of Practice and Development,* 6 (4).

Times: various dates

Tonnies, F (1957) *Community and society (gemeinschaft und gesellschaft).* East Lansing, MI: The Michigan State University Press.

Topss (2002) National occupational standards for social work. **www.topssengland. net/files/ SW%20NOS%20doc%20pdf%20files%20edition%20Apr04.pdf**

Townsend, P (1979) *Poverty in the United Kingdom.* London: Allen Lane.

Tumin, M (1953) Some principles of stratification: a critical analysis. *American Sociological Review,* 18(4), 387–94.

Twelvetrees, AC (2001) *Community work.* Basingstoke: Palgrave.

UNICEF (2007) *An overview of child welfare in rich countries.* **www.unicef.org/media/files/ ChildPovertyReport.pdf**

Utting, D, Monteiro, H and Ghate, D (2007) *Interventions for children at risk of developing anti-social personality disorder.* London: Policy Research Bureau. **www.cabinetoffice.gov.uk/ upload/assets/www.cabinetoffice.gov.uk/strategy/anti social.pdf**

Waterhouse, S (2004) Deviant and non-deviant identities in the classroom: Patrolling the boundaries of the normal social world. *European Journal of special Needs Education,* 19(1), 69–84.

Webb, D (1996) Regulation for radicals: The state, CCETSW and the academy. In Parton, N (ed.) *Social work, social theory and social change.* Abingdon: Routledge.

Webster, P (2001) Blair sets 2003 Euro deadline. *Times,* 8 February 2001.

Whelan, R (2001) *Helping the poor: Friendly visiting, dole charities and dole queues.* London: CIVITAS.

Whitty, G (2001) Education, social class and social exclusion. *Journal of Education Policy,* 16(4) (1 July), pp287–95.

Williams, F (1992) Somewhere over the rainbow: universality and diversity in social policy. *Social Policy Review* (4), 1992.

Williams, F (1998) Agency and structure revisited: Rethinking poverty and social exclusion. In Barry, M and Hallett, C (eds) *Social exclusion and social work.* Dorset: Russell House Publishing.

Winder, R (2004) *Bloody foreigners: The story of immigration to Britain*. London: Little, Brown.

Wright, C, Standen, J, German, G and Patel, T (2005) *School exclusion and transition into adulthood in African-Caribbean communities*. York: JRF.

Young, M and Young, P (1962) *Family and kinship in East London*. London: Penguin.

Index

Added to the page number, 't' denotes a table.